LIBRARY OF NEW TESTAMENT STUDIES

650

Formerly the Journal for the Study of the New Testament Supplement Series

Editor
Chris Keith

Editorial Board
Dale C. Allison, Lynn H. Cohick, R. Alan Culpepper,
Craig A. Evans, Jennifer Eyl, Robert Fowler, Simon J. Gathercole,
Juan Hernández Jr., John S. Kloppenborg, Michael Labahn,
Matthew V. Novenson, Love L. Sechrest, Robert Wall,
Catrin H. Williams, Brittany E. Wilson

The Transformational Role of Discipleship in Mark 10:13-16

Passage Towards Childhood

Katherine Joy Kihlstrom Timpte

LONDON • NEW YORK • OXFORD • NEW DELHI • SYDNEY

T&T CLARK
Bloomsbury Publishing Plc
50 Bedford Square, London, WC1B 3DP, UK
1385 Broadway, New York, NY 10018, USA
29 Earlsfort Terrace, Dublin 2, Ireland

BLOOMSBURY, T&T CLARK and the T&T Clark logo are trademarks
of Bloomsbury Publishing Plc

First published in Great Britain 2022
This paperback first published in 2023

Copyright © Katherine Joy Kihlstrom Timpte, 2022

Katherine Joy Kihlstrom Timpte has asserted her right under the Copyright,
Designs and Patents Act, 1988, to be identified as Author of this work.

For legal purposes the Acknowledgments on p. ix constitute
an extension of this copyright page.

All rights reserved. No part of this publication may be reproduced or
transmitted in any form or by any means, electronic or mechanical, including
photocopying, recording, or any information storage or retrieval system,
without prior permission in writing from the publishers.

Bloomsbury Publishing Plc does not have any control over, or responsibility for,
any third-party websites referred to or in this book. All internet addresses given
in this book were correct at the time of going to press. The author and publisher
regret any inconvenience caused if addresses have changed or sites have ceased
to exist, but can accept no responsibility for any such changes.

A catalogue record for this book is available from the British Library.

Library of Congress Cataloging-in-Publication Data
Names: Timpte, Katherine Joy Kihlstrom, author.
Title: The transformational role of discipleship in Mark 10:13-16 : passage
   towards childhood / by Katherine Joy Kihlstrom Timpte.
Other titles: Passage towards childhood
Description: London ; New York : T&T Clark, 2022. | Series: Library of New
Testament studies, 2513-8790 ; 650 | Revision of author's thesis (doctoral)–Princeton
   Theological Seminary, 2017, titled Passage towards
   childhood : the transformational role of discipleship in Mark 10:13-16. |
Includes bibliographical references and index. | Summary: "Katherine Joy Kihlstrom
Timpte employs socio-literary methods to show the radical nature of transformation
   that Jesus requires in his followers in Mark 10 in order to enter the
   kingdom "as a child""– Provided by publisher.
Identifiers: LCCN 2021025379 (print) | LCCN 2021025380 (ebook) |
ISBN 9780567699701 (hardback) | ISBN 9780567699718 (pdf) |
ISBN 9780567699732 (epub)
Subjects: LCSH: Bible. Mark, X, 13-16–Social scientific criticism. |
   Discipling (Christianity)–Biblical teaching. | Children–Religious
   aspects–Christianity. | Christian life–Biblical teaching.
Classification: LCC BS2585.6.C48 T56 2022 (print) | LCC BS2585.6.C48
   (ebook) | DDC 226.3/06–dc23
LC record available at https://lccn.loc.gov/2021025379
LC ebook record available at https://lccn.loc.gov/2021025380

ISBN:	HB:	978-0-5676-9970-1
	PB:	978-0-5676-9974-9
	ePDF:	978-0-5676-9971-8
	ePUB:	978-0-5676-9973-2

Series: Library of New Testament Studies, volume 650
ISSN 2513-8790

Typeset by Integra Software Services Pvt. Ltd.

To find out more about our authors and books visit www.bloomsbury.com
and sign up for our newsletters.

To Ryan, my Beloved:
You are the Reason.

When you are old and grey and full of sleep,
And nodding by the fire, take down this book,
And slowly read, and dream of the soft look
Your eyes had once, and of their shadows deep;

How many loved your moments of glad grace,
And loved your beauty with love false or true,
But one man loved the pilgrim soul in you,
And loved the sorrows of your changing face;

And bending down beside the glowing bars,
Murmur, a little sadly, how Love fled
And paced upon the mountains overhead
And hid his face amid a crowd of stars.
W.B. Yeats

Contents

Acknowledgments		ix
List of Abbreviations		x
List of Abbreviations of Ancient Sources		xiii
1	Introduction and Scholarly Overview	1
	Introduction	1
	History of Scholarship	2
	Overview of the Current Project	25
2	"Like a Child": Perceptions of Children in the Ancient World	27
	Negative Characteristics of Children	27
	Positive Characteristics of Children	39
	Death and the Child: Unfulfilled Hopes	48
	Conclusion and Summary	55
3	*Rites of Passage* and Entrance into Adulthood	57
	Van Gennep and the *Rites of Passage*	58
	Victor Turner's Analysis of the Liminal	61
	Mary Douglas	65
	The Assumption of the *Toga Virilis* as a Rite of Passage	68
	The Wedding Ceremony as a Rite of Passage	74
	Summary and Conclusion	84
4	*Rites of Passage* and Entrance into the Kingdom of God	87
	Mark 10:13-16	87
	Mark 10:13-16 Parallels	91
	Complementary Passages in Mark	95
	Summary and Conclusion	100
5	To Become Like a Child: Children and Childish Characters in Mark	101
	Healing Narratives with Children: Children as Vulnerable, Liminal, and Cherished	103
	Jesus's Teachings about Discipleship	109

	The Disciples and Jesus: The Struggle to Understand True Discipleship	112
	Conclusion and Summary	135
6	Conclusions and Looking Forward	137
	Looking Forward	139
Bibliography		142
Index		154

Acknowledgments

Writing a book is a process that cannot happen in a vacuum: countless people have helped in equally countless ways to encourage, critique, and dialogue with me. Doubtless I will fail to mention everyone who deserves it. However, I will endeavor to name a few.

First, this book began as a doctoral dissertation submitted to the faculty at Princeton Theological Seminary in 2018. I am grateful to my many colleagues and professors at Princeton Theological Seminary for their help and support. I am especially thankful to my dissertation committee for their tireless reading, and re-reading of many drafts, and their help in crafting my thoughts. Thanks go to Clift Black. His wit and sympathy, as well as keen intellect and sheer weight of knowledge, helped guide me through twists and turns, revisions and roadblocks. I count myself deeply lucky to have studied under a Markan scholar of such caliber as him. Shane Berg noticed my potential before I did, and set me on the road of graduate work, and has mentored me through all that life and academia can throw at a person. In so many ways he is the reason I have made it as far as I have. Jacqueline Laspley, likewise, fanned my love of literary analysis during my PhD studies and has been an invaluable dialogue partner.

Beyond my institution, several others aided in my research. Jason Hickel has been my dear friend for nearly two decades and is the person who first turned my attention to anthropology. Without his expertise in his field, I would have missed great insight in my own. I am grateful for the dialogue we have maintained across continents. I am grateful as well to my colleagues and students at St. Mary's College of California, all of whom have encouraged me in my work and acted as sounding boards as I thought and wrote.

Finally, my family deserves deepest thanks. Both my parents are inspirations as professors and mentors. My mom, Kim Kihlstrom, passed away during the early stages of my research, but was unwavering in her faith in me, and left my dad, Ken Kihlstrom, to take up the mantle of an encourager. I am so grateful to have the examples of two such warm and kind people, who see their intellect as one of the many venues to make the world a better place. My children, Beckett and Orin, were born in the midst of graduate work and manuscript editing and have been the cause of a transformation in my own thinking about children and potential. I delight in discovering the people they are and are becoming.

Finally, to Ryan, to whom this book is dedicated. Your love of children, and fierce insistence on their value, planted the seeds of my interest in the topic. Your creativity and intelligence nourished my mind and gave room for my ideas to sprout and grow. You weeded through hundreds of my footnotes. You were there to stand with me in the storms of my sorrows and my fears, keeping me deeply rooted. And you are here now that "the winter is past, the flowers have come, and the time of singing is at hand" (Song of Songs 2:12). You are the reason.

Abbreviations

AGJU	Arbeiten zur Geschichte des antiken Judentums und des Urchristentums
ANTC	Abingdon New Testament Commentaries
AT	Author's translation
AYB	The Anchor Yale Bible
AThR	Anglican Theological Review
BBR	Bulletin for Biblical Research
BTB	Biblical Theology Bulletin
BI	Biblical Interpretation
Bib	Studia Biblica et Orientalia
CBET	Contributions to Biblical Exegesis and Theology
CBQ	Catholic Biblical Quarterly
ChrCent	Christian Century
CEV	Contemporary English Version
CPh	Classical Philology
CurTM	Currents in Theology and Mission
EMC	Echos du Monde Classique
EvQ	Evangelical Quarterly
EvT	Evangelische Theologie
ExpTim	Expository Times
G&R	Greece and Rome
HDR	Harvard Dissertations in Religion
HTR	Harvard Theological Review
HUCA	Hebrew Union College Annual
Interp	Interpretation
JAAR	Journal of the American Academy of Religion

JoRS	*The Journal of Roman Studies*
JSJSup	Supplements to Journal for the Study of Judaism
JSNT	*Journal for the Study of the New Testament*
JSNTSup	Journal for the Study of the New Testament: Supplement Series
JBL	*Journal of Biblical Literature*
JETS	*Journal of the Evangelical Theological Society*
JTS	*Journal of Theological Studies*
JTSA	*Journal of Theology for Southern Africa*
JSHRZ	*Jüdische Schriften aus hellenistisch-römischer Zeit*
JSPSup	*Journal for the Study of the Pseudepigrapha Supplement Series*
KJV	King James Version
LNTS	Library of New Testament Studies
LXX	Septuagint
ms.	manuscript
NA²⁸	*Novum Testamentum Graece,* Nestle-Aland, 28th ed.
NIBC	New International Biblical Commentary
NICNT	New International Commentary on the New Testament
NIDB	*The New Interpreter's Dictionary of the Bible.* Edited by Katharine Doob Sakenfeld. 5 vols. Nashville: Abingdon, 2006–9
NovT	*Novum Testamentum*
NovTSup	Novum Testamentum Supplements
NRSV	New Revised Standard Version
NT	New Testament
NTSup	Supplements to Novum Testamentum
OT	Old Testament
PG	Patrologia graeca. Edited by J.-P. Migne. 162 vols. Paris, 1857–86.
PTS	Patristische Texte und Studien
ResQ	*Restoration Quarterly*
SC	Sources chrétiennes. Paris: Cerf, 1943–
SemeiaSt	Semeia Studies

SNTSMS	Society for New Testament Studies Monograph Series
StPatr	Studia Patristica
TDNT	*Theological Dictionary of the New Testament*
TheoT	*Theology Today*
TSK	*Theologische Studien und Kritiken*
TynBul	*Tyndale Bulletin*
TZ	*Theologische Zeitschrift*
WBC	Word Biblical Commentary
WUNT	Wissenschaftliche Untersuchungen zum Neuen Testament
WW	*Word and World*
ZNW	*Zeitschrift für die neutestamentliche Wissenschaft und die Kunde der älteren Kirche*
ZTK	*Zeitschrift für Theologie und Kirche*

Abbreviations of Ancient Sources

Ant.	Josephus, *Jewish Antiquities*
Cels.	Origen, *Contra Celsum*
Div.	Cicero, *De divinatione*
Ep.	Seneca, *Epistulae morales*
Eug.	*Eugnostos*
Hist. eccl.	Eusebius, *Historia ecclesiastica*
Inst.	Gaius, *Institutiones*
Jos. Asen.	*Joseph and Aseneth*
J.W.	Josephus, *Jewish War*
LAE	*Life of Adam and Eve*
Let. Aris.	*Letter of Aristeas*
Lucil.	Seneca, *Ad Lucilium*
Marc.	Tertullian, *Adversus Marcionem*
Metam.	Apuleius, *The Golden Ass*
M. Ket	Mishnah, Ketubot
M. Sot.	Mishnah, Sotah
QG	Philo, *Questions and Answers on Genesis*
Sat.	Juvenal, *Satirae*

1

Introduction and Scholarly Overview

Introduction

In recent decades the subject of ancient conceptions of the child has begun to catch the attention of the scholarly world. Both in classical studies[1] and in biblical studies,[2] there has been an increase of articles, monographs, and collections attempting to ascertain what the social context of a child would have been; how they were thought of; how they interacted with other children, siblings, parents, and adults; and how they were educated. In Markan studies specifically there are very few articles and books studying the role of the child.[3] Mark 10:13-16 represents a passage with especially untapped potential in biblical scholarship: a metaphorical use of "child" is imbedded in a story containing children as literary characters.[4] Moreover, this passage is one of the key texts highlighting the Kingdom of God and how one is to receive it.

---

[1] Note such collections as Jenifer Neils and John H. Oakley, eds., *Coming of Age in Ancient Greece: Images of Childhood from the Classical Past* (New Haven: Yale University Press, 2003); K. R. Bradley, *Discovering the Roman Family: Studies in Roman Social History* (New York: Oxford University Press, 1991); Andre Burguiere et al., eds., *A History of the Family, Volume I: Distant Worlds, Ancient Worlds* (Cambridge: Belknap, 1996); as well as monographs such as Suzanne Dixon, *The Roman Family* (Baltimore: Johns Hopkins University Press, 1992).

[2] For example, Peter Balla, *The Child-Parent Relationship in the New Testament and Its Environment* (Peabody: Hendrickson, 2006); Marcia J. Bunge, Terence E. Fretheim, and Beverly Roberts Gaventa, eds., *The Child in the Bible* (Grand Rapids: Eerdmans, 2008); Marcia J. Bunge, ed., *The Child in Christian Thought* (Grand Rapids: Eerdmans, 2001); Cornelia B. Horn and Robert R. Phenix, eds., *Children in Late Ancient Christianity* (Tübingen: Mohr Siebeck, 2009); Hans Ruedi Weber, *Jesus and the Children: Biblical Resources for Study and Preaching* (Atlanta: John Knox Press, 1994).

[3] Notable among these are Sharon Betsworth, *The Reign of God Is Such as These: A Socio-Literary Analysis of Daughters in the Gospel of Mark* (New York: T&T Clark, 2010), as well as Judith Gundry-Volf, "Mark 9: 33-37," *Interp* 53 (1999): 57–61; Gundry-Volf, "Putting *The Moral Vision of the New Testament* into Focus: A Review," *BBR* 9 (1999): 277–87; Gundry-Volf, "To Such as These Belongs the Reign of God: Jesus and Children," *TheoT* 56 (1999): 469–80; Gundry-Volf, "The Least and the Greatest: Children in the New Testament," in *The Child in Christian Thought*, 29–60; Gundry-Volf, "Children in the Gospel of Mark, with Special Attention to Jesus's Blessing of the Children (Mark 10: 13-16)and the Purpose of Mark," in *The Child in the Bible* (eds. Marcia J. Bunge, Terence E. Fretheim, and Beverly Roberts Gaventa. Eerdmans, 2008).

[4] Cf. Judith Gundry, "Children in the Gospel of Mark," in Bunge, Fretheim, and Gaventa, *The Child in the Bible*, 143–76.

In this book, I propose to fill a gap in scholarship by attempting to answer the dual questions: "In what way is a child supposed to be the model recipient of the Kingdom of God?" and "What is intended by the phrase 'whoever does not receive the kingdom *as a child* shall never enter into it'?" I will argue that the image of entering the Kingdom of God as a child involves entering in a state of dependence, but it is *also* an image of the radical transformation needed to enable that entrance—a transformation that both mirrors and reverses the traditional *rites of passage* by which a child became an adult. Anthropologists such as Arnold Van Gennep, Victor Turner, and Mary Douglas have carefully defined "*rites of passage*" as a set of rituals (birth, initiation, marriage, death) that follow a common structure of separation, transition, and reincorporation. These rites are seen as vitally important, verifying the transition from one state of being to another that is fraught with danger. Van Gennep drew a particularly close link between those rites transitioning children to their standing as adult and entrance into a cult/group/religion, labeling both under the category "initiation rite." Jesus, by insisting on entering the Kingdom of God as a child, invokes two interlacing images. First, the transformational element of initiation: to enter the Kingdom of God, one must be transformed. There really are insiders and outsiders, and to be an insider, more than a cursory commitment is needed. Second, this initiation rite is a reversal of the normal child-to-adult initiation rite, emphasizing the radical reversal seen throughout Mark between the way the Kingdom of God operates and the way of the social world of the time. This is why the child is invoked in Mark 10:13-16. To become like a child, one must strip off the things one gained by leaving childhood behind: wealth, power, family, respect.

History of Scholarship

There is a particular challenge in the project set forth, in that research on the child has only recently begun to gain interest in both the classical and biblical world, and children are being studied from wide-ranging perspectives. Studies of children, both within Markan and broader biblical scholarship, as well as in the contemporaneous Greco-Roman and Judaic cultures, are important for understanding the ways in which children were viewed and treated in the ancient world. Furthermore, "child" is both a term denoting one of a certain age (as opposed to "adult") as well as a term relating to familial roles (vis-à-vis "parent"). Although I will be limiting my scope primarily to children as contrasted to adults, a survey of scholarship on the family in Mediterranean antiquity will help more firmly place children within their social context.

Children in Classical Studies

The most famous early study of children is Phillippe Ariès's *Centuries of Childhood*.[5] His essential thesis is that childhood as a concept is modern, dating to about the

---

[5] Philippe Ariès, *Centuries of Childhood: A Social History of Family Life* (trans. Robert Baldick; New York: Vintage Books, 1962).

sixteenth and seventeenth centuries. Before this era, he argues, children, particularly of lower classes, would have mixed with adults as young as seven years old, joining the workforce and being functionally indistinguishable from adults.[6] With the rise of interest in education in the sixteenth and seventeenth centuries, however, a new conception of children as beings in need of moral and spiritual formation became normative.[7] Ariès's work stands preeminent in studies on children, and while routinely praised as such, he is often critiqued on his main argument. This, however, is generally simplified by others, and therefore misinterpreted. His position on the genesis of the concept of "children" is nuanced, and he specifically argues that the Hellenistic period, with its emphasis on education, conceived of a person in several discreet learning stages corresponding to age. For Ariès, this represented a more defined sense of "child" or "childhood" although it did not match perfectly with a modern sentiment. During the Middle Ages, the importance of educating children diminished. This led to children entering the workforce at an early age, resulting in their social invisibility and the loss of the developmental stage of "child/youth."

Works discussing children often focus on the family more broadly. Two sets of multi-volume works offer glimpses into the breadth of possibilities in researching children and families. The two-volume work, *A History of the Family*,[8] written in the mid-1990s, represents an assemblage of scholars generally using a historical-anthropological lens to examine families in their contexts, from Babylon and ancient Egypt through the modern era. The three-volume *Encyclopedia of Children and Childhood*[9] seeks to be an encyclopedic compendium on children. Organized alphabetically and containing more than 445 articles, it draws from almost all cultures and almost all time periods. It particularly focuses on visual representations of childhood, although literary material is also included, making it a useful companion to the work *Coming of Age in Ancient Greece* (see below). Its scope is massive, but its depth is shallow, giving a general introduction to a variety of topics and thinkers. A similar but less comprehensive[10] endeavor is a single-volume work entitled *The Child: An Encyclopedic Companion*.[11] This compendium tends to emphasize modern and global topics more than historical ones, although it covers some of both.

Classical studies began to be interested in the family, and the child specifically, at the end of the 1960s; concentrated scholarship on the subject arose in the 1980s and 1990s. There are a few notable works on the family and children in ancient Greece and Rome. Many focus on the family broadly; a few are interested in children specifically. Generally speaking, those authors interested in children address the question of whether perceptions of children and childhood either did or did not change significantly over

---

[6] Ibid., 411.
[7] Ibid., 412.
[8] Andre Burguiere et al., eds., *A History of the Family, Volume I: Distant Worlds, Ancient Worlds*, and *A History of the Family, Volume II: The Impact of Modernity* (Cambridge: Belknap, 1996).
[9] Paula S. Fass et al., eds., *Encyclopedia of Children and Childhood in History and Society*, Vols. I–III (New York: Macmillan Reference USA, 2004).
[10] "Less comprehensive" is a relative comparison. The work is just over 1,000 pages.
[11] Richard A. Shweder et al., eds., *The Child: An Encyclopedic Companion* (Chicago: University of Chicago Press, 2009).

a specified number of centuries of Greco-Roman history (usually from the classical to the Hellenistic period in Greece, or in the first four centuries CE in Rome). Authors interested in children tend to rely either on primarily literary evidence or on evidence from visual images, sometimes in combination with inscriptions (e.g., a funerary relief and inscription). All are of interest to this present work, as the number of reputable works on children in the ancient world still remains relatively small.

Mark Golden's comprehensive *Children and Childhood in Classical Athens* considers ancient conceptions of children and childhood. As the title suggests, he focuses on Athens from about 500 to 300 BCE,[12] concentrating on both the private and public lives of children. His first chapter details specific ancient perceptions of characteristics of children, grouping them into neutral, negative, and positive. Generally, he concludes that the child was thought of as inferior to an adult in every way—mentally, physically, morally—but this did not mean that they were not also loved.[13] Each of Golden's subsequent chapters is devoted to the relationship of a child to various things: the household, the community, parents, siblings, outsiders. Golden notes the transition that comes as a young boy becomes an adult male or as a young girl becomes a wife.[14] Golden, in general, is not interested in establishing a case for changing perceptions of childhood over time, and largely ignores the issue. His final chapter concludes that, while there is certain evidence that could support a case for a change in attitudes about children, the scarcity of resources leads him to adopt a "selective skepticism" on that issue.[15] Golden has written numerous articles on the subject of children, notably "Did the Ancients Care When Their Children Died?,"[16] which covers the idea of parental affection (or the lack thereof) toward children. His work provides excellent groundwork for the present study, even though the region and chronological period on which he focuses do not exactly correspond to my own interests.

Sarah B. Pomeroy also writes about children and families in Greece in her volume *Families in Classical and Hellenistic Greece: Representations and Realities*.[17] She limits her inquiry to 500–30 BC[18] and attempts to explore the Greek family chronologically, and whether there was any substantial change "shapes, structures, values and behavior"[19]

---

[12] Mark Golden, *Children and Childhood in Classical Athens* (Baltimore: Johns Hopkins University Press, 1993), xiii.
[13] Ibid., 11.
[14] Note that these categories are intentionally not parallel, because perceptions of gender were not parallel. A man could do and be so much more than merely a husband, and therefore a boy could be considered a man without being married. But a woman's highest goal was conceived of entirely in terms of her ability to be a wife and mother. Furthermore, as will be addressed in Chapter 3, marriage for women generally happened around puberty, and therefore acknowledgment of their "coming of age" was rolled up into the marriage ceremony. But a man might marry in his twenties or thirties, and therefore for men there was a stronger sense of "coming of age" apart from the marriage ceremony.
[15] Ibid., 171.
[16] Mark Golden, "Did the Ancients Care When Their Children Died?" *Greece and Rome* 35.2 (1988): 152–63.
[17] Sarah B. Pomeroy, *Families in Classical and Hellenistic Greece: Representations and Realities* (Oxford: Oxford University Press, 1997).
[18] Ibid., 13.
[19] Ibid., 1.

in those centuries. Specifically interested in the female, but expanding her search in this book to the family as such, she examines the family generally in Athens, referring to Sparta as the "exception that proves the rule."[20] She primarily argues that, rather than the usual division of male versus female, which also is traditionally correlated with public life versus private life, there is a threefold social division: public, domestic/public, and domestic/private.[21] Only in the second and third do women appear at all, and only the third most intimately "accommodates women and children freely."[22] While her scholarship is of the highest quality, her emphasis is on family units as such. She devotes little attention to biological children; rather, she stresses kinship among family members, paying particular attention to the practice of endogamy among the Greeks. Her particular emphasis on classical and Hellenistic Greece, an important background for the present study, is not the era with which I am most concerned.

Thomas Wiedemann, in his *Adults and Children in the Roman Empire*, attempts a similar project as Pomeroy, but focuses his attention to the first four centuries CE in Roman Italy. He attends less to women than to children specifically. He relies primarily on literary evidence, studying philosophers' treatises, letters, and personal reflections ranging from Pliny to Cicero to Seneca to Augustine. He summarizes his findings by relating attitudes toward children to their exceptionally high mortality rate. He says that while high mortality remains consistent throughout the four centuries, "the way in which people came to terms with that fact"[23] changed significantly. In the classical period they did so "by excluding children from civic life,"[24] whereas "Jews and Christians responded by giving not just the youngest child, but even the child in the womb, the same right to a place within the religious community as any adult."[25]

Beryl Rawson has written several volumes on the family in ancient Rome, all of which at least touch on children. In two of these works, *The Family in Ancient Rome* and *Marriage, Divorce, and Children in Ancient Rome*, she amasses articles on the family from scholars such as Susan Treggiari, K. R. Bradley, Suzanne Dixon, and Richard Saller. *The Family in Ancient Rome* presents the proceedings of a seminar in Australia in July 1981, but the edited volume has been crafted with an attempt at internal cohesion.[26] The articles cover a range of topics on the family, focusing on women, theories of conception, parenting, and finances. In *Marriage, Divorce, and Children in Ancient Rome*, Rawson's own essay, "Adult–Child Relationships in Roman Society,"[27] covers the interaction between children and their caregivers, noting that conditions like death, divorce, abandonment, and slavery suggest the

---

[20] Ibid., 17.
[21] Ibid., 19.
[22] Ibid., 18.
[23] Thomas Wiedemann, *Adults and Children in the Roman Empire* (New York: Routledge, 1989), 204.
[24] Ibid.
[25] Ibid.
[26] Beryl Rawson, ed., *The Family in Ancient Rome* (Ithaca: Cornell University Press, 1986). See, especially, the introduction.
[27] Beryl Rawson, "Adult-Child Relationships in Roman Society," in *Marriage, Divorce, and Children in Ancient Rome* (ed. Beryl Rawson; Oxford: Oxford University Press, 1991), 7–30.

need for a broader term than "parent" to describe a caregiver.[28] She also details the several life stages of a child (unborn, newborn, postnatal, developing, and transition to adulthood), emphasizing transitions and rites associated with each. She argues in parallel with Emiel Eyben that, particularly for the elite male, there was a protracted sense of "adolescence," whereby young men were legally adults but barred from public office and not expected to marry or begin a family.[29] For young men of lower classes and young women of all classes, "adulthood" was functionally achieved at a much younger age: women married in their very early to late teens (depending on social class), and the poorer classes were known to work for their living as early as age ten.[30] Suzanne Dixon's essay "The Sentimental Ideal of the Roman Family"[31] argues that, whatever the reality might have been, beginning in the late Republic there was an *ideal* of sentimental love for spouse and children.[32] Children were described in diminutives like *dulcis*, *suauis*, and *mellitus*[33] (all three roughly meaning "sweet"). She argues that letters, inscriptions, and orations described children as pleasurable in themselves, not only as potential adults or for their future ability to provide for their parents. While the reality may have been much harsher, she argues that the persistence of the ideal of harmony in the family is worthy of note. In "Fathers and Sons,"[34] Emiel Eyben writes about the relationship between sons and fathers, not only in childhood but also through adolescence and young adulthood. Literature details the love of fathers for their sons (and daughters as well), regardless of their intellectual, moral, or physical prowess.[35] The opposite was true as well: the "severe father" was a common literary trope.[36] Most Roman authors, however, appreciated a "golden mean" whereby discipline and affection were balanced, although they argued over what the balance looked like in practice.[37] Richard Saller similarly covers the topics of *pietas* ("filial devotion," although Saller argues for a more reciprocal sense of affection than others assume) and *uerbera* ("beatings") in the Roman household, both in regard to slaves and sons.[38] He draws a distinction between slaves and sons: slaves were thought to be primarily driven to obedience by fear of punishment, whereas sons could be reasoned with and encouraged by their fathers, and therefore should not be treated with the same degrading physical punishment.[39]

---

[28] Ibid., 7.
[29] Ibid., 28.
[30] Ibid.
[31] Suzanne Dixon, "The Sentimental Ideal of the Roman Family," in Rawson, *Marriage, Divorce, and Children in Ancient Rome*, 99–113.
[32] Ibid., 99.
[33] Ibid., 103.
[34] Emiel Eyben, "Fathers and Sons," in Rawson, *Marriage, Divorce, and Children in Ancient Rome*, 114–43.
[35] Ibid., 118–19.
[36] Ibid., 121.
[37] Ibid., 142.
[38] Richard Saller, "Corporal Punishment, Authority, and Obedience in the Roman Household," in Rawson, *Marriage, Divorce, and Children in Ancient Rome*, 146.
[39] Ibid., 164–5.

Rawson's most comprehensive work on children is entitled *Children and Childhood in Roman Italy*. Here she considers four centuries of Roman history, beginning in the first century BCE and finishing in the early third century CE.[40] Her scope, therefore, is similar to Wiedemann's, as is her argument: change in thought about children is discernible in those first few centuries CE.[41] She argues that the first half of the first century BCE was a period of transition, and with Augustus in the first century CE, there was a period of consolidation.[42] She argues not that families had greater love for their children but that with legislation by Augustus in 18 BCE and 9 CE, both encouraging families to have many children, there were both "more occasions and ways of expressing family sentiment."[43] Her book is divided into two major parts: "representations" of children and "life course" of a child. In the first section, "representations" of children, she studies visual portrayals of children in monuments, coins, and busts, seeking to get at the "diversity of ways in which children were perceived and represented—by a variety of people and a variety of sources."[44] In the second section, she looks at the "life course" of a child—the welcoming, rearing, education, and commemoration of children. Here she is indeed trying to reconstruct what it might be like to grow up as a child and what children experienced.[45] Rawson is rightly known as one of the key writers on children in the Greco-Roman world. This work offers invaluable background for my own project.

Suzanne Dixon's edited work *Childhood, Class and Kin*[46] has a similar scope to Rawson's edited volumes: Dixon seeks to explore childhood and its social components in Rome in the first two centuries CE. The essays' topics are very similar to those in Rawson's volume. The section on children covers such topics as children and dreams,[47] child exposure,[48] and children as cultural symbols.[49]

Numerous articles and books cover aspects of Greco-Roman social life that sometimes touch on childhood in the ancient world. While the literature on women in Greece and Rome is too numerous to even begin listing, several works cover marriage, particularly highlighting the transition of a young girl to woman. Susan Treggiari's seminal *Roman Marriage*[50] looms large, while other studies take up related issues: Richard Frank on Augustus' marriage legislation;[51] Archie C. Bush and Joseph

---

[40] Beryl Rawson, *Children and Childhood in Roman Italy* (Oxford: Oxford University Press, 2003).
[41] Ibid., 3.
[42] Ibid., 5.
[43] Ibid., 5–6, 8.
[44] Ibid., 92.
[45] Ibid.
[46] Suzanne Dixon, ed., *Childhood, Class and Kin in the Roman World* (London: Routledge, 2001).
[47] Keith Bradly, "Children and Dreams," in Dixon, *Childhood, Class and Kin*, 43–51.
[48] Mireille Corbier, "Child Exposure and Abandonment," in Dixon, *Childhood, Class and Kin*, 52–73. Also on this topic see W. V. Harris, "Child-Exposure in the Roman Empire," *JoRS* 84 (1994): 1–22.
[49] Beryl Rawson, "Children as Cultural Symbols: Imperial Ideology in the Second Century," in Dixon, *Childhood, Class and Kin*, 21–42.
[50] Susan Treggiari, *Roman Marriage Iusti Coniuges from the Time of Cicero to the Time of Ulpian* (Oxford: Oxford University Press, 1991).
[51] Richard I. Frank, "Augustus' Legislation on Marriage and Children," *Cal Studies in Classical Antiquity* 8 (1975): 41–52.

J. McHugh on Roman marriage from the perspective of social bonds, surveying marriage between social classes and relatives;[52] M. K. Hopkins on "The Age of Roman Girls at Marriage";[53] and later Brent Shaw on "The Age of Roman Girls at Marriage: Some Reconsiderations."[54] Fanny Dolansky's 1997 master's thesis, "Coming of Age in Rome: The History and Social Significance of Assuming the *Toga Virilis*,"[55] looks at the ceremony whereby a Roman boy would be formally proclaimed an adult. Her work will be discussed at length in Chapter 3.

Finally, works like *Coming of Age in Ancient Greece: Images of Childhood from the Classical Past*[56] and *Constructions of Childhood in Ancient Greece and Italy*[57] emphasize scholarly examinations of images of children in Greece and Rome.

In summary, there has been an increased interest in studying children in the Greco-Roman world, but the pool of scholarship is still relatively small. Many scholars are interested in families or in women, and tangentially mention children. Those works that focus on children themselves tend to group themselves into a few categories, many of which overlap with one another. Some focus on establishing a relationship between parents and children based on economic or social categories (e.g., inheritance, respect, and power). Others focus on the development (or the lack thereof) of socially acceptable affection between parents and children. Still others attempt to describe the perfection of stages in a child's life and traits associated with each stage. However, because the field is relatively small, the topical interest of articles covering the "child" in the Greco-Roman world is quite widespread.

Children in Biblical Studies

Studies on children in biblical studies have seen only a relatively recent surge in interest. Following the rise of an emphasis on women in the Bible, scholarship expanded on the roles of the families generally, but interest in the child as such, rather than in relation to the family unit, had been minimal.[58] One may consider this research in four subsections: children in the Hebrew Bible, children in the Christian Bible, children in the New Testament, and children in Markan studies.

---

[52] Archie C. Bush and Joseph J. McHugh, "Patterns of Roman Marriage," *Ethnology* 14.1 (1975): 25–45.
[53] M. K. Hopkins, "The Age of Roman Girls at Marriage," *Population Studies* 18.3 (1965): 309–27.
[54] Brent D. Shaw, "The Age of Roman Girls at Marriage: Some Reconsiderations," *JoRS* 77 (1987): 30–46.
[55] Fanny Dolansky, "Coming of Age in Rome: The History and Social Significance of Assuming the *Toga Virilis*" (Master's diss., University of Victoria, 1999).
[56] Neils and Oakley, eds., *Coming of Age in Ancient Greece*.
[57] Ada Cohen and Jeremy B. Rutter, eds., "Constructions of Childhood in Ancient Greece and Italy," *Hesperia Supplements* 41 (2007).
[58] See for instance Jan Willem Van Henten and Athalya Brenner, eds., *Families and Family Relations* (Netherlands: Deo Publishing, 2000). Of the six pairs of essays in the volume, none deals with nonadult children directly, although Ingo Kottsieper's contribution, "'We Have a Little Sister': Aspects of the Brother–Sister Relationship in Ancient Israel," comes closest.

Children in the Hebrew Bible

A handful of books examine children specifically from the perspective of the Hebrew Bible. One of the earliest is Shaye J. D. Cohen's edited work *The Jewish Family in Antiquity*, which aims to "stimulate interest in this underexplored field."[59] Throughout its essays a consistently reiterated theme is that "the Jewish family in antiquity seems not to have been distinctive by power of its Jewishness; rather its structure, ideals, and dynamics seem to have been virtually identical with those of its ambient culture(s)."[60] O. Larry Yarbrough's "Parents and Children in the Jewish Family of Antiquity" discusses parental obligation to the child (moral and religious education, teaching a trade, feeding and clothing him),[61] as well as a child's obligation to the parent (summed up by the commandment "honor your father and mother").[62] He also asserts that the marriage of a child functioned as roughly the dividing line whereby the direction of obligation was reversed: Before marriage a parent had more weighty obligations to the child; after marriage the child had more weighty obligations to the parent.[63] Adele Reinhartz's essay, "Parents and Children: A Philonic Perspective,"[64] covers similar topics specifically from the perspective of Philo. Her conclusions are similar to Yarbrough's, but she highlights Philo's explicit recognition of the inferiority of the child in the child-parent relationship.[65]

Laurel W. Koepf-Taylor's *Give Me Children or I Shall Die: Children and Communal Survival in Biblical Literature*[66] uses a sociohistorical lens to examine children in the Hebrew Bible. She looks at childhood as a social construct, pointing out the difference between modern and ancient views of children, particularly comparing the modern ideal of a child's value as "strictly emotional" as opposed to a hybrid economical/survival model from the ancient world.[67]

Julie Faith Parker examines children in the Hebrew Bible through linguistic and literary lenses in her book *Valuable and Vulnerable*,[68] arguing that it is possible to discern a concept of childhood from the Hebrew Bible and that by examining narratives about children, one's appreciation of the literature as a whole is enhanced.[69] She examines the variety of words used for children in the Hebrew Bible (considering children up until their marriage) and then focuses on key passages in 2 Kings to argue for how adults viewed children.

---

[59] Shaye J. D. Cohen, "Introduction," in *The Jewish Family in Antiquity* (ed. Shaye J. D. Cohen; Atlanta: Scholars, 1993), 2.
[60] Ibid., 2.
[61] Ibid., 48.
[62] Ibid., 49.
[63] Ibid., 48.
[64] Ibid., 61–88.
[65] Ibid., 66–9.
[66] Laurel W. Koepf-Taylor, *Give Me Children or I Shall Die: Children and Communal Survival in Biblical Literature* (Minneapolis: Fortress, 2013).
[67] Ibid., 23.
[68] Julie Faith Parker, *Valuable and Vulnerable: Children in the Hebrew Bible, Especially the Elisha Cycle* (Providence: Brown Judaic Studies, 2013).
[69] Ibid., 8–9.

Naomi Steinberg's *The World of the Child in the Hebrew Bible*[70] was published in the same year as Parker's book and covers similar territory. Steinberg employs a linguistic method to survey the semantic range of words for "child" in the Hebrew Bible, concluding that "child" can refer to a chronological period of time in a person's life (generally under twenty) or a social category that refers to various developmental stages related to the child's potential for economic contribution.[71] She then adopts a literary approach to key texts like Genesis 21 and 1 Samuel 1, showing how the term "child" could differ within a family, depending on a variety of factors. Steinberg also includes a section on the markers of transition between childhood and adulthood, arguing that being a parent more than anything else signals the complete transition to adult.[72]

In *Children in the Ancient Near Eastern Household*[73] Kristine Sue Hendrickson Garroway looks at both Ancient Near Eastern literature as well as tombs and other archeological materials from the seventeenth and thirty-third centuries BCE, respectively, to get a sense of the social status of a child. She draws from a variety of interpretive approaches, from archeological to anthropological to gender theory. She looks at such issues as adoption, slavery, and orphans. Ultimately, she argues that a child moved through several stages, from birth to full membership in society, and, therefore, that identity was fluid rather than fixed.

Finally, Stephen M. Wilson, in *Making Men: The Male Coming-of-Age Theme in the Hebrew Bible*,[74] takes up the theme of coming of age specifically in young men in the Hebrew Bible. He argues that the narratives of four Hebrew Bible characters (Moses, Samuel, David, and Solomon) exhibit the literary structures of Arnold van Gennep's *rites of passage*, showing their transition from boyhood to manhood. He furthermore argues that all four stories maintain a consistent set of both terminology and characteristics that apply to boyhood, and a separate set of terminology and characteristics that apply to manhood. Wilson also examines the characters (Samson and Jether) who fail to mature, both of whose liminal status reflect the greater narrative impression of the liminal status of Israel itself.[75] Wilson's work, which I only came across in the very latest stages of my own final edits of this book, has some strikingly similar interests to my own. His interest in *rites of passage*, liminality specifically, and narrative portrayals of children becoming adults all are very much in alignment with this book. He is, however, interested exclusively in the narration of male maturation, whereas I am interested in studying children of both sexes, and furthermore focuses on the Hebrew Bible, where I am interested in Mark's Gospel.

---

[70] Naomi Steinberg, *The World of the Child in the Hebrew Bible* (Sheffield: Sheffield Phoenix Press, 2013).
[71] Ibid., 18.
[72] Ibid., 68–73.
[73] Kristine Hendrickson Garroway, *Children in the Ancient Near Eastern Household* (Winona Lake: Eisenbrauns, 2014).
[74] Stephen M. Wilson, *Making Men: The Male Coming-of-Age Theme in the Hebrew Bible* (New York: Exoford University Press, 2015).
[75] Ibid., 147.

Children in the Christian Bible

One of the earliest essays engaging a theology of the child in the Bible is Karl Rahner's essay "Ideas for a Theology of Childhood."[76] He states that he is not aiming at pedagogical reflections but rather searching for what the Bible has to say about children themselves. More specifically, "In the intention of the Creator and Redeemer of children, what meaning does childhood have, and what task does it lay upon us for the perfecting and saving of humanity? That is the question before us."[77] He divides his work into three sections: "The Unsurpassable Value of Childhood," "The Christian Awareness of Childhood," and "The Fullness of Childhood Consists in Being Children of God." In the first section, he argues that, while most consider childhood a stage to grow out of and leave behind, "rather we go towards it as that which has been achieved in time and redeemed forever in time. We only *become* the children whom we *were* because we gather up time—and in this our childhood too—into our eternity."[78] Childhood is good in itself, not just as a symbol of what we will become.[79] Related to this, in the second section Rahner argues that the child is already fully a human—the child is "already in possession of that value and those depths which are implied in the name of man." By so arguing, he is strongly advocating for valuing the child as he or she is already. This does not mean for Rahner that the child has nothing to learn; instead, he uses language of "the already but not yet," which I too shall advocate. He says, "[W]hat is already present in the child has still to be realized, to become actual in experience."[80] Moving on to what the Bible values in a child, he argues that the New Testament never defines for us what a child is; rather, we know this implicitly and from our own experiences of children. Considering Jesus with the little child (Matthew 19, loosely interpreted), he argues that it is certainly *not* innocence which Jesus points to as important but rather a specific form of dependence: both knowing they have nothing intrinsically that makes them deserve and demand help and yet a carefree trust that God will nonetheless give it.[81] In his last section Rahner talks about how childhood is openness, *infinite* openness, and an openness that the "mature childhood of the adult" can practice through trust in God.[82] In this way the biological child can be both a model for the adult striving for childhood and one who is valued and treated with dignity because of his or her position as model recipient of the kingdom.

There are a few collected volumes on children in the Bible. Stephen Barton's edited volume, *The Family in Theological Perspective*,[83] generally focuses on centuries outside the purview of my own interests. However, James Francis's "Children and Childhood

---

[76] Karl Rahner, "Ideas for a Theology of Childhood," in *Theological Investigations*, Vol VIII: *Further Theology of the Spiritual Life II* (trans. David Bourke; New York: Herder and Herder, 1971), 33–50.
[77] Ibid., 33.
[78] Ibid., 36.
[79] Ibid., 37.
[80] Ibid., 38–9.
[81] Ibid., 41.
[82] Ibid., 48–9.
[83] Stephen Barton, ed., *The Family in Theological Perspective* (Edinburgh: T&T Clark, 1996).

in the New Testament"[84] is noteworthy for its broad focus on children in the Christian Bible, and notes the contextual assumptions that childhood differed essentially from adulthood,[85] as well as the countercultural ways in which Jesus uses children as a model for receiving the Kingdom of God.[86] He argues briefly that in Mark 10:15-16, as well as in the Lukan parallel, the implied characteristic of children invoked is "a sense of glad and wholehearted acceptance as a child receives a gift."[87] Ken M. Campbell's edited work, *Marriage and Family in the Biblical World*,[88] does a better job than Barton's volume at including children in its purview. Each essay follows a similar pattern of studying marriage and family in their respective contexts (Ancient Near East [ANE], Ancient Israel, Greek, Roman, Second Temple Judaism, and New Testament). Each dedicates a separate section to children, along with husbands, wives, and servants/slaves. The emphasis of the book tends to be on duties toward one another in the family; therefore, the section on children focuses on the general obligation of the child, male and female, to honor and respect one's parents, particularly his or her father. Each essay details specific betrothal and marriage ceremonies. Once again, the interest tends to be legal or cultural, rather than focusing on the transition of boys and girls from childhood to an adult role. All of the articles delve deeply into their respective fields. Both *Children in Late Ancient Christianity*[89] and *Children and Family in Late Antiquity*[90] express similar intentions. Both examine children from a variety of perspectives, such as children as literary characters, children as present in rituals, and children as understood by medical writers. *Children and Family in Late Antiquity* has an additional interest in health and death in late antiquity. Some of its essays intersect with interests of my own. For instance, Inta Ivanovska's study of "Baptized Infants and Pagan Rituals: Cyprian *versus* Augustine"[91] deals with the transition between children and adults via baptismal rites. She examines both Cyprian and Augustine, who have conflicting views of the qualities children lack when born, particularly owing to sin. However, both of these volumes concern themselves with children in centuries far too late to inform my own research directly.

The edited volume *Early Christian Families in Context: An Interdisciplinary Dialogue*[92] divides its constituents into sections like "Archeology of *Domos* and *Insulae*" and "Domestic Values: Equality, Suffering," as well as sections on women, slaves, and

---

[84] James Francis, "Children and Childhood in the New Testament," in Barton, *The Family in Theological Perspective*, 65–85.
[85] Ibid., 70–1.
[86] Ibid., 72–80.
[87] Ibid., 76.
[88] Ken M. Campbell, ed., *Marriage and Family in the Biblical World* (Downers Grove: InterVarsity, 2003).
[89] Horn and Phenix, eds., *Children in Late Ancient Christianity*.
[90] Christian Laes, Katarina Mustakallio, and Ville Vuolanto, eds., *Children and Family in Late Antiquity* (Interdisciplinary Studies in Ancient Culture and Religion 15; Walpole: Peeters, 2015).
[91] Inta Ivanovska, "Baptized Infants and Pagan Rituals: Cyprian *versus* Augustine," in Horn and Phenix, *Children in Late Ancient Christianity*, 46–73.
[92] David L Balch and Carolyn Osiek, eds., *Early Christian Families in Context: An Interdisciplinary Dialogue* (Grand Rapids: Eerdmans, 2003).

children. The section on children has two articles of note. Beryl Rawson[93] discusses customs of commemorating dead children ("Death, Burial, and Commemoration of Children in Roman Italy"). She notes that children aged approximately 3–10 are the "most heavily represented decadal group commemorated."[94] She examines Roman Christian inscriptions as well as those of Roman pagans, and while she nods toward a developing change in attitude toward children, she pushes against the idea that there was a substantially different attitude toward children adopted by Christians from their cultural context.[95] Christian Laes[96] examines the term *delicia* and its cognates, arguing that the "pet slave child" of the Roman household could take many forms, from grotesque novelty, to sexual plaything, to affectionate foster child. Laes makes the connection between children and slaves as marginal beings, but notes that upper-class freeborn children were not regarded as inferior or "lower beings" like slaves were, but, rather, were thought of with "high hopes."[97]

There are three collections of essays that specifically focus on the child and religion, all edited by Marcia Bunge: *The Child in Christian Thought*, *The Child in the Bible*, and *Children and Childhood in World Religions*. Much attention will be paid to *The Child in the Bible*, as its purview is the closest to that of my own, but the other two volumes are also important to mention and to summarize more briefly.

In *The Child in Christian Thought*, Bunge collects essays on the topic of children as seen through the lens of Christian theology throughout the centuries. Her stated purpose is "to offer a critical examination of past theological perspectives on children in order to strengthen ethical and theological reflections on children today and to contribute to the current academic and broader public discussion on children."[98] Engaging thinkers from Augustine to Calvin to Barth, modern authors draw attention not only to technical concepts like original sin and child development but also to practical matters like child-rearing and child abuse. Bunge divides this collection of essays into three general thematic topics: "contributions to the history of Christian thought and of conceptions of childhood,"[99] "perspectives on the nature of children,"[100] and "insights into obligations to children."[101] Of particular note in this collection is Judith Gundry's essay, "The Least and the Greatest: Children in the New Testament,"[102] which will be addressed in a later section devoted to her corpus of work, as well as Dawn DeVries's article, "'Be Converted and Become as Little Children': Friedrich

---

[93] Beryl Rawson, "Death, Burial, and Commemoration of Children in Roman Italy," in Balch and Osiek, *Early Christian Families in Context*, 277–97.
[94] Ibid., 279.
[95] Ibid., 296.
[96] Christian Laes, "Desperately Different? *Delicia* Children in the Roman Household," in Balch and Osiek, *Early Christian Families in Context*, 298–326.
[97] Ibid., 317.
[98] Bunge, ed., *The Child in Christian Thought*, 7.
[99] Ibid., 10.
[100] Ibid., 13.
[101] Ibid., 20.
[102] Judith M. Gundry-Volf, "The Least and the Greatest: Children in the New Testament," in Bunge, *The Child in Christian Thought*, 29–60.

Schleiermacher on the Religious Significance of Childhood."[103] One of DeVries's stated intents is to examine how Schleiermacher "defines the special gifts of childhood— the unique genius that characterizes this stage of human development."[104] She briefly recounts Schleiermacher's thoughts on Mark 10:13-16, essentially boiling down his understanding of children as model recipients in this passage to what he sees as innocent present-ness—being unconcerned by both past and future.[105] DeVries further explicates the religious significance of childhood for Schleiermacher as having two sides. First, children's relationship to their caregivers, particularly in their "utter vulnerability and dependence" as well as their ability to easily and painlessly accept such dependence, mirrors the ideal relationship between humanity and God.[106] Second, and coming from the adult perspective, child-rearing is of utmost importance, as a child can be formed in beneficial and harmful ways, deeply influencing and even causing either their connection to or alienation from God.[107]

With Don Browning, Bunge also edited a volume entitled *Children and Childhood in World Religions*.[108] In this volume, six of the world's major religions are considered: Judaism, Christianity, Islam, Hinduism, Buddhism, and Confucianism, and what they think about children as discovered through their "classic and formative texts."[109] Each article attempts to answer some or all of a set of guiding questions, which include topics such as a child's basic nature, their role in religious practices, and obligations to children, including moral and spiritual formation.[110] In the chapter on Christianity,[111] Marcia Bunge and John Wall survey texts from the New Testament as well as selections from periods of Christian history beginning with the early church and ending with the twentieth century. They argue that common themes emerge: A child's nature is a tension between the *imago Dei* and a fallen creature; parents have a responsibility to care for and train children; adults should morally and spiritually guide children and bring them into religious practice and activity.[112] However, particular manifestations of each of these themes are highly varied throughout the centuries and depend on one's core beliefs about sin, grace, and childhood itself. Each of the essays collected in this volume tends to be highly generalized due to the immense scope it undertakes, and yet the collection as a whole is valuable, blending multiple and religiously diverse strains of thought on children.

Finally, Marcia Bunge, along with Terence Fretheim and Beverly Gaventa, edited a collection of essays entitled *The Child in the Bible*.[113] This collection is one of the

---

[103] Dawn DeVries, "'Be Converted and Become as Little Children': Friedrich Schleiermacher on the Religious Significance of Childhood," in Bunge, *The Child in Christian Thought*, 329–49.
[104] Ibid., 331.
[105] Ibid., 339.
[106] Ibid., 348.
[107] Ibid.
[108] Don S. Browning and Marcia J. Bunge, eds., *Children and Childhood in World Religions* (New Brunswick: Rutgers University Press, 2009).
[109] Ibid., 2.
[110] Ibid., 5–6.
[111] Marcia J. Bunge and John Wall, "Christianity," in Browning and Bunge, *Children and Childhood in World Religion*, 83–149.
[112] Ibid., 85–7.
[113] Marcia J. Bunge, Terence E. Fretheim, and Beverly Roberts Gaventa, eds., *The Child in the Bible* (Grand Rapids: Eerdmans, 2008).

best and most comprehensive groups of essays on the topic of children in the biblical text. It boasts some of the central names in biblical scholarship: Terence Fretheim, Jacqueline Lapsley, Beverly Gaventa, and Walter Brueggemann, whose contributions are arranged in sections of Hebrew scriptures, New Testament texts, and thematic essays. Jacqueline E. Lapsley argues[114] that while it may seem at first as though children are in the background of Isaiah, they, however, are very much in the foreground, serving partially as indicators of Israel's relationship with God. Even more, she says that "they are not simply barometers; rather, children in the book of Isaiah are signs of and, in an important way, constitutive of the flourishing that God would have for Israel, and by extension, for all humanity."[115] Judith Gundry's essay[116] is sufficiently important to warrant, along with another article, its own section, and will be discussed later at length. In "'What Then Will This Child Become?': Perspectives on Children in the Gospel of Luke,"[117] John T. Carroll surveys children in the Gospel of Luke, generally associating them with low status and humbleness and insisting that "in the upside-down, inside-out world of reversal that is God's dominion, children—like others among the socially marginalized—will be specially honored guests."[118] He tentatively posits that a child's ability to play may give a sense of the hospitality of a community (citing Luke 7:31-35). Carroll finally notes that the Gospel of Luke, while sympathetic to children, can be uncompromising about biological family relationships: familial bonds are to be rejected in favor of those formed in the family of Christ. Both Beverly Gaventa[119] and Reidar Aasgaard[120] examine children within Paul's letters. Gaventa catalogues the few implied and explicit references to children before identifying some of the ways Paul employs metaphorical language about children. This primarily exists in Paul's use of a parent-child relationship when referring to himself and the church to which he is writing. She finishes by using Pauline theology to reconstruct modern views of children and family. Reidar Aasgaard similarly explores Paul's rhetorical use of childhood, primarily employing the four categories of semantic fields that Peter Müller uses to outline the word "child" in the New Testament[121] (viz., kinship, social position, formation, and belonging) to talk about Paul's metaphorical language of childhood. In many cases, Paul's use of metaphorical language adheres to conventional ancient conceptions of children: innocent, beloved, weak, unformed, and in need of care. Aasgaard points out the surprising way that Paul describes himself as an infant. Finally, and most important for the purposes of my project, Aasgaard mentions the ideas of the child as marginal

---

[114] Jacqueline E. Lapsley, "'Look! The Children and I Are as Signs and Portents in Israel': Children in Isaiah," in Bunge, Fretheim, and Gaventa, *The Child in the Bible*, 82–102.

[115] Ibid., 83.

[116] Judith M. Gundry, "Children in the Gospel of Mark, with Special Attention to Jesus's Blessing of the Children (Mark 10: 13-16) and the Purpose of Mark," in Bunge, Fretheim, and Gaventa, *The Child in the Bible*, 143–76.

[117] John T. Carroll, "'What Then Will This Child Become?': Perspectives on Children in the Gospel of Luke," in Bunge, Fretheim, and Gaventa, *The Child in the Bible*, 177–94.

[118] Ibid., 192.

[119] Beverly Roberts Gaventa, "Finding a Place for Children in the Letters of Paul," in Bunge, Fretheim, and Gaventa, *The Child in the Bible*, 233–48.

[120] Reidar Aasgaard, "Like a Child: Paul's Rhetorical Use of Childhood," in Bunge, Fretheim, and Gaventa, *The Child in the Bible*, 249–77.

[121] Peter Müller, *In der Mitte der Gemeinde: Kinder im Neuen Testament* (Neukirchen-Vluyn: Neukirchener, 1992), 165–200.

and transitioning within the context of formation. One ancient view of children is that of immaturity—physical, mental, moral—congruent with the idea of the child as unfinished.[122] Forming a child into the ideal—an adult male—took effort and training, primarily in the form of education. Paul uses many of the traditional pedagogical tools and language within his letters for training the congregations he writes.

Aasgaard's particular connection between the unformed, transitional child and the language of already-but-not-yet within the Christian life is rare and occurs only in one or two other places. One such place is found in a footnote of Keith White's article "'He Placed a Little Child in the Midst': Jesus, the Kingdom, and Children,"[123] which is likewise found in *The Child in the Bible*. The majority of White's essay is focused on children in Matthew, emphasizing children *qua* children, rather than as metaphors or symbols. He argues that children in Matthew most fully illustrate and realize the nature of God's kingdom. He identifies both play and a child's status as liminal as among the ways they are uniquely able to identify and show Jesus's message. In a footnote (33), he says that, while it is not a major part of his argument here, "one fruitful line of inquiry concerns the congruity between the kingdom of heaven, which is both 'now and not yet,' and children, who are also fully human and yet still in the process of becoming mature adults."[124]

In addition to his piece in *The Child in the Bible*, Reidar Aasgaard's helpful article, "Children in Antiquity and Early Christianity: Research History and Central Issues,"[125] surveys research on children in both antiquity and early Christianity. He both details some of the methodological challenges inherent to studying children in the ancient world (e.g., the extremely limited nature of general material from the ancient world and an even greater paucity of material referring to or focusing on children),[126] and identifies six distinct research areas (including formation, family roles, and cultural roles).[127] Briefly detailing the research both in the Greco-Roman/Jewish field and that of early Christianity, he also summarizes the basic findings in each of his six research areas, as well as points out some of the problematic definitions. For instance, in his section on attitudes toward children, he points out the ambiguity of the word "attitude": Was there only *one* attitude? Was there a difference between attitudes about children as a concept versus the practical reality of the social role they were given? How would one measure attitudes?[128] Here, too, he states the point, made in his later essay in *The Child in the Bible*, about children as unfinished humans, as liminal beings.[129] This article is concise, comprehensive, and extremely useful in laying out the major issues surrounding studies on children.

---

[122] Reidar Aasgaard, "Like a Child," in Bunge, Fretheim, and Gaventa, *The Child in the Bible*, 260.
[123] Keith White, "'He Placed a Little Child in the Midst': Jesus, the Kingdom, and Children," in Bunge, Fretheim, and Gaventa, *The Child in the Bible*, 353–74.
[124] Ibid., 367.
[125] Reidar Aasgaard, "Children in Antiquity and Early Christianity: Research History and Central Issues," *Familia* 33 (2006): 23–46.
[126] Ibid., 24–5.
[127] Ibid., 25.
[128] Ibid., 31.
[129] Ibid.

Angela Shier-Jones's edited volume, *Children of God: Towards a Theology of Childhood*,[130] looks at children in all stages. The essays cover a variety of interesting topics, including the pain and potential of birth,[131] the role of education for forming a child,[132] and two treatments of the transition between childhood and adulthood. In "Maturity, Delinquency and Rebellion," Sheryl Anderson questions the usual association between teenage rebellion, sin, and puberty. While acknowledging that some argue that teenage rebellion is a post–Second World War construct, she argues that "from the earliest of times societies have struggled to manage the behavior of the young, particularly young men."[133] She briefly quotes Hesiod and then uses Augustine as her primary point of reference.[134] Similarly Jocelyn Bryan's essay, "Being and Becoming: Adolescence,"[135] on its face has a strikingly similar interest to my own. She is interested in the process by which adolescents become adults, and even briefly mentions "markers" that transition children to adulthood, like "*rites of passage* and training in preparation for new responsibilities."[136] However, rather than delving into anthropology, as one might expect, or mentioning any *rites of passage* other than the Bar Mitzvah, which she fails to locate in history, she proceeds to Erik Erikson, connecting his theories to the Prodigal Son. Her methodology, therefore, is far from my own. This holds true for Shier-Jones's *Children of God* as a whole. While the topics are similar to my own interests, the approaches of these articles are not those of a biblical specialist. Consequently, the articles tend to lack careful exegesis or historical context.

Theology Today devoted its January 2000 issue[137] to articles about children, mostly covering modern topics like youth ministry or Christian education. A few articles, like Judith Gundry-Volf's article,[138] to be reviewed below, focus on children in the Bible. Similarly, the April 2001 issue of *Interpretation*[139] focuses on children in the Bible, with articles covering topics in the Old and New Testaments, as well as articles on theology of childhood and modern social issues like children in gangs.

Children in New Testament Studies

S. Legasse's *Jesu et l'enfant: "Enfants", "petits" et "simples" dans la tradition synoptique*[140] looks at a variety of texts in the Synoptic Gospels that either refer to biological children

---

[130] Angela Shier-Jones, ed., *Children of God: Towards a Theology of Childhood* (Peterborough: Epworth, 2007).
[131] Esther Shreeve, "Birth: Pain and Potential," in Shier-Jones, *Children of God*, 21–40.
[132] David Deeks and Angela Shier-Jones, "Moulding and Shaping: Education," in Shier-Jones, *Children of God*, 63–83.
[133] Sheryl Anderson, "Maturity, Delinquency and Rebellion," in Shier-Jones, *Children of God*, 119.
[134] Ibid., 119–20.
[135] Jocelyn Bryan, "Being and Becoming: Adolescence," in Shier-Jones, *Children of God*, 135–58.
[136] Ibid., 138.
[137] *TheoT* 56 (2000).
[138] Judith Gundry-Volf, "To Such as These Belongs the Reign of God: Jesus and Children," *TheoT* 56 (2000): 469–80.
[139] *Interp* 55 (2001).
[140] S. Legasse, *Jesu et l'enfant: "Enfants", "petits" et "simples" dans la tradition synoptique* (Paris: Librairie Lecoffre, 1968).

or use terms like "small" or "least." He uses a redaction-critical lens, attempting to assign sayings to Jesus himself or to the writer of each respective Gospel. In the latter case he makes arguments about problems in the Evangelists' churches that caused certain things to be written (for instance, the "little ones" of Matthew 10:42 and the original context of Mark 9:36-37 may refer to somewhat troublesome missionaries). He addresses Mark 10:13-16 several times, ultimately identifying Mark 10:15 to a Markan insertion. He scoffs at the idea that the "child" here represents innocence or something of that nature, but rather firmly thinks that the child represents helplessness and dependence. He tentatively assigns a positive sense of "trusting faith" to children: as children trust in parents to help them, so, too, the gift of the kingdom is given freely to those who do not deserve it. Hans-Hartmut Schroeder, writing just a few years later, studied the parent-child relationship in his monograph *Eltern un Kinder in der Verkundigung Jesu: Eine hermeneutische und exegetische Untersuchung*. His interest is in family relationships and whether there is, in his words, an "Intention" in the New Testament texts at changing the parent-child relationship.[141] Essentially he argues that while Jesus says some radical things about separating from family (in particular, Mark 3:20-21, 31-35, and 10:28-30), these were not to be taken as normative, nor did the early church understand them as such. He shows little interest in examining the child as such; his concern lies in the child's position in the family structure.

Peter Müller's work *In der Mitte der Gemeinde: Kinder im Neuen Testament*[142] is one of the rare full monographs examining children in the New Testament. He begins with a study of Mark 10:13-16, calling it the "exemplarischen" text. He essentially argues that children in this passage function in two interrelated ways. First, they represent a "Modell des Glaubens," as those who cannot do anything to earn God's favor; Jesus embraces them out of their lack and dependence.[143] Second, Müller argues that children can function on a social level similar to that of the "little ones" or "sinners and tax collectors"—namely, those who have not. Müller argues that the community of faith, particularly in the world of the writers of the New Testament, was in need of reminding that members are not to vie for power or authority. Rather, "Das Kind in der Mitte der Jünger ist eine Absage an deren Streben um die guten Platze, in der Gemeinde ebenso wie im Himmel."[144] Children, therefore, are not just models for faith but also models of ideal community interaction. Müller carefully examines the Greco-Roman and Jewish literature on children, moving from Mark 10:13-16 to examine children in the Synoptic Gospels, as well as in the New Testament letters, particularly the household code material. He argues that there is a consistent, broadly construed theme of welcoming children throughout both Gospels and Epistles, and that this theme reflects the problems early Christian communities experienced with agreeing on the position of children in the church. His interest in discerning the problems of the first-century communities of faith branches off from my own interest, but his

---

[141] Hans-Hartmut Schroeder, *Eltern un Kinder in der Verkundigung Jesu: Eine hermeneutische und exegetische Untersuchung* (Theologische Forschung 53; Hamburg-Bergstedt: Reich, 1972), 10.
[142] Müller, *In der Mitte der Gemeinde*.
[143] Ibid., 287-8.
[144] Ibid., 287.

scholarship on children in the ancient world, as well as careful analysis of Mark 10:13-16, closely aligns his work with my own.

In *When Children Became People: The Birth of Childhood in Early Christianity*,[145] O. M. Bakke traces the developing notion of the child through the Greco-Roman and patristic periods. His twofold quest is (1) to ascertain how Christians thought about children and (2) how this developing theology about children affected their practical education and treatment.[146] Beginning with concepts of children in the Greco-Roman world, he moves through the works of authors such as Plato, Aristotle, Cicero, Pliny, Pseudo-Plutarch, and Quintilian. Bakke emphasizes the philosophical tradition as mainly seeing the child as the negative counterpart of the adult male. Children lack what the ideal male have: reason, strength, courage. He notes that if they are seen as interesting, it is in their potential to become and develop into the ideal male.[147] Moving on to patristic notions of children's "nature" and "qualities," Bakke begins by discussing the fathers' interpretation of the biblical metaphors of children and childhood as models for Christian life.[148] Surveying the works of Clement of Alexandria, Origen, Chrysostom, and Augustine, Bakke argues that some of the qualities ascribed to children are that of simplicity, loyalty, and obedience to their fathers, and unconcern for the cares of the world. Origen highlights the idea of the lack of sexual desire; Augustine, their physical weakness. A major concern for Bakke is the patristic understanding of the child and original sin: Is the child "innocent"?[149] Augustine is particularly famous for his affirmation of the infant's ability to be greedy and selfish, limited only by his or her physically and mentally underdeveloped state.[150] However, prior to Augustine, especially in Eastern sources, there is a sense of a child's innocence. Clement of Alexandria, for instance, insists that a child's "simplicity" is at the heart of Mark 10:15. Bakke argues that Clement is specifically responding to the sense of the Greco-Roman world that children were unable to reason and replacing that negative characteristic with the positive sense of "innocence."[151] His work offers useful background for the present project: he brings forward some of the earliest Christian voices interpreting the biblical understanding of the child, including that of Mark 10. He furthermore takes time to lay out some of the predominant Greco-Roman sources mentioning children. On the converse side, he may overstate the effects of Christianity on the child's place in society. Furthermore, his survey of both Greco-

---

[145] O. M. Bakke, *When Children Became People: The Birth of Childhood in Early Christianity* (Minneapolis: Augsburg Fortress, 2005).
[146] Ibid., location 165 of 5462.
[147] Ibid., location 342 of 5462.
[148] Ibid., location 861 of 5462.
[149] Ibid., location 853 of 5462.
[150] Sample quotes from the *Confessions* are illuminating: "Who remindeth me of the sins of my infancy? For in Thy sight none is pure from sin, not even the infant whose life is but a day upon the earth... what then was my sin? Was it that I hung upon the breast and cried?... what I then did was worth reproof, but since I could not understand reproof, custom and reason forbade me to be reproved... the weakness then of infant limbs, not its will, is its innocence. Myself have seen and known even a baby envious; it could not speak, yet it turned pale and looked bitterly on its foster brother." Augustine, *Confessions* (trans. Edward Pusey. Uhrichsville: Barbour, 1984), 10.
[151] Bakke, *When Children Became People*, location 921 of 5462.

Roman and patristic sources tends to leave significant gaps in source material without making clear why certain philosophers or theologians are excluded. Finally, because his interest lies in the first five centuries of Christianity, the latter two-thirds of his book have little bearing on the present project.

Another full-length work devoted to exploring childhood throughout the first few centuries CE is William Strange's *Children in the Early Church*.[152] Strange first takes a cursory look at Greco-Roman and Jewish presentations of children. He considers a child's life stages (birth, naming, education, coming of age[153]), as well as features attributed to children. He also brings up issues of infanticide and abuse. He tends to speak in extremes in regard to the Greco-Roman context, arguing for both "tenderness" but also intense cruelty.[154] He speaks more favorably of Jewish habits and perspective, highlighting a greater concern for the life and education of its children.[155] Strange moves on to identify children in the Gospels, from Jesus as infant and child to the interactions of children with adults like Jesus, the disciples, and parents. Here he notes that, while Jesus clearly valued children and used them as examples, he did not treat them on the same level as adults. In fact, the parents are always the ones spoken to, rather than the children themselves.[156] Strange's book has the merit of focusing specifically on children, exploring the background of the New Testament world, and explicating the words of Jesus in reference to children. In addition, he touches (albeit briefly) on transitional rites to adulthood. However, his work tends to operate on a general, rather than a specialized, level, leaving much to be desired in terms of careful, well-documented scholarship, and deep engagement of each individual topic. In addition, some of his characterizations of Greco-Roman ideology and behavior are both sensationalized and dated,[157] undermining further his book's place in a serious scholarly discussion of children in the New Testament.

Keith White, whose chapter in *The Child in the Bible* has already been mentioned, also has two works worth citing. The first is an unpublished address[158] (November 9, 1999) entitled, "Childhood and the Kingdom of God." In it he mentions the idea of the resonance between the "now" and "not-yet" of the kingdom and the nature of a child as both fully human and also in the process of becoming.[159] He urges a dialogue of theology with sociology, and notes the fact that even in sociology, the interest in children is surprisingly recent. Second, in his full-length work *Entry*

---

[152] William A. Strange, *Children in the Early Church: Children in the Ancient World, the New Testament and the Early Church* (Carlisle: Paternoster, 1996).

[153] He does a particularly nice, although brief, job of noting the rituals associated with the transition from childhood to adulthood.

[154] Ibid., 37.

[155] Ibid.

[156] Ibid., 64.

[157] His brief thoughts on infant exposure in particular bear the markers of emotional, rather than informed research. Cf. Strange, *Children in the Early Church*, 21–2; Harris, "Child-Exposure in the Roman Empire," 1–22; D. Engels, "The Problem of Female Infanticide in the Greco-Roman World," *CPh* 75 (1980): 112–20; Golden, "Did the Ancients Care When Their Children Died?," 152–63, among many others.

[158] Many thanks to Keith White, who emailed me a copy directly.

[159] White, "Childhood and the Kingdom of God," 3.

Point: Towards Child Theology with Matthew 18,¹⁶⁰ co-authored with Haddon Willmer, he aims at examining Matthew 18:1-14, specifically calling their book "neither critical commentary nor pure exegesis… [but] rather an essay, venturing ideas; our daring is greater than our competence."¹⁶¹ Taking seven key words ("child," "kingdom," "temptation," "disciple," "humility," "reception," "father"), they muse on the nature of Matthew 18, ultimately ending up in a place very similar to that of Judith Gundry (see below). The child represents the way of the cross, a way of humility and self-denial.¹⁶² Equally important to their view of the child in Matthew 18 is that the child must be *received*. The child, as a representation of all who are alienated, is nonetheless a whole and complete person, and much be accepted as such.¹⁶³ White is clear that he is not aiming at critical scholarship, and he certainly does not attain it. However, his general sense of the child is admirable, and he comes closest to my own understanding of the transitional nature of the child of almost any work I have found. In some respects, the present book offers a theoretical scaffold for White's tentative thesis.

Edmund Newey's book, *Children of God: The Child as Source of Theological Anthropology*,¹⁶⁴ examines what it means for a person to be called a "child of God," coming at the question from the perspective of theological anthropology. He uses key figures like Traherne, Rosseau, Schleiermacher, and Peguy to hold up different views of what qualities are associated with the "child." His interest is on the changing associations with childhood throughout the modern era. His contribution to the field of childhood is important, but his interests rarely intersect with my own.

Children in Marcan Studies

Andreas Lindermann's essay "Die Kinder und die Gottesherrschaft: Markus 10,13-16 und die Stellung der Kinder in der späthellenistischen Gesellschaft und im Urchristentum"¹⁶⁵ notes the paucity of references to biological children in the New Testament and compares the general sense of how children were treated in late Hellenistic thought with several New Testament texts that engage with children. He argues that the Hellenistic age showed a change in thinking about the child from that of the previous era: children were now merely considered "unfertig" rather than "unzureichendes Wesen."¹⁶⁶ He argues that, in general, Hellenistic, Roman, Jewish, and Christian sources have a similar viewpoint on children, but that Mark 9:33-37

---

¹⁶⁰ Keith White and Haddon Willmer, *Entry Point: Towards Child Theology with Matthew 18* (London: WTL Publications) 2013.
¹⁶¹ Ibid., 11.
¹⁶² Ibid., 15–17, 112.
¹⁶³ Ibid., 17, 150–4.
¹⁶⁴ Edmund Newey, *Children of God: The Child as Source of Theological Anthropology* (Surrey: Ashgate, 2012).
¹⁶⁵ Andreas Lindermann, "Die Kinder und die Gottesherrschaft: Markus 10, 13-16 und die Stellung der Kinder in der späthellenistischen Gesellschaft und im Urchristentum," in *Die Evangelien und die Apostelgeschichte: Studien zu ihrer Theologie und zu ihrer Geschichte* (WUNT 241; Tübingen: J. C. B. Mohr, 2009).
¹⁶⁶ Ibid., 113.

and Mark 10:13-16 (and their Synoptic parallels) show surprising and different perspectives on children. His analysis of Mark 10:13-16 addresses the debate as to whether child baptism motivated that passage. He finishes by asking what 10:15 intends by "as a child." His conclusion is that "Jesus hat (v. 14c) den Kindern die βασιλεία zugesprochen—gegen äußere Widerstände."[167] That is, Lindermann thinks the child is completely passive but represents one whom others try to deny access to Jesus. Jesus defends such and makes access possible.

Two authors' contributions to the subject of children in the Gospel of Mark stand above all others, and they are similar to the task and purpose of this book. These are Sharon Betsworth's book *The Reign of God Is Such as These: A Socio-Literary Analysis of Daughters in the Gospel of Mark* and Judith Gundry's several essays: "Mark 9:33-37," "To Such as These Belongs the Reign of God: Jesus and Children," "Putting *The Moral Vision of the New Testament* into Focus: A Review," "The Least and the Greatest: Children in the New Testament," and "Children in the Gospel of Mark, with Special Attention to Jesus' Blessing of the Children (Mark 10:13-16) and the Purpose of Mark."

In *The Reign of God Is Such as These*, Betsworth tackles the project of analyzing daughters in Mark. Her work follows a socio-literary approach, analyzing Mark's literary use of daughters while also comparing them to other, contemporaneous literary documents in which daughters play a role. She first dedicates a chapter "reconstructing the life of daughters in the Greco–Roman world,"[168] which she summarizes by saying that they held a "socially tenuous position."[169] By way of their gender, daughters had a higher risk of infant exposure, tended to receive less education compared to sons, and were married at a far younger age.[170] The rearing of a daughter tended to focus on her potential for marriage and motherhood: she was kept closely watched to maintain her virginity and purity, which limited her exposure to the world outside her house, and taught by her mother necessary domestic tasks and skills such as weaving.[171] Daughters were simultaneously esteemed by their fathers and held to a strict standard: utter submission was expected, as was chastity before marriage and perfect fidelity thereafter.[172] While Betsworth's reconstruction of the social location of daughters gives a picture of a rather stark, sheltered, and powerless existence, in Chapter 3 she argues that literary representations of daughters often push the boundaries of traditional roles for girls. For instance, they are given names and voices, sometimes they are the primary focus of literary texts, they often are separated from their families, and they are vulnerable to threats and yet are protected by deities.[173] This boundary-pushing had limits, however: the literary texts uphold the vital importance of chastity before and fidelity after marriage for these young women.[174] In Chapter 4, she argues that Mark follows a similar pattern of boundary-pushing in regard to daughters. In

---

[167] Ibid., 132.
[168] Sharon Betsworth, *The Reign of God* (New York: T&T Clark, 2010), 27.
[169] Ibid., 59.
[170] Ibid.
[171] Ibid., 46.
[172] Ibid., 56.
[173] Ibid., 95.
[174] Ibid., 96.

Mark daughters are shown as protected by Jesus (as demonstrated by his healing of them), and, therefore, included in the reign of God. She argues that they in particular represent the last or the least and that, as such, they also represent the ones who will be first in God's kingdom.[175] It will become clear that Betsworth's approach and focus are similar to the project proposed in this book; however, there are a few key ways in which her work differs from my own. First, her focus is on women, given the epithet "daughter"; her study is not confined to the young. Moreover, she does not consider stories of male children or stories where the child's gender is unspecified. Finally, while referring to Mark 10:15 in her book's title, her interest does not lie in explicating its full meaning; rather, she uses it as a touchstone for her own interest in daughters.

Betsworth's later book, *Children in Early Christian Narratives*,[176] expands her interest in children to include an examination of all four Gospels, as well as the *Infancy Gospel of Thomas*, and the *Protevangelium of James*. She includes a chapter titled "Children in the Ancient Mediterranean Context," which details aspects of a child's life, including her transition to adulthood, and specifically notes that "ritual frequently marked the transition."[177] Her methodology and basic thesis are consonant with those of her earlier, published dissertation: children throughout the Gospels are represented as important and worthy of attention. The Gospels issued from a social context in which children occupied a place in society where they were loved and important in certain sectors but not valued by others.[178] A similar dichotomy exists in the Gospels: children are specifically included in the new family of Jesus, just as other marginalized figures were, and yet Jesus also brings a "disruption" to biological families.[179]

In her various articles and essays, Judith Gundry continuously insists on not only the importance of children as a metaphorical model for adults but also for the importance of children in and of themselves. Her thesis in her article "Children in the Gospel of Mark" is as follows:

> I will argue that Mark depicts Jesus as overcoming the religious and cultural obstacles to embracing children's full and equal participation in the eschatological reign of God, and so motivates the audience of the Gospel likewise to overcome the religious and cultural obstacles to faith in the crucified Jesus and their own participation in the eschatological reign of God.[180]

Gundry specifically focuses on the particular way Mark represents the Kingdom of God throughout the Gospel. She argues that Jesus both inaugurates the Kingdom of God, through healings, teaching exorcisms, and his death and resurrection, but also that the kingdom is yet to come in full power.[181] She argues, too, that there is a distinction

---

[175] Ibid., 142.
[176] Sharon Betsworth, *Children in Early Christian Narratives* (New York: Bloomsbury, 2015).
[177] Ibid., 37.
[178] Ibid., 2–3.
[179] Ibid., 4.
[180] Gundry, "Children in the Gospel of Mark," in Bunge, Fretheim, and Gaventa, *The Child in the Bible*, 143.
[181] Ibid., 151.

between *receiving* the Kingdom of God, an action related to the present, and of *entering into it,* one reserved for the future.[182] It is interesting that she does not make the further connection to the child's unique transitional nature: one tied both to the present and to the future. The connection she does make, instead, is the child's ownership of the kingdom as a function of need—the same need, Gundry argues, as that of the tax collectors and sinners in Mark 2.[183] She believes that need, and need alone, can explain their particular relationship to the kingdom. Even in the stories in Mark when miracles are done to children, she emphatically notes that not only are the children silent and passive throughout these (Jairus's daughter is already dead, and the Syrophoenician's daughter is not even present) but that even after the healing, the child seems to have no "attitudinal response" to Jesus.[184] Finally, following Willi Egger, she asserts that part of the way one must be childlike to enter the Kingdom of God is to be understood by way of Jewish apocalyptic literature and later works like the Talmud. Jesus, Egger argues, employs a distinct formula in Mark 10:15 for conditions to enter the Kingdom of God. Generally the conditions found in Talmudic and Jewish apocalyptic literature involved fulfillment of the law in some kind and degree. However, by contrast, Jesus holds up a child—a "non-doer of the law"[185]—as the entrance requirement, thereby stressing dependence on God and God alone.[186] Furthermore, Egger argues (and Gundry agrees) that Jesus echoes Old Testament imagery of God's choosing the small/weak/helpless *child* Israel as God's own—again emphasizing Israel's radical dependence on God. Gundry concludes by proposing that "Jesus brings this Old Testament prophetic tradition to a climax by asserting that *only* those who stand in the least palatable, most shameful and unenviable position of dependence on God, namely, that of a little child, will enter the Kingdom of God."[187] Moreover, she asserts, this is intended as a liberating statement: *anyone* might enter.[188]

Gundry argues much the same point in her earlier article, "To Such as These Belongs the Reign of God: Jesus and Children."[189] Here her formulation is slightly different: she argues that entering the reign of God as a child "seems to involve *both* a certain status—actual dependence on God—*and* a corresponding quality—trust—that are both 'childlike.'"[190] Furthermore, in this article she highlights children as models of humility especially appropriate for church leaders, children as particularly important to serve as the "least," children as representatives of Jesus as the "suffering Son of Man," and children as capable of true confession of Jesus as Christ.[191]

---

[182] Ibid., 151, footnote 30.
[183] Ibid., 151.
[184] Ibid., 152.
[185] Ibid., 169. This point of being a "non-doer" is important, as Egger/Gundry argue that Judaism understands children to be too young to be held to obedience to the law.
[186] It is important to note that Gundry attempts to avoid anti-Jewish tendencies in this statement, noting (p. 170) the varied and diverse senses in which works of the law can be understood.
[187] Gundry, "Children in the Gospel of Mark," 172.
[188] Ibid.
[189] Gundry-Volf, "To Such as These Belongs the Reign of God," 469–80.
[190] Ibid., 474.
[191] Ibid., 480.

In "The Least and the Greatest: Children in the New Testament," Gundry again continues her theme of emphasizing the importance of children in the texts of the Bible itself, as well as the importance of children as models for adults to emulate. She takes more time than usual in this article to contextualize the New Testament passages on children within both a Hellenistic as well as Old Testament and early Jewish context. Here as well, the precise formation of her consistent thesis across all of her writings is that there are five main ways Jesus emphasizes the significance of children: including them in the reign of God, making them models of entering that reign, portraying them as models of greatness, serving them as a sign of greatness, and equating service of them with receiving Christ himself.[192]

Overview of the Current Project

As has been seen, there is an increased interest in studying children in Greco-Roman and biblical contexts. This interest, however, is relatively new, and while scholars are now investigating various aspects of childhood, much remains to be studied. In Mark 10:13-16 Jesus reproaches his disciples for denying children access to him, and he insists that adults must enter the Kingdom of God like these children. My book aims to answer the question of what Jesus means by entering the kingdom of God "like a child."

In Chapter 2, I survey contemporaneous Greco-Roman and Jewish literature using a sociohistorical lens. I look at the ways children are spoken of, what characteristics they are believed to exhibit, and, in particular, the ways in which adults are compared to children. Children in the ancient world were thought to have both negative and positive characteristics; however, their negative characteristics tended to be far more prominent. In general, they were thought to be "undeveloped" physically, intellectually, and morally, and basically inferior to adults in a culture whose mature, well-born males set the standard. The positive characteristics of children tend to be narrowly conceived: charming actions, endearing speech, and pleasant appearance. Such characteristics tended to be age-appropriate, normally not admirable when imposed on an adult. Chapter 2 also notes the difficulty ancient thinkers had in accounting for the transition between childhood and adulthood. How is it that a young boy, so devoid of the virtues of an adult male, is able to develop into the latter? As we shall see, the quality of "potential" often addresses this question, sometimes in reference to the lost potential of a child's untimely death.

Chapter 3 develops the topic of the transition from childhood to adulthood, drawing from the theories of seminal anthropologists such as Arnold van Gennep and Victor Turner. Attention will be paid to *rites of passage*, which include separation from previous modes of being, transition from one state of being to the next, and reincorporation into a new state of being. The middle, or transitional, stage emerges as especially interesting: in Turner's terms, it is an unstable period of "liminality" that affects both individuals and the incorporative group into which children and

---

[192] Gundry-Volf, "The Least and the Greatest," 36.

other novitiates must be initiated. The ceremony of the *toga virilis* and the wedding ceremony were occasions of momentous transformation for, respectively, young boys and young girls.

In Chapter 4, we move to the Markan material itself, applying these socio-anthropological approaches to the Gospel. I first examine Mark 10:13-16, noting the exegetical difficulty raised by Jesus's admonition, ὃς ἂν μὴ δέξηται τὴν βασιλείαν τοῦ θεοῦ ὡς παιδίον, οὐ μὴ εἰσέλθῃ εἰς αὐτήν (emphasis mine). I argue that Mark should be understood from the perspective of a *rite of passage*—with a twist. Jesus speaks of entering the kingdom and of the conditions necessary to enter it. By identifying a child as the model entrant into the kingdom—one who is intellectually or morally inferior—Jesus radically, even shockingly, signals the kingdom's values, which run diametrically opposite to those of the Gospel's social world. Cognate values of humility and social reversal are suggested by the Matthean and Lukan parallels to Mark 10:13-16, as well as Mark 9:33-37, Matthew 18:1-5, and John 3. For Mark, the ideal member of the kingdom looks much more like a child than a mature adult. The initiation rites into the kingdom represent a radical reversal of social expectations.

In Chapter 5, I turn from the steps necessary to enter the kingdom to what an exemplary kingdom member looks like. Mark 10:13-16 serves as a key by which to understand Mark: an exemplary member of God's kingdom looks like a child. Drawing on both negative and positive associations with children in Mark's social world, I examine the characterizations of Jesus and of his disciples throughout Mark's Gospel. Discipleship is a notoriously tricky topic in Mark: the twelve whom Jesus chooses seem to be anything but exemplary. Furthermore, they seem to go from mediocre to worse: instead of improving, morally or intellectually, throughout the narrative, they appear more and more foolish, until the story ends with their scattering and denying Jesus at his arrest and trial. Scholarship has struggled to account for why the disciples are portrayed in such negative terms. I argue that it is possible to view the disciples as acting in ways that correlate well, albeit ironically, with contemporaneous literature's description of children. The purpose of such a literary twist would be twofold. First, the disciples' childish behavior serves as a literary foil to Jesus's own actions, allowing him to shine as the competent, wise, and a faithful teacher or parent. Second, the disciples' childish conduct engages and challenges the implied audience, which must be prepared to look as foolish and uncomprehending as the disciples.

Chapter 5 also maps the qualities of children onto Jesus himself throughout the narrative. His passion and resurrection predictions correspond to the tripartite structure of a funerary *rite of passage*. More pointedly in Mark, it is Jesus himself who functions as the model of true discipleship. As such, he is consistently identified in childlike terms: either as the "Son of God" or as the "Son of Man." Moreover, Jesus constantly proclaims the importance of childlike behavior: the hierarchy of the kingdom favors the lowly and the servants. He insists on breaking down normal social connections, rejects his own biological family, and asks his followers to give up wealth and status—in all cases invoking characteristics of dependence, inferiority, and humility commonly associated with children. Jesus's childlikeness culminates at the cross: apparently ineloquent and incompetent while on trial, ridiculed and disowned at his crucifixion. At Golgotha he dies stripped of all respect, honor, social connections, and even apparent connection with God.

2

"Like a Child": Perceptions of Children in the Ancient World

How were children generally regarded in the Greco-Roman and Jewish world near the date of the composition of Mark's Gospel? This is a complicated question, as children are not featured prominently in classical literature. The ideal figure was the educated, elite male; anything that was not that—slaves, women, and children—was not worthy of much attention. Children tend to be mentioned or described only in passing in philosophical texts, personal letters, educational materials, gravestones, and occasional poetry. Furthermore, from the little that was recorded about them, there was a variety of thoughts about children. Philosophers, in particular, occasionally used children as examples of growth; *how* they grew up and were transformed into adults were matters of debate.

This chapter summarizes general impressions about children, focusing in particular on the ways in which children were used metaphorically. Special attention will be given to the less common but valuable use of the child as a transitional figure in philosophical works. In particular, some works by Cicero and Seneca will be examined, each of whom lived and wrote in the century surrounding Jesus and the writing of Mark, and each of whom refers to this sense of the child's ability to grow and change. Their work serves as a bridge to the third part of the chapter—examination of funerary inscriptions and epitaphs of children. Among the themes present about children, their capacity for transformation—for growing up and changing—will be highlighted. However, unlike what we find with Cicero and Seneca, in funerary inscriptions this ability is mourned: the child will never grow up and do the things as an adult that his or her parents dreamed about. Plutarch's *Consolation to His Wife*, with its theme of grief at the death of his little girl, will be examined for its close connection to grief over a child and for his unusual understanding of the ways in which his daughter should be mourned.

Negative Characteristics of Children

While individual children may have been enjoyed and loved, children in ancient literature are typically considered in a derogatory sense. Both "childish" and "puerile"[1]

---

[1] Puerile, clearly, comes straight from the Latin with which we are dealing.

are English adjectives that communicate this metaphorical sense in the Hellenistic world. In Hellenistic usage there are many negative associations with children and "childishness," encompassing nearly every aspect of a child's existence. In Mark Golden's apt summary, children are thought to be "physically weak, morally incompetent, mentally incapable."[2] While these categories are useful for organization and division (and will be used throughout this chapter and beyond), it should also be noted that these things flow together—it is partially *because* a child is physically weak that she is morally weak as well. Ancient Greco-Roman society did not have the neat division of attributes that modern Americans generally employ; for the Greco-Romans, mind, body, and soul were interconnected. Children are commonly paired with adults, either to contrast the behavior of one to the other or to embarrass the adult by comparison with the child. Lucretius, in *De Rerum Natura*, expresses this perfectly:

> Besides, we feel that the mind is begotten along with the body; with the body, and grows up with it, and with it grows old. For as toddling children have a body infirm and tender, so a weak intelligence goes with it. Next, when their age has grown up into robust strength, the understanding too and the power of the mind is enlarged. Afterwards, when the body is now wrecked with the mighty strength of time, and the frame has succumbed with blunted strength, the intellect limps, the tongue babbles, the intelligence totters, all is wanting and fails at the same time.[3]

Lucretius throughout *De Rerum* is interested in easing the fear of death that is so common. He argues that the body is the vessel of both mind and spirit, and that when the body dies, the mind and spirit both dissipate. Death is not to be feared, therefore, since it is unknowing, unfeeling emptiness. In arguing this, he argues for a deep interconnection of the body, soul, and mind. It is natural, therefore, for him to portray children as both mentally and physically weak in the same breath. There is a similar reference point going on when the Apostle Paul closes his famous 1 Corinthians 13: "When I was a child, I spoke like a child, I thought like a child, I reasoned like a child; when I became an adult, I put an end to childish ways." A child is the incomplete version of an adult on all levels.

The Child as Physically Frail

Children were known to be weaker physically. Lucretius, as we have just seen, references a child's weak and delicate bodies. This observation rarely comes up so directly in ancient literature because it is so obvious. The idea, however, is made clear in unfavorable comparisons with adult males. Plutarch speaks of the assumed belief that fathers could harm their children just by looking at them, based on the difference of strength:

---

[2] Mark Golden, *Children and Childhood in Classical Athens* (Baltimore: Johns Hopkins University Press, 1993), 5.
[3] Lucretius, *De Rerum Natura*. 222–3 (Rouse, LCL).

We know that some men by looking upon young children hurt them very much, their weak and soft temperature being wrought upon and perverted, whilst those that are strong and firm are not so liable to be wrought upon.[4]

The phrase "even a child" was sometimes used to get at the physical weakness of children. Columella, in his book *On Agriculture*, talks about clearing a field, writing that "the fern is more easily destroyed by sowing and manuring; but even if you cut it down with the sickle (which is work even a child could do) as it sprouts out from time to time, within the aforesaid period its vigor is spent."[5] Here he assumes that child's physical frailty is sufficient for the task. Plutarch argues in his essay "On the Control of Anger" that well-chosen words can avert wrath. In bolstering his point, he quotes an ancient Greek fragment, saying, "For not a woman only, even a child, tickling the bristly boar with tender hand, may throw him easier than a wrestler might."[6] The underpinnings of this example are based in a child's physical weakness—the child is weaker than a woman, who, in turn, is weaker than a man. The example in context is used to show the importance of things other than strength, but the negative assumption of children's frailty is nonetheless clear. Sometimes, too, the phrase "even a child" was used to degrade an adult's victory or take away the honor of his death. Plutarch, attempting to undermine the death of Lysander, says, "But Lysander threw away his life ingloriously, like a common targeteer or skirmisher… where not only an ordinary man, but even a child or a woman may chance to smite and slay the mightiest warrior, as Achilles, they say, was slain by Paris at the gates."[7]

In medical writing, too, there are occasional signs of a child's physical weakness in contrast to an adult's. Celsus, for instance, writes, "Neither should we listen to those who would fix numerically how many times a patient is to be stroked; for that is to be regulated by his strength."[8] He argues that the physician should evaluate the individual patient to know how many strokes to give but that, in general, "the hand is to be passed even fewer times over a woman than over a man, fewer over a child or old man, than over a young adult."[9] This quotation of Celsus is further informative in showing the pairing of the physical strength of the elderly and children. This was a fairly common motif in the ancient world[10] and was used to highlight the bodily decline of the elderly.

---

[4] Plutarch, Quaestiones Convivales 5.7 (Goodwin, Perseus). [cited 5 March 2018]. Online: http://www.perseus.tufts.edu/hopper/text?doc=Perseus%3Atext%3A2008.01.0312%3Abook%3D5%3Achapter%3D7. This translation gets at the general comparison. However, ὑγρότητι is translated as "soft" where it could also be translated as "moist." A brief explanation of the moist/dry physiological dichotomy will be addressed later, but a child's moist nature stood in an important contrast to the adult male's dry one, and was one of the root causes of the child's general weakness.
[5] Columella, *On Agriculture*. 116–17 (Ash, LCL).
[6] Plutarch, Moralia. On the Control of Anger. 148–9 (Helmbold, LCL).
[7] Plutarch, Lives. Comparison of Lysander and Sulla. 452–3 (Perrin, LCL).
[8] Celsus, *On Medicine*. 178–9 (Spencer, LCL).
[9] Ibid.
[10] A particularly beautiful version of this theme is found in Aeschylus's *Agamemnon*: "But we, who because of our ancient flesh could not then contribute to the force in support, and were left behind, remain here, guiding our childlike strength upon staffs. For the immature marrow that rules in a child's breast is like that of an old man, and there is no Ares in that realm; while extreme old age, its leaves already withering, walks its way on three feet, no stronger than a child, a dream-vision wandering through the day" (Aeschylus, *Agamemnon*. 10–13 [Sommerstein, LCL]).

Cicero writes in *Pro Sestio*, "If you were to give a sword to a little boy or a weak, feeble old man, he would hurt no one by his own effort, but if he approaches a defenseless man, even though one of the bravest, he may be able to wound him by the sharpness and force of the weapon alone."[11] Seneca the Younger talks about his own aging body and reports a trip to his country home. Seneca mocks an old, decrepit slave stationed at the door, and the slave responds back that he is the former favorite of Seneca's youth. "The man is clean crazy," I remarked. "Has my pet slave become a little boy again? But it is quite possible; his teeth are just dropping out."[12] The slave has reverted to childhood in his toothless visage. Juvenal picks up this theme and develops it with vivid ferocity. He snidely writes that while young men are individuals and varied in their accomplishments or good looks or strength, "old men all look alike, with tremulous limbs and voices, bald pates, wet runny noses, like a baby's, and toothless gums with which they must mumble their bread."[13] The elderly revert back to their childhood, losing the individuality and looks and strength that they once did, becoming just like a snotty baby.

The Child as Morally Undeveloped

In addition to the physical frailty of children, childhood is commonly associated with an undeveloped or nonexistent sense of virtue. Where a modern audience would consider many of the following examples to be "undeveloped" or "immature" emotions, for the ancients, this is rather counted and condemned as inferiority and immorality. Children are often compared with animals, women, and slaves, all of which are considered morally inferior to the adult male.[14] In fact, "animals and children are as inferior to adults as bad and foolish men are to good and wise ones."[15]

Part of the moral trouble with women and children in the ancient world is that their bodily makeup was different that of the adult (free) male. Dale Martin in *The Corinthian Body* explains the radically different way Greco-Romans understood the body from a modern conception. While Greco-Roman conceptions did include a dichotomy of "body/soul," he argues that the context behind these words betrays stark differences from what a modern reader might assume. Other modern categories, like "natural/supernatural," would be utterly foreign to a Greco-Roman audience.[16] The human body, instead, was not just similar to the broader world, it "*was* a microcosm—a small version of the universe at large."[17] Two important assumptions of the Greco-Roman world resulted from this: first, the outer world constantly influenced the human body via *poroi* ("pores") because of their direct correlation; second, the physical body was

---

[11] Cicero, *Pro Sestio*. 64–5 (Gardner, LCL).
[12] Seneca, *Epistles*. 66–7 (Gummere, LCL).
[13] Juvenal, *The Sixteen Satires* (trans. Peter Green; London: Penguin Books, 1998), 81.
[14] For instance, "Many have pardoned their enemies; shall I not pardon the lazy, the careless, and the babbler? Let a child be excused by his age, a woman by her sex, a stranger by his independence, a servant by the bond of intercourse" (Seneca, *Moral Essays. De Ira.* 316–17 [Basore, LCL]).
[15] Golden, *Children and Childhood in Classical Athens*, 7.
[16] Dale Martin, *The Corinthian Body* (New Haven: Yale University Press, 1995), 3.
[17] Ibid., 16.

a direct reflection of the inner person, and therefore could be analyzed to get an understanding of the person's inner qualities, good and bad.[18] Blood, in particular, was thought to be connected to "the state of the soul and both to the surface of the body."[19] The nature of the blood could be analyzed by various dyads; Martin quotes Elizabeth Evans, who writes that "blood is conceived of as hot or cold, thick or thin, moist or dry, swift or slow. These qualities in the blood characterize the physiology of the soul and its activities. Such activities in turn affect the behavior of man and his outward appearance."[20] Finally, Martin explains that all human bodies in the ancient world (male or female) were conceived of on a single spectrum: masculinity occupied one pole, femininity the other.[21] While ancient writers conceived of a fundamental imbalance between men and women ("an axis where the telos is male"[22]), movement along that axis was possible (particularly downward toward the female), and one's place alongside axis had to do with bodily makeup.

The most common dyads used by ancient physicians formed a four-part spectrum, with two axes: hot/cold, moist/dry.[23] The adult male is dry; women and children are moist. Again, while the value judgment associated with what was considered "good" was somewhat arbitrary, the analysis of physiology came from external observation: women and children's bodies tend to be literally softer (softer muscles, a higher fat concentration), whereas men's bodies tended to be leaner and more muscular. In this understanding women and children's bodies retained more water, and therefore were "moister." Aristotle compares women and children's bodies: "Nor does hair grow upon women and children, both of whom are moist and not dry."[24] Similarly Galen pairs children and women over against young men, arguing for different treatments for each based on the mixture of their inner constitution:

> children and women, and those with soft flesh, contrasting these with young men, farmers and people who earn their living from the sea. It is not because of the moistness of the *krasis*[25] in children and women that he has seen such medications as highly regarded, nor again is it because of the dryness that he is able to recognize others suitable for reapers and sailors.[26]

While this pairing of wet versus dry with women/children and men is consistent throughout medical texts like those mentioned, there was great disagreement over

---

[18] Ibid., 18–19. Martin references the *Physiognomics*, a Pseudo-Aristotelian text from roughly the third century CE which analyzes physical characteristics to reveal a person's character.
[19] Ibid., 19.
[20] Ibid., 19. Quoted from Elizabeth C. Evans, *Physiognomics in the Ancient World* (Philadelphia: American Philosophical Society, 1969), 23.
[21] Ibid., 32.
[22] Ibid.
[23] Fairly frequently "hard/soft" was used as well.
[24] Aristotle, *Problems*. 148–9 (Mayhew, LCL).
[25] *Krasis* means something like "mixture" or "internal makeup." The original translation leaves the word in Greek so as to preserve the ambiguity of the word, which features prominently in Galen.
[26] Galen, *Method of Medicine*. 298–9 (Johnston and Horsley, LCL).

whether women and children were considered hot or cold. What *is* consistent is that the adult man is always classified as the opposite and that this difference accounts for the superiority of the man over the women/child. Aristotle, for instance, says, "Children, because they are moist and hot, are in a state of excessive boiling, because they are not cooled."[27] Later too, he betrays this assumption: "Why is it that children, who have a hot temperament, are not fond of wine… Is it because… children are hot and moist?"[28] Galen, on the other hand, varies on this point. Sometimes he agrees that children are hot: "for example, the *krasís* of children, being moist and hot,"[29] while at other times, he contrasts the warm and dry young man with the moist and cold child: "so that one is a young man, hot and dry in nature… whereas the other is a child in age, moist and cold in custom."[30]

Bodily makeup had a direct relationship to moral and immoral actions. Galen, for instance, argues that excess heat of the heart results in anger. "However, if heat reaches a greater amount, there is sudden anger and crazy rashness… Further, in the case of a heart that is hot to the highest degree, the whole body also becomes hot, unless the liver acts strongly in opposition."[31]

This perception is directly related to the child's inability to perceive and to attain virtue. Philo sums up neatly the common association of children with vice: "For when the life of man begins, from the very cradle till the time when the age of maturity brings the great change and quenches the fiery furnace of the passions, folly, incontinence, injustice, fear, cowardice, and all the kindred maladies of soul are his inseparable companions."[32] Because of this association between children and vice, unvirtuous men are degraded by being likened to children. Thus, Plutarch writes, "Do you come whining like a child,"[33] to emphasize how outrageous it would be if his interlocutor had actually been upset. Philo does not confine the word "child" to the young alone but rather argues that the Scriptures use the term allegorically. He says that throughout Genesis the words "child" or "the younger" connote the less developed virtues of two people: by comparison with his older half-brother Ishmael, Isaac is "the generic form of happiness, of the joy and gladness which belongs to those who have ceased from the manner of women [Gen. 18:11] and died to the passions—Isaac, whose heart is in the pursuit of no childish sports, but those which are divine."[34] So, too, in *On Sobriety* Philo argues, "And indeed in the Greater Song, he[35] calls the whole people when they shew a rebellious spirit, by the name which belongs to the age of folly and babyhood, that is 'children.'"[36] A few sentences later he picks up the same rhetoric: "We see clearly that

---

[27] Aristotle, *Problems*. 22–3 (Mayhew, LCL).
[28] Ibid., 106–7.
[29] Galen, *Method of Medicine*. 534–5 (Johnston and Horsley, LCL).
[30] Ibid., 440–1.
[31] Ibid., 197.
[32] Philo, *On the Birth of Abel and the Sacrifices Offered by Him and Cain*. 102–3 (Colson and Whitaker, LCL).
[33] Plutarch, *Moralia. How a Man May Become Aware of His Progress in Virtue*. 444–5 (Babbitt, LCL).
[34] Philo, *On the Cherubim*, 227 (Colson and Whitaker, LCL).
[35] "He" is Moses, according to Philo, who is taking quotations from the Torah.
[36] Philo, *On Sobriety*. 446–7 (Colson and Whitaker, LCL). The Loeb translation uses "bairns" instead of "children," but I have updated the language to sound contextually appropriate.

he has given the name of 'children' to men within whose souls are grounds for blame, men who so often fall through folly and senselessness and fail to do what the upright life requires."[37] Here he again uses the example of Isaac and Ishmael to exemplify this distinction: "Accordingly when Ishmael had apparently lived about twenty years, Moses calls him a child by comparison with Isaac, who is full grown in virtues."[38] The Apostle Paul chastises the Corinthians by saying, "And so, brothers and sisters, I could not speak to you as spiritual people, but rather as people of the flesh, as infants in Christ" (1 Corinthians 3:1).

Plutarch uses the child's volatile emotions as another example of the morally underdeveloped person. In his essay *How a Man May Become Aware of his Progress in Virtue*, he argues that a person may become so accustomed to acting or thinking in the right way that even when the body or mind is given freedom to do otherwise, it is so conditioned to do right that it does not take the opportunity to do wrong. The body can be conditioned to fail to lust even at the sudden appearance of a very attractive person. In the realm of the mind, sleeping for Plutarch counts as a place of relaxation, where a person cannot exercise the same mental control as when awake. Therefore, dreams can give people a sense of how far they have progressed: if they are untroubled in their sleep, they are making good progress, but, for those less far along the path:

> torturing memories, perturbations, ignoble desertions, and childish transports of joy and sorrow, such as are experienced in dismal or abnormal dreams, are like to billows that break and toss, inasmuch as the soul does not yet possess the power to keep itself in order, but is still being molded by external opinions and laws, and when it gets farthest away from these during the hours of slumber, it is again made free and open to other influences by the emotions.[39]

In brief, a child is prone to be overcome by emotions, unable to exercise self-control and to restrain oneself. Livy continues this theme when describing the volatile nature of Antiochus in all matters:

> Antiochus, setting up an ivory chair in the Roman fashion, would administer justice and adjudge disputes on the most trifling matters. And so incapable was his mind of sticking to any station in life, as it strayed through all the varieties of existence that it was not really clear either to himself or to others what kind of person he was. It was his habit not to speak to his friends, to smile at mere acquaintances in a most friendly way, and with an inconsistent generosity to make himself and others laughing-stocks; to some, men of distinction who held themselves in high esteem, he would give childish presents, as of food or toys, others, who expected nothing, he would make rich. And so he seemed to some not to know what he wanted; some said that he was playing childish tricks, some that he was unquestionably insane.[40]

---

[37] Ibid.
[38] Ibid.
[39] Plutarch, *Moralia. How a Man May Become Aware of His Progress in Virtue*. 444–5 (Babbitt, LCL).
[40] Livy, *History of Rome, Volume XII*. 248–9 (Sage and Schlesinger, LCL).

Not only does Antiochus behave like a child in his vacillating emotions and actions but he also behaves like a child in the scope of his imagination.

Children's lack of adult virtue is manifested by their inability to control their anger. In an essay *On Anger*, Seneca associates anger, and a weak or inferior moral sense, with women and children. Arguing that feeling anger at all is wrong for anyone, he personifies extremes with which all his readers would agree:

> On the other hand, to be constantly irritated seems to me to be the part of a languid and unhappy mind, conscious of its own feebleness, like folk with diseased bodies covered with sores, who cry out at the lightest touch. Anger, therefore, is a vice which for the most part affects women and children. "Yet it affects men also." Because many men, too, have womanish or childish intellects.[41]

Plutarch picks up this theme as well, showing both how susceptible to anger an adolescent was and the dire results: "his[42] son, who was hardly a boy anymore, in a fit of angry displeasure caused by some trivial and childish grievance, threw himself headlong from the roof and was killed."[43]

Children are also described as being unusually fearful and lacking courage. When Seneca wants to show how silly an adult is acting, the reader is reminded that children fear ridiculous things. "So, too, anger is in itself hideous and by no means to be feared; yet it is feared by many, just as a hideous mask is feared by children."[44] Later he makes even more explicit the connection between children's fears and those of an inferior mind: "Foolish creatures are frightened by foolish things:... elephants are frightened at the cries of pigs: and so also we fear anger just as children fear the dark, or wild beasts fear red feathers: it has in itself nothing solid or valiant, but it affects feeble minds."[45] Lucretius, writing a century earlier, likewise identifies children's silly fear of the dark. "For just as children tremble and fear all things in blind darkness, so we in the light fear, at times, things that are no more to be feared than what children shiver at in the dark and imagine to be at hand."[46]

In a different context Seneca compares an adult fear of death with other childish fears: "Boys fear trifles, children fear shadows, we fear both."[47] So, too, Plutarch, arguing against Epicurean beliefs, says, "The great majority, however, have an expectation of eternity undisturbed by any myth-inspired fear of what may come after death; and the love of being, the oldest and greatest of all our passions, is more than a counterpoise for that childish terror."[48] When Pliny the Elder dismisses the common beliefs in the

---

[41] Seneca, *Moral Essays. De Ira.* 160–5 (Basore, LCL).
[42] This quote refers to Dion, a disciple of Plato. The story is that Dion saw a terrible vision of a woman/fury, and feared for his own life, but then it was his son who in fact died.
[43] Plutarch, *Lives, Volume VI: Dion and Brutus.* 116–17 (Perrin, LCL).
[44] Seneca, *Moral Essays. De Ira.* 188–93 (Basore, LCL).
[45] Ibid.
[46] Lucretius, *De Rerum Natura.* 98–9 (Rouse, LCL).
[47] Seneca, *Epistles, Volume I.* 14–15 (Gummere, LCL).
[48] Plutarch, *Moralia, That Epicurus Actually Makes a Pleasant Life Impossible.* 130–1 (Einarson and de Lacy, LCL).

afterlife, in expressing the reasoning behind his scorn for the persistence of this belief, he says that they are "fictions of childish absurdity, and belong to a mortality greedy for life unceasing."[49] While he clearly has adults in mind here, rather than children, his point is to unfavorably compare adults to childish actions. In this case, again, the fear of death in an adult is childish and silly—betraying a lack of courage, as well as a fragility of thought.

The Child as Mentally Undeveloped and Naïve

Another frequently found trope of childhood is that of naïveté, in a rather specific sense. Here the basic difference is between the earnestness of the child and the ability to attain it. While a child might take some endeavor with utter seriousness or believe her efforts to be accomplishing something great, in fact the child accomplishes nothing substantial. In his work *On the Sublime*, Longinus discriminates good from bad. The bad can take many forms, one of which is timidity: "For many times they seem to themselves to be inspired, but rather than caught up in Bacchean frenzies, they are instead childishly playing."[50] Later, he further explicates:

> But while tumidity seeks to outdo the sublime, puerility is the exact opposite of grandeur; utterly abject, mean spirited, and in fact the most ignoble of faults. What then is puerility? Is it not obviously an idea born in the classroom, whose overelaboration ends in frigid failure?[51]

Plutarch, too, shows his disgust of poets by comparing them to the works of children: "but the works of poets are nothing but childish."[52]

Children could be credulous in a more general sense as well, willing to believe absurd things. Here again the child's mental abilities are in question—they are not developed enough to distinguish impossibilities from reality. Wisdom 12:24-25 gets at this sense when talking about the belief in false gods: "For they went far astray on the paths of error, accepting as gods those animals that even their enemies despised; they were deceived like foolish infants. Therefore, as though to children who cannot reason, you sent your judgment to mock them." Pliny the Elder gives another example of the scorn associated with a child's mental abilities. While exposing a belief of Sophocles he finds to be utterly absurd, he says, "Can one imagine, one wonders, a mind so childish and naïve as to believe birds that weep every year or that shed such large tears or that once migrated from Greece, where Meleager died, to the Indies to mourn for him?"[53] Pliny's point is twofold. First, a childish mind is credulous, willing to believe almost

---

[49] Pliny the Elder, *Natural History*. 634–5 (Rackham, LCL).
[50] Longinus, *On The Sublime*. 168–9 (Fyfe, LCL). Rites surrounding Bacchus tended to involve wild ecstasies caused by Bacchus himself. The line between divinely inspired and ridiculously foolish was a narrow one.
[51] Ibid., 169–70.
[52] Plutarch, *Moralia. Were the Athenians More Famous in War or in Wisdom?* 520–1 (Babbitt, LCL).
[53] Pliny the Elder, *Natural History*. 194–5 (Eichholz, LCL).

anything, no matter how absurd. In addition, a childish mind is unintelligent in a more general way: "Yes; but that anyone should seriously tell such a story regarding such a substance as this… is a gross insult to man's intelligence and an insufferable abuse of our freedom to utter falsehoods."[54] It is not merely that only a thoroughly childish and naïve mind would believe this but also that the sort of person who would *tell* such a lie has such a low view of humanity that the liar views humanity's intelligence on par with a child's. The writer of Ephesians gets as a similar point when urging, "We must no longer be children, tossed to and fro and blown about by every wind of doctrine, by people's trickery, by their craftiness in deceitful scheming" (Ephesians 4:14).

Finally, there is a sense in the ancient world of the naïveté of the child in terms of their innocence of the way the world actually works. In his *Discourses*, Epictetus speaks of virtue and of beliefs he feels are correct. Although the general public would disagree, he urges that it is wise to forbear from constantly correcting them:

> What then? Must I say these things to the multitude? For what purpose? Is it not sufficient for a man himself to believe them? For example, when the children come up to us and clap their hands and say, "To-day is the good Saturnalia," do we say to them, "All this is not good?" Not at all; but we too clap our hands to them. And do you too, therefore, when you are unable to make a man change his opinion, realize that he is a child and clap your hands to him; but if you do not want to do this, you have merely to hold your peace?[55]

Here he uses the example of children, engaging in holiday mirth, who are unaware of the greater misery that exists in the world. Rather than expose their naïveté, one plays along with them, returning their greeting with the appropriate response. When encountering adults who are unable to grasp one's superior position, Epictetus counsels that treating them as one would treat a child is best, either by engaging them on their own level or by, at least, not rudely correcting them.

Belief in children's naïveté accompanies a sense of their undeveloped mental functions. Children are frequently interested in small or petty things, as they lack a sense of the greater world and its importance. In this case there is a slight blurring with the child's moral development, but in general the emphasis here is that he or she is unable to recognize or understand what is truly worthwhile rather than that he or she chose badly. Plutarch combines both a mental and moral sense in his essay *On Brotherly Love*. He urges that brotherly contention should be noticed and addressed even from childhood, for here dissention begins and can increase over time.

> For having once begun to differ in childish matters, about the care of animals and their fights, as, for instance, those of quails or cocks, they then continue to differ about the contests of boys in the palaestra, of dogs on the hunt, and of horses at

---

[54] Ibid., 194–5.
[55] Epictetus, *Discourses*. 190–1 (Oldfather, LCL).

the races, until they are no longer able to control or subdue their contentious and ambitious spirit in more important matters.⁵⁶

He continues: "It is therefore of no slight importance to resist the spirit of contentiousness and jealousy among brothers when it first creeps in over trivial matters, practicing the art of making mutual concessions."⁵⁷ Plutarch identifies a progression and maturation of interests: children are interested in small things like animals and little fights; boys in more mature contests in the palestra; adults, in hunting and horse races.⁵⁸ Mirroring the maturation of interests, he argues that anger and contention can also grow and mature, such that true adult hatred and division can spring up from small disagreements. Plutarch's implication is that children are focused on small things because their mental faculties are small. In a similar vein, Arrian has one adult male chastise another who ought to know better for his "childish" intellectual faculties. "Nearchus replied that he was childish, if he was ignorant of Alexander's purpose in dispatching the expedition."⁵⁹

Sometimes a historical figure will reveal his future greatness through his wisdom and maturity even while a child. This usage, while unusual, acts as the exception that proves the rule about children and their immaturity. Truly great figures are so great that *even as children* they can rise above their (inferior) station. Their true worth is apparent to preternaturally shine through despite the lowest circumstances. So, Alexander the Great as a child is described by Plutarch as being wise beyond his years, not limiting his questions to the small and insignificant things children would normally ask:

> The desire which he cherished to accomplish this task was implanted in him from childhood, and was fostered and increased with the years that passed. Once, when ambassadors came from the Persian king to Philip, who was not at home, Alexander, while he entertained them hospitably asked no childish questions, as the others did, about the vine of gold or the Hanging Gardens, or how the Great King was arrayed; but he was completely engrossed with the most vital concerns of the dominion.⁶⁰

Alexander did not merely avoid asking childish questions; even though he was, in fact, a child, he also avoided asking the sorts of childish questions that *other adults around him* were asking.

Finally, children are represented as having generally minimal mental faculties. They have a very limited grasp on ideas and the way the world works. This sentiment often manifests itself through rhetoric. Philo argues that the Bible uses the word "child" or

---

⁵⁶ Plutarch, *Moralia. On Brotherly Love*. 300–1 (Helmbold, LCL).
⁵⁷ Ibid.
⁵⁸ It should be noted that even here, interest in the horse races is often treated with scorn as a low and immature hobby (cf. Pliny the Younger, *Letters, Volume II*. 86–9 [Radice, LCL]). Nonetheless it is associated with adults, rather than children.
⁵⁹ Arrian, *Indica*. 402–3 (Brunt, LCL).
⁶⁰ Plutarch, *Moralia. On the Fortune or the Virtue of Alexander*. 470–1 (Babbitt, LCL).

"younger" as a derogatory statement (as seen above). This applies to an estimation of an adult's mental facilities as well: "And in this he had no thought of literal age in the sense in which we use it of the bodies of the young, but of their truly infantine lack of a reasonable understanding."[61] When an author wants to push forward just how obvious a point he is making, he will rhetorically question, Is not this "so obvious that even a child could not avoid seeing it?"[62] Likewise the converse: a point will be so obviously wrong that "even a young child, educated in liberal studies would immediately recognize it."[63] In each case, once again, the purpose is to show that the most basic intellect, that of a child, is able to grasp the truth of the matter (and therefore so should the reader be that much more able to see the truth or error of the statement). Paul writes in 1 Corinthians 14:20, "Brothers and sisters, do not be children in your thinking; rather, be infants in evil, but in thinking be adults."

The intellectual deficiencies of a child are manifest in the mental decline of the elderly. Just as it was seen to be a common trope that the old physically weaken until they are not stronger than children, so, too, their mental facilities are described as "childlike." When Plutarch describes a Roman festival and explains the history and symbolism of the procession, he says:

> Romulus also celebrated a triumph for this victory on the Ides of October, having in his train, besides many other captives, the leader of the Veientes, an elderly man, who seems to have conducted the campaign unwisely, and without the experience to be expected of his years. Wherefore to this very day, in offering a sacrifice for victory, they lead an old man through the forum to the Capitol, wearing a boy's toga with a bulla attached to it.[64]

The symbol of the leader's folly is that he acted in a childish manner, and therefore he is clad the visible markers of children in the Roman world—the *bulla* and *toga praetexta*. The leader is therefore reduced to a childish state. This was clearly intended to shame the leader, and the triumph of Romulus continues to be celebrated by reenacting this victory procession. In perhaps an even clearer example, Plutarch argues in his essay *Old Men in Public Affairs* that the elderly must continuously use their intellects and bodily strength, lest they lose them. He uses a general named Lucullus as an example, saying that well into his old age, he was an able general "when he combined thought with action." However, "when he gave himself up to a life of inactivity and to a home-keeping and thought-free existence, he became a wasted skeleton, like sponges in calm seas."[65] He is then taken advantage of by a wicked servant until he is rescued by his brother, who "managed and tended him like a child the rest of his life, which was not long."[66] The mental and physical degradation happens simultaneously: Lucullus is helpless and must be cared for as a child.

---

[61] Philo, *On Sobriety*. 448–9 (Colson and Whitaker, LCL).
[62] Cf. Galen, *On the Natural Faculties*. 148–9 (Brock, LCL).
[63] Galen, *Method of Medicine*. 34–5 (Johnston and Horsley, LCL).
[64] Plutarch, *Lives. Theseus and Romulus*. 170–1 (Perrin, LCL).
[65] Plutarch, *Moralia. Whether an Old Man Should Engage in Public Affairs*. 124–5 (Fowler, LCL).
[66] Ibid.

Strabo in *Geography* talks about how myths are useful for coaxing children into learning, as children find myths enjoyable. However, these myths should only be used for a time. "At the beginning we must make use of such bait for children, but as the child advances in years we must guide him to the knowledge of facts, when once his intelligence has become strong and no longer needs to be coaxed."[67] Strabo assumes that a child's intelligence is initially limited but can also grow. Strabo goes on to compare the illiterate, uneducated, and "half-literate" man to a child, both for his taste for stories but also because "for his reasoning faculty has not been fully developed, and, besides, the mental habits of his childhood persist in him."[68]

In summary, the child was thought in every way—physically, morally, mentally—the inferior of the adult male. A modern audience would understand the child's physical, mental, and moral states as developing, and therefore that they might be *age appropriately* strong or wise or moral. An ancient audience would not use such a description. Women, slaves, and children were all inferior to adult freeborn men. While there may be reasons to explain why this is so (fundamental incapacity, bodily makeup, lack of education), ultimately causation was less important than the "facts" of their inferiority.

Positive Characteristics of Children

Associations of children with negative characteristics abound; positive estimations of the child are far less common. Such positive traits tend to be superficial and specific to actual individuals, rather than used as analogies for the behavior of adults. However, there are a few instances where adjectives like "childlike" are used favorably when applied to adults. Furthermore, in his *The Orator's Education*, Quintilian takes the time to describe children, and in these, his descriptions express a far more gracious and positive estimation of the child than is common.

Occasionally, specific characteristics of children were described as pleasing to adults. The most common of these occasional references is to mention that the childish voice and childish faces are pleasing. Quintilian, describing his own sons, says of the younger, "What beauty he showed in his face, what charm in his talk."[69] Similarly of the elder, he notes that he had "a clear and pleasant voice, a sweetness of speech, and an exact pronunciation of every letter in either of the two languages."[70] Seneca the Younger, in *De Consolatione ad Helviam*, speaks to his mother Helvia about her living grandson Marcus. He says that in the presence of the boy no sorrow can be felt: "Whose heart contracted by pain will his lively prattle not release... Whom intent upon his own thoughts will he not attract to himself and divert by the chatter that no one will weary of?"[71] On a tombstone inscription of a teenage boy, the opening line is,

---

[67] Strabo, *Geography*, Volume I. 68–9 (Jones, LCL).
[68] Ibid.
[69] Quintilian, *The Orator's Education, Volume III*. 12–13 (Russell, LCL).
[70] Ibid., 13–14 (Russell, LCL).
[71] Seneca, *Moral Essays. De Consolatione ad Helviam*. 478–81 (Basore, LCL).

"Eustathius, sweet is thy image, but I see thee in wax, and no longer doth that pleasant speech dwell in thy mouth."[72] So too, in Martial's epigrams, a girl of seven years old is mourned: "But death hurried to close the channel of her sweet voice, lest her tongue should prevail to sway the pitiless goddesses."[73] While Quintilian valued the precision of his son's speech, the "childish lisp" was also commented upon and enjoyed.[74] Sweet breath was also ascribed to children—a girl is said to have breath "ten times sweeter than perfume."[75]

Children were thought to be individually adorable and charming in their behavior. A girl named Hymnis is described as "Evander's daughter, ever the loveable pet of his house, the coaxing nine-year-old girl."[76] Seneca the Younger further describes the boy Marcus to Helvia by saying he is "a most winsome lad, the sight of whom no sorrow can possibly withstand.... Whose tears would his merriment not stay... whom will his playfulness not provoke to mirth?"[77] In *Heroides*, Ovid has Hermione speak of growing up without her mother.[78] "You were not near in my first years, O my mother, to receive the caressing prattle from the tripping tongue of the little girl; I never clasped about your neck the little arms that would not reach, and never sat, a burden sweet, upon your lap."[79] Pliny describes a young girl who has died saying that he "never saw a girl so gay and lovable... She would cling to her father's neck, and embrace us, his friends, with modest affection."[80]

A child's antics could be praised as pleasing to the gods. In an ode to the goat, the children play at adult games and do so with a charming zeal for the amusement of the god: "The children, billy goat, have put purple reins on you and a muzzle on your bearded face, and they train you to race like a horse round the god's temple that he may look on their childish joy."[81] This is a rare case where παιδεύουσι is used favorably, rather than with scorn: the sense is that the children are delightful and charming in their mimicry of adult endeavors. Similarly, Pliny the Elder uses the adjective *simplicitas*—simplicity—favorably in conjunction with children. He describes a sculpture of "Two Children, in which the carefree simplicity of childhood is clearly displayed."[82]

---

[72] *The Greek Anthology, Volume II: Book 7.* 322–3 (Paton, LCL).

[73] Martial, *Epigrams, Volume III: Book 11.* 74–5 (Bailey, LCL).

[74] See for instance Seneca's long repetition of Euripides. In the quote, the greedy speaker argues that money is better than anything "Money, that blessing to the race of man,/Cannot be matched by mother's love, or lisp/Of children, or the honour due one's sire" (Seneca, *Epistles, Volume III.* 328–9 [Gummere, LCL]). See also, below, Hermione's reference to the "caressing prattle from the tripping tongue of the little girl."

[75] It is unclear how old this girl is, and she clearly is being courted romantically. The whole of the poem is, "Isias, though your breath is ten times sweeter than perfume, awake and take this garland in your dear hands. Now it is blooming, but as dawn approaches you will see it wilting—a symbol of your youth" (*The Greek Anthology, Volume I: Book 5.* 278–9 [Paton, LCL].)

[76] *The Greek Anthology, Volume II: Book 7.* 344–5 (Paton, LCL).

[77] Seneca, *Moral Essays. De Consolatione ad Helviam.* 478–81 (Basore, LCL).

[78] Her mother being Helen of Troy. Hermione complains of having neither father nor mother near her, because of the war.

[79] Ovid, *Heroides.* 104–5 (Showerman, LCL).

[80] Pliny the Younger, *Letters.* 378–9 (Radice, LCL).

[81] *The Greek Anthology, Volume I: Book 6.* 468–9 (Paton, LCL).

[82] *Et pueros duos, in quibus spectatur securitas aetatis et simplicitas* (Pliny the Elder, *Natural History.* 312–13 [Rackham, LCL].)

All of these descriptions of children tend to focus on their appearance, their voice, their speech, and their antics. Children rarely are commented on positively at all in ancient literature, and when they are, the references are almost characteristics that are charming only in an age-appropriate context. Children may be adorable, but not often admirable.

However, there are a very few times where adults are compared favorably to children. Pliny the Younger, for instance, uses "childlike" in a positive circumstance. In a letter congratulating a friend for their choice of son-in-law, Pliny praises the fiancé, saying, "He belongs to one of our noble families and his father and mother are both highly respected; while he himself is scholarly, well read, and something of an orator, and he combines a childlike frankness and youthful charm with mature judgement." Here we see a blending of boyhood, youth, and mature adulthood: this young man brings good from each stage of life. Childlike frankness (*puer simplicitate*), or artlessness, is praiseworthy in Pliny's mind and worth highlighting in another.[83]

Plutarch uses "childlike" or "childish" to paint a scene of sweet innocence. A young lady named Perigune flees from Theseus, as Theseus has just killed her father. She attempts to hide in shrubbery, "and with exceeding innocence and childish simplicity was supplicating these plants, as if they understood her, and vowing that if they would hide and save her, she would never trample them down nor burn them."[84] While her behavior is comical, it is not meant to be sneered at: she instead appears gentle and simple. Her nature wins the favor of Theseus, who promises not to harm her, and she goes on to bear him a son. Contextually, παιδικῶς is associated with innocence and naïveté in a favorable way. So, too, Paul in 1 Corinthians 14:20 makes the distinction between being "infants in evil," which is laudable, and "children in thinking," which is to be avoided.

Quintilian claims a higher viewpoint of a child than many of his contemporaries. While most assume that only a few people are quick learners, he says that the majority of children are instead "quick to reason and prompt to learn."[85] This is the very nature of humanity—they are reasonable. Children are the proof of this, he says. While many children show great promise, this promise often fades. This is not, however, because their true nature is developing but rather because they have failed to be nurtured correctly.[86]

Quintilian consistently argues for the needfulness of nurturing the child. It is easier to corrupt good than correct bad, he says, and therefore great care should be taken from the very beginning to craft a child so that they might thrive. For instance, he strongly urges against beating children to help them to learn, arguing that this method

---

[83] The idea of the *puer senex* (literally "old [person] child") is a trope in ancient literature much talked about by modern scholars. Pliny uses the phrase to praise a dead young woman about to be married: "She had not yet reached the age of fourteen, and yet she combined the wisdom of age and dignity of womanhood with the sweetness and modesty of youth and innocence." (Pliny the Younger, *Letters*. 378–9 [Radice, LCL].) C.f. Teresa C. Carp, "'Puer senex' in Roman and Medieval Thought," *Latomus* 39.3 (1980): 736–9.
[84] Plutarch, *Lives. Theseus and Romulus*. 18–19 (Perrin, LCL).
[85] Quintilian, *The Orator's Education, Volume I*. 64–5 (Russell, LCL).
[86] Ibid.

causes children to wilt rather than grow. Educational practices in the ancient world were methodical and often brutal. Alan Booth writes a brief article[87] cataloguing corporeal punishment of students, beginning with Aristotle and Plato, both of whom assume that a child is inferior and can only learn through threats of punishment.[88] He aptly summarizes the literature: "I have no doubt that the descriptions of the irascible, whip-wielding teacher have elements of a literary commonplace, but there is sufficient evidence to show that teacher with his rod is no mere literary fiction."[89] He argues that the first century saw a softening of educational theory: authors like Plutarch and Seneca argue for mildness in teaching, but each argues that some amount of fear or punishment can be useful for teaching.[90] Similarly, Raffaella Cribiore has a section on corporal punishment in the ancient classroom in *Gymnastics of the Mind*.[91] She contextualizes the brutality of the classroom within the "universality of violence in the ancient world," and references the idea that "Greeks and Romans considered it normal to beat children and slaves, who could not be controlled by rationality and occupied an intermediate position between human and beast."[92] Quintilian's thoughts, therefore, are not unique, but they are rare, and are particularly emphatic in their opposition to physical punishment. Beating a child can result in a child being so fearful that they can become depressed and unable to learn properly. Quintilian is passionately disapproving of this practice: "I blush to mention the shameful purposes." Instead, "It is enough to observe that no one ought to be allowed too much power over helpless and easily

---

[87] Alan D. Booth, "Punishment, Discipline, and Riot in the Schools of Antiquity," *EMC* 17 (1973): 107–14.

[88] Plato's rhetoric is particularly illuminating here: "just as no sheep or other witless creature ought to exist without a herdsman, so children cannot live without a tutor, nor slaves without a master. And, of all wild creatures, the child is the most intractable; for in so far as it, above all others, possesses a fount of reason that is as yet uncurbed, it is a treacherous, sly and most insolent creature. Wherefore the child must be strapped up, as it were, with many bridles—first, when he leaves the care of nurse and mother, with tutors, to guide his childish ignorance, and after that with teachers of all sorts of subjects and lessons, treating him as becomes a freeborn child. On the other hand, he must be treated as a slave; and any free man that meets him shall punish both the child himself and his tutor or teacher, if any of them does wrong. And if anyone thus meets them and fails to punish them duly, he shall, in the first place, be liable to the deepest degradation; and the Law-warden who is chosen as president over the children shall keep his eye on the man who has met with the wrong-doings mentioned and has failed either to inflict the needed punishment at all, or else to inflict it rightly. Moreover, this Law-warden shall exercise special supervision, with a keen eye, over the rearing of the children, to keep their growing natures in the straight way, by turning them always towards goodness, as the laws direct." (Plato, "Laws 7.808d-809a" in Plato, *Plato in Twelve Volumes, Volumes 10 & 11* (trans. R. G. Bury; Cambridge: Harvard University Press; London: Heinemann, 1967 & 1968.). In a footnote to Plato's text in the above quote, "On the other hand, he must be treated as a slave," the translator R. G. Bury, writes, "The child is of two-fold nature,—semi-rational; as such he needs a double 'bridle,' that of instruction (proper to free men), and that of chastisement (proper to slaves)" (f1, Plato, *Laws* 7.808e).

[89] Booth, "Punishment, Discipline, and Riot," 108.

[90] Ibid. See Plutarch, *Moralia, The Education of Children*. 40–1, 56–9 (Babbitt, LCL). and Seneca, *De Ira*. 208–11 (Basore, LCL).

[91] Raffaella Cribiore, *Gymnastics of the Mind: Greek Education in Hellenistic and Roman Egypt* (Princeton: Princeton University Press, 2001), 65–73. See also Stanley F. Bonner, *Education in Ancient Rome: From the Elder Cato to the Younger Pliny* (Berkeley: University of California Press, 1977), 143–5.

[92] Ibid., 69.

victimized young people."[93] Part of Quintilian's disgust with physical punishment as a means of teaching is that he, unlike many authors, distinguishes between children and slaves. In emphasizing why he disagrees with beating children, he says that "it is humiliating and proper only for slaves; and certainly it is an infringement of rights (as it is agreed to be at a later age)."[94] There were laws against striking a free adult; Quintilian thinks this should apply to children as well.

It is not that Quintilian thinks that all children are alike in promise. Some children are smarter and better than others, and it is the teacher's job to analyze this and proceed accordingly.[95] In Book 1.3 of the *Orator's Education*, he spends time detailing the way in which an educator can assess promise in a child. Children's intellectual capabilities vary, which requires of their teacher a variety of educational methods. Some children respond well to pressure, while others do not; some are restrained by fear, while others are paralyzed by it.[96] He still prefers a particular kind of student who is intelligent and eager. Not all these mental traits are equally admirable, but there does seem to be both knowledge of and tolerance for variety, which is unusual.

Quintilian has a strong sense of an infant's ability to learn. While urging parents to take care in choosing a nurse, he says, "We naturally retain most tenaciously what we learned when our minds were fresh: a flavor lasts a long time when the jar that absorbs it is new, and the dyes that change wool's pristine whiteness cannot be washed out."[97] Memory is at its most retentive in the earliest years.[98] Memory in particular is one of the few faculties that a very young child possesses and that a teacher is able to develop. Quintilian also insists here on combining moral lessons with rote memorization—crafting the child both morally and mentally simultaneously:

> I should like to suggest that the lines set for copying should not be meaningless sentences, but should convey some moral lesson. The memory of such things stays with us till we are old, and the impression thus made on the unformed mind will be good for the character also... Memory (as I shall show in due time) is very necessary to the orator; there is nothing like practice for nourishing and strengthening it, and, since the age-group of which we are now speaking cannot as yet produce anything on its own, it is almost the only faculty which the teacher's attention can help to develop.[99]

Quintilian, therefore, goes against mainstream educational philosophies in a variety of ways, which evidence a more optimistic opinion of children and childhood. In describing his methods for education, he shows a fondness for children, a confidence

---

[93] Quintilian, *The Orator's Education, Volume I*. 102–3 (Russell, LCL).
[94] Ibid., 100–1.
[95] Ibid., 98–9. For instance, some children had an elasticity of mind, a care in thought which showed them to be above average compared to their peers.
[96] Ibid.
[97] Ibid., 66–7.
[98] Ibid., 72–3.
[99] Ibid., 80–1.

in the reasonableness of children, and an awareness not only of the spectrum of abilities of children but of it being worthwhile to cater learning to each child's individual needs.

The Child as Capable of Development

Another important exception to the often-negative characterization of children is the way in which they are believed to grow into adulthood. As we have seen, the Hellenistic world did not generally think well of children and correlated them frequently with beasts, women, and slaves. Golden observes that a slave was called *pais*, "child," in ancient Greece to signify his status as inferior and not worthy of the name "adult": another denigration of those who are not actually children by imbuing them with childish (i.e., inferior) characteristics. Golden notes, however, a difference between children and slaves. Slaves were considered persistently inferior. The situation of actual children was more complicated. "They were expected to change their statuses, to become adults. This resulted in their interesting hybrid nature, sharing some of the characteristics of the grown-ups they would be, although less fully developed."[100] This was more specifically applied to well-born boys, as they specifically could transform so starkly from children to elite adult men.

An unusual mechanism for this transition can be found in Epicurean writings. Thomas Wiedemann notes therein the metaphor of "sparks of manliness" for a child's potential, citing both Lucretius *De Rerum Natura* and Cicero's *De Finibus*.[101] Cicero's work is worth considering in detail, for his various and interlacing metaphors for a child's potential for virtue are useful. Cicero argues that if only from the moment of birth one could know himself and the various parts of his nature, he would be "incapable of error in anything."[102] However, "But as it is, our nature at all events at the outset is curiously hidden from us, and we cannot fully realize or understand it."[103] This metaphor of human nature being hidden, needing to be discovered, continues as his argument develops. At first, just like animals, infants desire only to be safe. Infants are helpless; as they grow, they discover their abilities.[104] Cicero then moves on to another metaphor of great interest: the seed that sprouts. A person is fundamentally constituted toward virtue, and children, "hence children, without instruction, are actuated by semblances of the virtues, of which they possess in themselves the seeds, for these are primary elements of our nature, and they sprout and blossom into virtue."[105] Children, according to Cicero, do not have these virtues in their entirety from the moment of conception. There is the seed of virtue, but it must grow. Cicero comes back to the

---

[100] Mark Golden, "Childhood in Ancient Greece" in *Coming of Age in Ancient Greece: Images of Childhood from the Classical Past* (eds. Jenifer Neils and John H. Oakley; New Haven: Yale University Press, 2003), 14.

[101] Ibid., 23, footnote 39. Weidemann cites Cicero, who can be used positively, but the quote he references is in fact negative—"it is a difficult matter to praise a boy; for praise must then be given to hope, not to achievement" (Cicero, *On the Republic*. 284–5 [Keyes, LCL]).

[102] Cicero, *On Ends*. 440–1 (Rackham, LCL).

[103] Ibid.

[104] Ibid.

[105] Ibid., 442–3.

idea of virtue's being hidden from children, using the idea of fog: "the powers of our nature are clouded by a mist."[106] Finally, switching the metaphor once more, he uses the idea of fire to bring his point home: *in pueris virtutum quasi scintillas videmus,* "we can see in children as it were the spark of virtue,"[107] which then can be ignited into a full-blown fire "from which the philosopher's torch of reason must be kindled."[108] This nature, however, must be sought after, discovered, and adhered to, since by itself it remains incomplete. Through these metaphors of fog, seed, and flame, Cicero argues that children already have within them virtue, but in each case, time and training are needed to actualize and to realize this potential. Here Cicero evinces a rather high view of a child's desire to learn, insisting that, even when driven away with punishments, still a child will come back to learn.[109]

Seneca, on the other hand, has a lower view of a child's development toward an adult. A child is irrational, and children are constantly used with reference to those adults who fail intellectually and morally to behave as they should. Seneca struggles to account for the transition between a child and adult, therefore, and yet references it on several occasions. In *Letter* 118 he is engaged in defining what is "the Good." Separating it from the Honorable, which is the perfect Good, the Good, he decides, is more than just "according to nature" (as some others believe), but rather that which is *perfectly* in accordance with nature.[110] Some things, Seneca argues, change as they grow. Children exemplify this phenomenon. He argues that "he who was a child, becomes an adult, his peculiar nature is transformed; for the former is irrational, the latter rational. Certain things increase not only in size, but grow into something else."[111] As children grow into young adulthood, they are transformed. How does this transformation happen? Is it not simply, as Cicero suggests, that the potential is always there but needs to be activated? Seneca seems to think not. In continuing his theme on "the Good," he attempts to explain how something could be transformed at all. Some things, he argues, grow but do not change into something different. Wine, no matter what it is put in, stays wine, and no matter how much or little there is, it always stays the same. Seneca argues that some things do indeed remain the same no matter how much or little there is of it—simple addition does not change the thing. Other things, however, are different:

> There are others, however, which, after many increments, are altered by the last addition; there is stamped upon them a new character, different from that of yore.

---

[106] Ibid. Rackham's translation reads "are discerned as through a mist," which I have updated to communicate better the predicament.
[107] Ibid.
[108] Ibid.
[109] Ibid., 448–9.
[110] "*Si perfecte secundum naturam est.*" "Only if it is completely according to nature" Seneca, *Letters*. 366–7 (Gummere, LCL). I prefer to translate *prefecte* with "perfectly."
[111] Ibid., 118.14, translation my own. Gummere translates it similarly "A person, once a child, becomes a youth; his peculiar quality is transformed; for the child could not reason, but the youth possesses reason. Certain things not only grow in size as they develop, but grow into something else." Seneca, *Letters*. 368–9 (Gummere, LCL). I have opted for "adult" rather than "youth" in translating pubes.

One stone makes an archway—the stone which wedges the leaning sides and holds the arch together by its position in the middle. And why does the last addition, although very slight, make a great deal of difference? Because it does not increase; it fills up.[112]

In this example Seneca underscores the idea of transformation: something becomes something else entirely. Stones are just stones, and a stack of them remains a stack, even if they are being built into an arch. An arch does not properly come into existence, however, until the last stone, the keystone, is put into place. Suddenly the whole is transformed. So, too, things can be according to nature but can be altered by "greatness" until it is transformed into something else and now is a Good.

Seneca thinks this way about children. They cannot be called "Good" as such, because of their lack of reason. In *Letter* 121 he continues the theme of the "Good," again using children (and animals) as prime examples. Here, Seneca is specifically arguing with Lucilius about character: one can only find out what to do when one studies a human's nature. This leads to a discussion of animals and children. Seneca proposes that animals by instinct move with grace; they do not need to be trained, but rather from birth immediately can do so. People will object that they are driven by fear; Seneca counters that this is not true, because even when it is painful to move as they naturally should, they struggle to do so even then. Proving this point, he uses the example of a child's learning to walk: "Thus the child who is trying to stand and is becoming used to carry his own weight, on beginning to test his strength, falls and rises again and again with tears until through painful effort he has trained himself to the demands of nature."[113] Another objection is posed: if animals have a "consciousness of their physical constitution," then should not humans, from birth, have an understanding of their own inner constitution? How can this possibly be, when philosophers spend so much time trying to grasp it? Seneca refutes this objection by differentiating "a definition of" their constitution from their "actual constitution."[114] A child may not know the definition of things (like how to define "animal") but knows instinctively, "understands," that he or she is an animal. A child may understand he or she has a soul, but: "only understands confusedly, cursorily, and darkly."[115] *Even children* and animals have a sense of their "principal part" but "it is not clearly outlined or portrayed."[116]

Continuing his argument, Seneca again betrays his assumptions that a child is incapable of reason, while also hinting at, without fully explaining, the transformation a child can undergo. Again anticipating an objection, he has his imaginary interlocutor posit that a man[117] is a reasoning being in addition to a living one. How, then, the interlocutor asks, can a child adapt himself to a reasoning constitution when the child

---

[112] Seneca, *Letters*. 366–7 (Gummere, LCL).
[113] Seneca, *Letters*. 400–1 (Gummere, LCL).
[114] Ibid., 400–3.
[115] Ibid., 402–3.
[116] Ibid.
[117] Presumably he actually means "man," although he uses the generic "hominis."

is not yet rational?[118] Seneca does not object to the child as irrational, but instead pushes the idea of a transforming constitution. Each age—infant, boy, old person—has a unique constitution, different from another, yet each age is adapted to its own constitution. A child starts without teeth, and he or she is "fitted to this condition."[119] Then teeth grow, and the child is also fitted to this condition as well. Like Cicero, Seneca uses a metaphor of vegetation to connect with the child's growth: each stage of a plant's development is different from the last, and yet each stage has a specific constitution, and at each stage the plant conforms to it.[120] The fact that each age has a distinct constitution, however, does not mean that a person is completely divided. While the infant, boy, youth, and old person have distinct periods, it is still the same person throughout. And the process of adaptation in each stage is the same as well—it is simply that what one adapts to changes. Here Seneca touches again on something that came up in *Letter* 118, although in this case he concentrates on a different issue. In both cases, he can maintain that a later state might be better than a previous one, yet that the previous one can be "according to nature." "For even if there is in store for him any higher phase into which he must be changed, the state in which he is born is also according to nature."[121]

In an earlier letter, Seneca both notes clear distinctions between children and adults and, like Paul, also warns of slipping back into a childish state.[122] *Letter* 4 refers to the ceremony of the *toga virilis*, a ceremony that will be considered in the next chapter. This ceremony formally acknowledges the young boy as a man, removing the toga of the child, and donning the toga of the adult. This symbolically and arguably ontologically marked the putting aside of childish ways and truly *becoming* an adult. Here, however, Seneca notes the ways in which backsliding can occur, particularly in reference to a fear of death. Writing again to Lucilius, he says:

> You remember, of course, what joy you felt when you laid aside the garments of boyhood and donned the man's toga, and were escorted to the forum; nevertheless, you may look for a still greater joy when you have laid aside the mind of boyhood and when wisdom has enrolled you among men. For it is not boyhood that still stays with us, but something worse—boyishness. And this condition is all the more serious because we possess the authority of old age, together with the follies of boyhood, yea, even the follies of infancy. Boys fear trifles, children fear shadows, we fear both.

Here we see several things. First, there is a natural progression one ought to follow: just as a boy grows into a man, so, too, ought the mind progress from the boyish state to a mature one. This was seen clearly in the previously discussed letters: "the Good" was seen as each thing lives into what it ought to be, and a child's progression to an

---

[118] Ibid.
[119] Ibid., 404–5.
[120] Ibid.
[121] Ibid.
[122] 1 Corinthians 3:1-3. See also 1 Corinthians 13:11, 14:20.

adult involves not only physical but also moral and intellectual progress. Second, while the progression of boy to man is automatic, the maturation of the mind is not. Physical progress requires some amount of effort, demonstrated by the child's painful determination to learn to walk (*Letter* 118). Yet this progress is by nature or instinct, just as animals by nature or instinct are able to jump, leap, growl, or squeak. On the other hand, the highest good an adult (male) can achieve in mind and morals requires a different sort of effort, one neither automatic nor often recognized. Indeed, "What does the virtuous life look like, and how does one attain it?" are the fundamental questions of all of the philosophical schools in Seneca's era. Third, the state of living with a man's body but a child's mind is far worse than being a child with a child's mind, because the former possesses the "authority" of old age, mixed with the "follies" of boyhood. This to Seneca is a potent combination.

Death and the Child: Unfulfilled Hopes

A vivid and poignant example of the potential of children in ancient literature is expressed at their death, and their parents grieve what could have been.[123] This is seen clearly both in funerary inscriptions and in consolation literature. This is also demonstrated in letters and personal reflections of one's own children, such as Quintilian in his *Orator's Education*. Quintilian takes time to enumerate his griefs, beginning with his young wife, and moving on to his two children. The younger son died first, and Quintilian says of the child: "what flashes of intellect, what solid possession of a calm and even at that age almost unbelievably lofty mind? The child would have deserved love, even if he had been another's."[124] After the younger son dies, Quintilian says, "Henceforward, I depended entirely on the hopes and delights given to me by my little Quintilian. He could be comfort enough. He had shown not just promising flowers, like his brother, but, by the time he entered his tenth year, sure and well-formed fruits."[125] The older brother, too, falls sick and dies after a prolonged illness. Quintilian says he almost should have anticipated this death, as the child was so full of promise: "it has often been observed that early ripening means a quicker fall, and that there is some envious power that cuts short great promise, presumably to prevent our blessings being prolonged beyond what man is allowed to enjoy."[126] Quintilian uses several turns of phrase that will be commonly found in funerary inscriptions—the loss of hopes for their child, the promise of talent cut short, the comparison of a child to a blooming or fruitful tree, cut down too soon.

---

[123] See Richard Saller, *Patriarchy, Property and Death in the Roman Family* (Cambridge: Cambridge University Press, 1994), in particular part 1, for simulations on life expectancy and infant mortality. He essentially argues that about half of babies would die in infancy, another half would die by puberty. If one made it to puberty, however, that person had a reasonable chance of making it to middle age.
[124] Quintilian, *The Orator's Education, Volume I*. 12–13 (Russell, LCL).
[125] Ibid., 14–15.
[126] Ibid.

Mirroring what has been seen from Quintilian's writings, one of the most common themes in funerary inscriptions for children is that with their death, so, too, the parent's hope for them has died. Sometimes this takes the form of a general, sad expression of lost hope:

> I wept for the death of my Theonoe, but the hopes I had of our child lightened my grief. But now envious fate has bereft me of the boy, too. Alas my child, all that was left to me, I am cheated of thee! Persephone, give ear to the prayer of a mourning father, and lay the child in the bosom of its dead mother.[127]

> Who is there that has not suffered the extremity of woe, weeping for a son? But the house of Posidippus buried all four, taken from him in four days by death, that cut short all his hopes of them. The father's mourning eyes drenched with tears have lost their sight, and one may say that a common night now holds them all.[128]

At other times the grief is over a more concrete hope that will now be unrealized. Sometimes this unfulfilled hope is that of being born at all. One such inscription bemoans the marriage bed, because it led to the child's conception. It goes on to say: "Three days passed and ever the babe remained with unfulfilled hope of its being born. The womb, O babe, instead of the dust rests lightly on thee, for it enwraps thee and thou hast no need of earth."[129] More usually, these concrete hopes focus on activities a child may have accomplished had they lived. Many inscriptions are from parents, wailing that it should be their children burying them in their old age, not the reverse. "Five daughters and five sons did Bio bear to Didymon, but she got no joy from one of either. Bio herself so excellent and a mother of such fine babes, was not buried by her children, but by strange hands."[130] Children were to be a joy to their parents in their life, a support in their old age, and to bury and mourn them in their death. A child's untimely death destroys all these hopes.

A common theme of concrete unrealized hopes is that of a girl dying before she was able to be married. Sometimes these are general, expressing sadness that the young girl never grew up enough to be married and have children. One such is of the tomb of Helen, whose mother is said to be mourning twice over: for her and for her previously deceased brother. Helen's suitors are mentioned as well: "To her suitors I left a common grief; for the hope of all mourned equally for her who was yet no one's."[131] Similarly a mother mourns, "Alas! Aristocrateia, thou art gone to deep Acheron, gone to rest before thy prime, before thy marriage; and naught but tears is left for thy mother,

---

[127] *The Greek Anthology, Volume II: Book 7.* 206–9 (Paton, LCL).
[128] Ibid., 208–9.
[129] Ibid., 312–13.
[130] Ibid., 264–5.
[131] Ibid., 104–5. See also 266–7, "I bewail virgin Antibia, eager to wed whom came many suitors to her father's house, led by the report of her beauty and discretion; but destroying Fate, in the case of all, sent their hopes rolling far away."

who reclining on thy tomb often bewails thee."[132] Especially poignant are those that proclaim that the girl was on the very eve of her bridal night.

> [As she had just loosed her maiden zone] Death came first and took the maidenhood of Crocale. The bridal song ended in wailing, and the fond anxiety of her parents was set to rest not by marriage but by the tomb.[133]

> No husband but Death did Clearista receive on her bridal night as she loosed her maiden zone. But now at eve the flutes were making music at the door of the bride, the portals of her chamber echoed to knocking hands. And at morn the death wail was loud, the bridal song was hushed and changed to a voice of wailing. The same torches that flamed round her marriage bed lighted her dead on her downward way to Hades.[134]

> But now the sweet flute was echoing in the bridal chamber of Nikippis, and the house rejoiced in the clapping of hands at her wedding. But the voice of wailing burst in upon the bridal hymn, and we saw her dead, the poor child, not yet quite a wife. O tearful Hades, why didst thou divorce the bridegroom and bride, thou who thyself takest delight in ravishment?[135]

A few things are noteworthy. First, each of these examples uses irony in the juxtaposition of expectations and actualities. Where the parents had intended flutes for joyful music, instead they are used for mourning. Singing, too, abruptly changed from a bridal hymn to a dirge. Where a human bridegroom was expected, Hades, god of the dead, instead became the bridegroom. Second, this irony is used to show bitter anguish. It is not merely that a young girl has died but rather that she has died at just the time where her parents' hopes were to be realized. At the moment of greatest joy comes the moment of absolute sorrow. Finally, there is an interesting commonality between the rituals surrounding marriage and death. This is how the irony can be highlighted so starkly: musical instruments, sung hymns, lighted candles/torches, processions—all of these are employed for both bridal and funerary observances.[136]

The other major unrealized hope for young girls' tombs is that of motherhood: because of their untimely death, they will never bear children for their parents.

> Fate carried me off but fourteen years old, the only child that Thalia bore to Didymus. Ah, ye Destinies, why were ye so hard-hearted, never bringing me to the bridal chamber or the sweet task of conceiving children? My parents were on the

---

[132] Ibid., 488. See also 486–7.
[133] Ibid., 104–5.
[134] Ibid., 102–5.
[135] Ibid., 106–7.
[136] See Andrzej Wypustek, *Images of Eternal Beauty in Funerary Verse Inscriptions of the Hellenistic and Greco-Roman Periods* (Boston: Brill, 2013), 118–21 for a discussion on the similarities between the two rites. He is however, dismissive of any deep correlation, arguing that the connections between two are "superficial" (118).

point of leading me to Hymen, but I went to loathed Acheron. But, ye gods, still, I pray, the plaints of my father and mother who wither away because of my death.[137]

While the sorts of unrealized hopes for young girls tended to center on marriage and motherhood, there were many more specific and concrete hopes lost for young boys. Fronto's tomb, found in Cyzicus, is a long and detailed example of the sorts of unfulfilled hopes a parent might bemoan on a boy's tomb:

Cruel fate, why didst thou show me the light for the brief measure of a few years? Was it to vex my unhappy mother with tears and lamentations owing to my death? She it was who bore me and reared me and took much more pains than my father in my education. For he left me an orphan in his house when I was but a tiny child, but she toiled all she could for my sake. My desire was to distinguish myself in speaking in the courts before our righteous magistrates, but it did not fall to her to welcome the first down on my chin, herald of lovely prime, nor my marriage torches; she never sang the solemn bridal hymn for me, nor looked, poor woman, upon a child of mine who would keep the memory of our lamented race alive. Yea, even in death it grieves me sore, the ever-growing sorrow of my mother Politta as she mourns and thinks of her Fronto, she who bore him short-lived, an empty delight of our dear country.[138]

Fronto's mother mourns her son's distinguishing himself as an adult before magistrates, but she also specifically mourns important rites that signal his progression into adulthood—his first beard, his marriage,[139] and his future children, the symbol of the continuity of the family line. Each of these represents moments of great joy, moments anticipated and hoped for, and all have failed to come to be. Here we also see the disappointment of hopes expressed through the futile effort she put into raising him and giving him an education. She has put in effort, saying that she "toiled all she could," yet Fate taunts and torments her with his death instead of granting her the expected realization of her efforts. So, too, in the tomb of Rufinus, the inscription states: "I was born of a noble mother, but in vain was I born; for after reaching the perfection of

---

[137] *The Greek Anthology, Volume II: Book 7*. 314–15 (Paton, LCL).
[138] Ibid., 178–81.
[139] Marriage and procreation was a blessing parents generally hoped for their children. However, there is an interesting vacillation on the subject. For instance, inscription #603 (ibid., 322–33), is written about a young man. It is written in a dialogue, where A mourns, and B contradicts A in an effort to give comfort (?). When it comes to being married, the inscriptions says "A. 'He knew not wedlock.' B. 'Nor the pains of wedlock.'" The marriage legislations of Augustus in 18 BCE and 9 CE show this—the push from the emperor betrays the lack of enthusiasm on the part of the nobility. See too Dio Cassius's rendition of Augustus's speech to his unmarried troops: "You talk, forsooth, about this 'free' and 'untrammelled' life that you have adopted, without wives and without children; but you are not a whit better than brigands or the most savage of beasts," (Dio Cassius, *Roman History, Volume VII*. 16–17 [Cary and Foster, LCL]) as well as his commendation of the married ones: "These, now, are the private advantages that accrue to those who marry and beget children; but for the State, for whose sake we ought to do many things that are even distasteful to us, how excellent and how necessary" (ibid., 8–9.)

education and youth, I carried, alas! my learning to Hades and my youth to Erebus."[140] Here the unrealized hope is expressed through the intended-versus-actual beneficiary: it is Hades, and not his mother, father, or country, who gains the benefit of his education.

Funerary inscriptions of the young were expressed in many beautiful and poignant metaphors. Many of these are found in nature, associating young boys and girls with growing trees, flowers, or fruit: "even as the whirlwind uproots a beautiful sapling,"[141] "in the bloom of his youth,"[142] "the flower in full bloom is defiled by the dust,"[143] and "Hades spoiled the ripe fruit of my youth."[144] Each of these continues the theme of destroyed potential—the flower/fruit/tree is destroyed before or just as it is able to reach its climax, its natural state of full growth.

The region of the dead and its various governors (especially Hades and Persephone) are often invoked, and they are said to enjoy that which the parents of the dead should have been enjoying.

> In unknown Acheron, Cleodicus, shalt thou bloom in a youth that never, never may return here…[145]

> Hades, inexorable and unbending, why hast thou robbed baby Callaeschron of life? In the house of Persephone the boy shall be her plaything, but at home he leaves bitter suffering…[146]

> I carried, alas! my learning to Hades and my youth to Erebus.[147]

> A. "Charon is savage." B. "Kind rather." A. "He carried off the young man so soon."[148]

Plutarch's *Consolation to His Wife*

One of the most poignant and beautiful ancient texts on death of children is Plutarch's *Consolation*. Plutarch writes to his wife from afar, having received word that their daughter had died at the age of two years. Plutarch writes in a typically consolatory style.[149] While it could cover many types of grief, death was the most common subject. George Parsenios notes that consolation literature arrived at its definitive form in the Hellenistic age.[150] Authors like Seneca and Plutarch wrote letters of consolation,

---

[140] *The Greek Anthology, Volume II: Book 7*. 300–1 (Paton, LCL).
[141] Ibid., 184–5.
[142] Ibid., 252–3.
[143] Ibid., 258–61.
[144] Ibid., 300–1.
[145] Ibid., 262–3.
[146] Ibid.
[147] Ibid., 300–1.
[148] Ibid., 322–3.
[149] Pseudo-Demetrius, writes in *On Style* that "the consoling type is written to people who have had something unpleasant happen (to them)" (trans. Hans-Josef Klauck and Daniel P.; *Ancient Letters and the New Testament: A Guide to Context and Exegesis*, 199).
[150] George Parsenios, *Departure and Consolation: The Johannine Farewell Discourses in Light of Greco-Roman Literature* (Boston: Brill, 2005), 29.

which contain remarkable stylistic and thematic similarities. However, "it is equally important to recognize that the consistent themes are present in the earliest stages of Greek literature."[151] Consolation literature in the Hellenistic age attempts to frame grief within a philosophical framework where the individual is strengthened to meet the challenges of life.[152] In this tradition, Plutarch's letter is as much about expressing grief and sympathy to his wife as it is encouraging her to grieve in the right way—with moderation and decorum. This does not lessen the grief he feels and expresses, but his philosophical convictions are a way of life to him and to his spouse. He finds it important, therefore, to rely on the things he finds true about the world in helping make sense of the present loss.

Plutarch's consolation is notable for its focus both on the loss of a daughter and on the loss of an infant.[153] The ancient world valued sons above daughters; indeed, daughters were often hardly worth mentioning. In this letter, however, not only does Plutarch mention that the daughter was especially longed for by his wife ("because after four sons the much-desired daughter was born to you")[154] but also that he himself took especial pleasure in her—partially as result of his wife's joy, partially because he was able to name her after his wife. Plutarch says that "this child was beloved by me above all."[155] Moreover, she is about two years old, an age young enough to preclude burial or the full range of funerary rites. Plutarch's interpretation of the law is that "[it] forbids this [full funerary rites] in the case of small children, holding it wrong [to show grief thus] towards those who have passed to a better and holier land and lot."[156] In her commentary on the letter, Sarah Pomeroy notes that "deaths of small children were too common to elicit the mourning and burial ceremonies deemed appropriate for an adult. Infants and small children were often buried in pottery containers, or in a group apart from adults."[157] Plutarch believes that he is not merely following the law; he urges that the parents' inner state be "even more unsullied and pure and modest"[158] than the law dictates. However, it is again notable that while making a show of adherence to the law, he is sufficiently distraught to pen the letter in the first place, then to publish it later.[159] That is to say, sadness

---

[151] Ibid., 31.
[152] C. E. Manning, *Seneca's "Ad Marciam"* (Mnemosyne Supplement 69; Boston: Brill, 1981), 12. See also Parsenios, *Departure and Consolation*, 29–31.
[153] "Infant" broadly defined. Plutarch notes that his daughter is about 2 years old.
[154] Plutarch, *Moralia. Consolation to His Wife*. 582.
[155] Plutarch, *A Consolation to His Wife*, trans. Donald Russel, in *Plutarch's Advice to the Bride and Groom and A Consolation to His Wife: English Translations, Commentary, Interpretive Essays, and Bibliography* (ed. Sarah B. Pomeroy; New York: Oxford University Press, 1999), 59.
[156] Ibid., 63.
[157] Sarah B. Pomeroy, "Commentary on Plutarch, A Consolation to His Wife" in Pomeroy, ed., *Plutarch's Advice to the Bride and Groom and A Consolation to His Wife: English Translations, Commentary, Interpretive Essays, and Bibliography*, 81.
[158] Plutarch, *Moralia. Consolation to His Wife*. 604.
[159] There is of course debate as to whether the letter is substantially as it would have originally been written, or indeed if the letter was only written much later. Pomeroy spends some time musing over the arguments, but ultimately (and correctly) admits that without any evidence of an earlier edition, the debate is somewhat academic (Pomeroy, "Reflections on Plutarch, *A Consolation to His Wife*" in Pomeroy, ed., *Plutarch's Advice to the Bride and Groom and A Consolation to His Wife: English Translations, Commentary, Interpretive Essays, and Bibliography*, 77).

over the death of his daughter was far from a fleeting occurrence. Rather, he feels pain, desires to share it with his wife, and later desired to share it with the general public. Richard Hawley makes this point as well, suggesting that, while consolation literature was common, "Plutarch's is the only surviving example written about the death of so young a child, thus emphasizing their grief."[160] There is something that resonates more universally about grieving the death of a child, even a female, even an infant, than burial laws and customs might reveal.

Plutarch's *Consolation* is also striking for the way in which he grieves for his daughter's virtuous qualities, while strongly urging his wife to avoid grieving the things the little girl will never do. Typical of consolation literature, he lists many qualities that are admirable in the departed one.[161] Little Timoxena was gentle, good, and free "from any crossness or complaint."[162] She responded happily to affection, and she was generous and kind.[163] She was also sweet to hear, see, and touch.[164] Notably absent from his letter, however, are refrains such as we found on many of the funerary inscriptions: Plutarch does not lament that she failed to grow up, get married, and have children. In fact, he specifically urges his wife to not think of these things: "if you feel pity for her, because she died unmarried and childless… they are not the sort of blessings that are important to those who are deprived of them."[165] She is now without pain, and therefore cannot be pained by what she does not have or will not have. Plutarch furthermore argues that her death in a state of relative immaturity is a blessing in two ways. First, she only had the capacity to experience small things.[166] Therefore, she cannot mourn the great things that she may have had, for "how can she be said to be deprived of things her senses and her mind never conceived?"[167] Second, Plutarch understands the soul as "immortal, and as like a captive bird."[168] If the soul has been captive for a long time, it becomes used to the cage, and it is much harder for the soul to be set free again. However, because the little girl died so very young, she did not resist letting go of the body, but rather her soul joyfully "leaps up towards its natural home," not having been "drugged, as it were, into a state of softness and fusion with the body."[169] Noting the absence of lament of the girl's future as a wife and mother, Hawley argues that Plutarch

---

[160] Richard Hawley, "Practicing What You Preach: Plutarch's Sources and Treatment," in Pomeroy, ed., *Plutarch's Advice to the Bride and Groom and A Consolation to His Wife: English Translations, Commentary, Interpretive Essays, and Bibliography*, 125.

[161] C.f. Seneca, *Moral Essays. De Consolatione ad Polybium.* 362–3 (Basore, LCL).

[162] Plutarch, *A Consolation to His Wife*, trans. Donald Russel, in Pomeroy, ed., *Plutarch's Advice to the Bride and Groom and A Consolation to His Wife: English Translations, Commentary, Interpretive Essays, and Bibliography*, 59.

[163] Ibid.

[164] Ibid., 60.

[165] Ibid., 62.

[166] "Your Timoxena is deprived of little things, for little things are all she knew and took delight in," Plutarch, *A Consolation to His Wife*, trans. Donald Russel, in Pomeroy, ed., *Plutarch's Advice to the Bride and Groom and A Consolation to His Wife: English Translations, Commentary, Interpretive Essays, and Bibliography*, 62.

[167] Ibid.

[168] Ibid.

[169] Ibid.

modifies this traditional motif. Rather than bemoan the young child's failure to achieve marriage and children, Plutarch instead focuses on how his wife *herself* achieved these things. Timoxena the elder is, in fact, envied for her own happiness. "Thus," Hawley suggests, "there is no negative string to his daughter's death, only the pathos created by vivid vignettes of her happiness (esp. 2, 3), and Timoxena once again satisfies the ideal by being admired for the three most important things in a woman's life."[170] In this way Hawley believes that Plutarch is able to promote both his daughter and his wife as "extraordinarily virtuous and fortunate."[171]

Keith Bradley considers *Consolation* as offering a rare glimpse into children in the ancient world, more specifically a rare perspective from an *adult-parent* of children in the ancient world. Bradley argues for Plutarch's "special sensitivity to the distinctiveness of the young child on the part of one highly educated individual at a particular moment of Roman imperial (and Greek) history."[172] Bradley emphasizes especially the passages that describe a child at play—in *Consolation* he notes the passage where Plutarch describes his daughter as sharing her food (i.e., the wet nurse) with various toys and dolls she particularly was fond of. For Bradley, Plutarch's comments on children at play reveal that the philosopher clearly understands children and their world on its own terms, distinct from those of an adult. The child has "its own activities, rituals, and *rites of passage*."[173] Bradley argues this to disprove many early studies on the history of children—most famously Philippe Aries's *Centuries of Childhood*—which argue that only with the early modern world did childhood begin to be understood as a "specifically demarcated stage of life."[174] Bradley highlights not only a lovely view of fond recollections of a departed child and her particular virtues but also the fact that Plutarch himself betrays through his writing a sensitive and engaging view of children and their unique world.

Conclusion and Summary

Throughout this chapter, I have explored various ways that children were conceived of and referenced in the approximate time period surrounding the writing of Mark's Gospel. Children were rarely the focus of attention of writers, but children sometimes featured in examples, especially in moral writings. Whenever compared to the ideal adult male, children come up as deficient. Children were characterized as having weak and underdeveloped bodies. Similarly, their mental and moral capacities were described as inferior. A child was known to understand little, betray petty anger, fear, and lack the

---

[170] Richard Hawley, "Practicing What You Preach," in Pomeroy, ed., *Plutarch's Advice to the Bride and Groom and A Consolation to His Wife: English Translations, Commentary, Interpretive Essays, and Bibliography*, 127.

[171] Ibid.

[172] Keith Bradly, "Images of Childhood: The Evidence of Plutarch," in Sarah B. Pomeroy, ed., *Plutarch's Advice to the Bride and Groom and A Consolation to His Wife: English Translations, Commentary, Interpretive Essays, and Bibliography*, 184–5.

[173] Ibid., 191.

[174] Ibid.

measured thoughtfulness that was aspired to. On the other hand, children as a group were enjoyed for small, adorable things: their prattling voices, their frank expressions of tenderness, even their sweet innocence. Furthermore, individual children could be prized and loved. Both consolation letters and epitaphs mourn specific children, and remember unique traits to each child. Many funerary inscriptions also mourn the potential of the child that has been lost to death: she will never grow up to marry; he will never grow up to claim honors in the forum. This ability of the child to change and grow is also commented upon by philosophers. It remains something of a mystery *how* this transformation takes place, but a child has the potential to become something more than he already is. In the following chapter, modern anthropologists will provide a useful rubric to describe this process of transformation, coined "*rites of passage*" by Arnold van Gennep. These *rites of passage* help guide a person from one state of being to another, effecting a complete transformation. After looking at the general category of *rites of passage*, I will examine specific ceremonies found in the first century and argue that these ceremonies fit the category of *rites of passage*, and help transform children into adults. Both the conceptual framework of how children were viewed and the process by which they became adults will be used to better understand what Mark intends when he asserts that one must enter the Kingdom of God "as a child."

3

Rites of Passage and Entrance into Adulthood

As we have seen from the last chapter, the ancient world conceived of children and adults in a crucially distinct way. Far from seeing children as already formed individuals, waiting to take their place in society, children in the ancient world were considered incomplete, vulnerable, and marginal. If the Greco-Roman ideal was the elite male, then all others—women, slaves, children, barbarians, animals—were to some degree simply "not-male." This did not mean they were unloved or unwanted, but it does mean that they were not regarded with high esteem or as worthy of emulation. We have also seen that children—certainly at minimum male freeborn children—had an interesting and unique quality: their *potential* to grow up into the ideal. The imagery used in funerary inscriptions was particularly instructive here. Much of the time, in an untimely death, the potential of the child was mourned. This was seen in the young girl's failure to be married and the young boy's failure to become a man, to gain the senatorial ranks, and to achieve greatness in arms. Most often this was seen in the lost potential of the child to continue the family's legacy and to care for the parents in their old age.

This chapter takes up the idea of potential. If a child has the potential to become a man or a woman, then how this potential was achieved—that is, how a boy attained manhood, how a girl attained womanhood—is of crucial importance here. This will not only show us the transition between a child and an adult—of key importance given the phrase "become like a child"—but also re-highlight the characteristics of children from the previous chapter. In this chapter, I will be drawing on the works of anthropologists who have been groundbreaking in their field in recognizing and defining a set of rites called *rites of passage*. These *rites of passage* are important in their ability to mark and guide the transition of a person from one state of being to another—in our case, the important one being the transition between a child and an adult. Having the structural framework in place, I will examine two *rites of passage*: one for boys becoming men (the *toga virilis* ceremony) and one for girls becoming women (the marriage ceremony). *Rites of passage* interact with the idea of "potential" in two interrelated ways. First, *rites of passage* function to safely transition a person from one state to another—activating their potential, while also acknowledging both the momentous quality of the moment and its danger. Second, *rites of passage* contain a middle stage where the person formally is neither what they were previously nor what they are about to become. This idea of "liminality" will come up as well, and is closely related to potential. Liminality is present in all *rites of passage*, but is particularly protracted in initiation rites. Anthropologists such as Arnold van Gennep, Victor Turner, and Mary Douglas mark and categorize *rites of passage*, showing both their importance in their well-defined structure and their notable qualities of transforming a person from potential into actuality, and in doing so fundamentally altering a person. This idea will be invaluable as I explore in Chapters 4 and 5 the idea of the Kingdom of God and how fundamental transformation of a person is necessary to enter it.

Van Gennep and the *Rites of Passage*

In a groundbreaking work,[1] Arnold van Gennep describes and connects several sets of rituals that he calls "*rites of passage*." Many before him had studied marriage rituals, initiation rituals, funerary rites, and rites surrounding pregnancy or birth. However, van Gennep's contribution was to identify that these rituals had a formal or structural similarity to one another. Terming them *rites of passage*, these rituals all involved a transition, specifically "a passage from one situation to another or from one cosmic or social world to another."[2] He further identified a consistent pattern in each rite: the "means of transition," so to speak. Such rituals always follow the same pattern, with three major phases: "rituals of separation, transitional rites, and rites of incorporation," or preliminal rites, liminal rites, and postliminal rites.

It is important to note that van Gennep understands "civilization" to lie on a spectrum.[3] While more "advanced" civilizations divide the secular from the sacred, he argues, as you "move downward on the scale of civilization,"[4] "the holy enters nearly every phase of a man's life."[5] Highlighting tribal societies in which the spiritual and holy are explicitly acknowledged in these rituals, he is able to draw clear lines of comparison between types of rituals. It is not that van Gennep thinks that modern Western society is devoid of the sacred in ritual. However, he is most interested in those rituals where the participants themselves, as well as the culture as a whole, acknowledge and expect a transition to happen. One is changed in a fundamental way, having gone through one of these rites.

This sense of fundamental change is stressed in the three stages of separation rites, transitional rites, and incorporation rites. In rites of separation, there is a sense of leaving behind and being severed from the past mode of being, which requires safe passage away from the old. Thus, the rite may include the severing of the umbilical cord in birth, "leaving" a house in a marriage ceremony, stripping away clothing, and so forth. The second stage, rites of transition, guides their participants through a stage where one is neither here nor there, neither this nor that. More will be presently said

---

[1] Arnold van Gennep, *The Rites of Passage* (trans. Monika Vizedom and Gabrielle Caffee; London: Routledge & Kegan Paul, 1960).
[2] Ibid., 10–11.
[3] For perhaps obvious reasons modern anthropologists reject this teleology.
[4] Ibid., 2. Again, this understanding of society is rejected by current anthropology.
[5] Ibid.

about this stage; for now, it is suffice to know that this is a stage of danger, characterized by intense camaraderie among those going through it at the same time. Finally, in rites of incorporation, there is a sense of welcoming and firmly binding the person into the new mode of being. One may be dressed in an attire that signals the new status as wife or adult or initiate, who physically enters a new space or dwelling or territory, and may receive a new name or title. At this point the transition is safely completed. Van Gennep is careful to note that, while the stages of separation, transition, and incorporation are to some extent present in each of the *rites of passage* he describes, for different rituals there is more emphasis on one of these stages and less on another. Funerals, for instance, usually place more emphasis on rites of separation; marriage, on rites of incorporation; and the movement from childhood to adulthood, or "social puberty,"[6] emphasizes transitional rites.

Having described the general phases of the *rites of passage*, van Gennep uses the rest of the book to exemplify his system. The chapters that are of most importance to us are those dealing with children: "Birth and Childhood" and, perhaps of even greater importance, "Initiation Rites."

In his chapter "Birth and Childhood," van Gennep primarily deals with the rites associated with a child's birth; he also touches on rites associated with becoming an adult (and continues the latter theme into a subsequent chapter). One of the more interesting aspects of the liminal period between the rites of separation and rites of incorporation—which can last in some cultures only a few moments, in others days and even years—is that in some cultures the child is considered not yet to have a soul. In this connection he cites an Ainu[7] saying:

> The Ainu gives the following reason for the liminal period in which mother, father, and child are maintained for the first days after birth: the mother gives the child its body and the father its soul but this occurs only gradually; the body is acquired during pregnancy and the soul comes into being during the twelve days following birth... only on the twelfth day is the child a complete and autonomous individual.[8]

This idea is startling, especially in contrast to modern, anti-abortion claims of the soul's formation at conception. It serves well to illustrate the degree to which the period of liminality creates a pause, even a gap in a person. Incorporation rites do more than give cursory titles; rather, they shift, from one perceived stage to another, the deepest part of who a being *is*.

---

[6] Van Gennep strongly argues that "physiological puberty" and "social puberty" are not the same thing, and only in extremely rare cases converge. In fact (*Rites of Passage*, 66), he specifically uses ancient Roman marriage customs to prove his point: the legal age of marriage for a girl in Rome was twelve, whereas the average age for the beginning of her menstrual period—the quintessential sign of female puberty—was usually between the ages of fourteen and sixteen. Soranus, in his *Gynecology*, asserts that "menstruation, in most cases, first appears around the fourteenth year, at the time of puberty and swelling of the breasts" (Soranus, *Gynecology*, trans. O Temkin; Baltimore: Johns Hopkins University Press, 1956), 17. See M. K. Hopkins, "The Age of Roman Girls at Marriage," *Population Studies* 18.3 (1965): 310, for a summary of the ancient discussion pinpointing menarche.
[7] The Ainu are a people indigenous to Japan and parts of Russia.
[8] Ibid., 53.

This trend is furthermore notable in van Gennep's chapter on "initiation rites," which describes multiple societies and their distinctive interpretations of initiation rites. Van Gennep has chosen this title carefully, as he is not merely interested in those "coming-of-age" rites by which a child passes into adulthood but, rather, sees an exact parallel between such rites and entrance into secret societies or the installation of a king. In each case the general phases of preliminal, liminal, and postliminal rites appear; however, the initiation rites are notable as a group for their visible and often protracted liminal period. In some tribes in Australia, the novice is secluded into the bush, separated from his mother and family. Such rites clearly lie in the category of separation; van Gennep notes that in many tribes the novice is considered dead. He "remains dead for the duration of his novitiate"[9] in the case of the Kwakiutl, for whom the transition from childhood to adulthood is symbolized by the exorcism of a "spirit" who personifies the previous world.[10] The in-between state is generally prolonged, often accompanied by activities designed to physically and mentally weaken the novice. This, van Gennep suggests, is "undoubtedly intended to make him lose all recollection of his childhood existence."[11] Finally, after the novitiate has been instructed in the mysteries and ways of the culture, an initiation ceremony is conducted, which often includes a special bodily mark (circumcision, a tooth removed) that symbolizes and visually demonstrates the inclusion of the novice into adult membership. Whereas the metaphor of death was used for the novice, he is now "resurrected." In the case of the Kwakiutl, the novitiate ends with the acquisition of the "spirit" protector of the tribe.

In this connection van Gennep describes rites of entering Christianity.[12] Admittedly, his view is imbalanced; it is clearly emblematic of a time where ancient Christianity's similarity to the mystery religions was overstated by then current scholarship. His source material, moreover, comes from the *ordo baptismi* from the eleventh century, as well as that found in the missal of Pope Gelasius II,[13] and therefore represents a specific, rather than general, rite of baptism. That said, van Gennep analyzes such rites with perspicuity. He considers the catechumen a liminal being. Rites accepting one as a catechumen include rites of separation, such as exorcism, and rites of incorporation that mark the catechumen state with prayer, the sign of the cross, and administration of salt. During one's time as a catechumen, repeated exorcisms were performed, and the person was permitted to go to the service and be taught, but was required to withdraw during the Mass. The length of time one stayed a catechumen was not fixed, and could last until death. One made the transition from the catechumenate stage by a final exorcism (separation), being anointed with oil (incorporation), and then the official baptism, at which point one "became *regeneratus*, or *conceived again*, according to the very terms of the prayer pronounced during the rite which followed."[14] One was

---

[9] Van Gennep, *Rites of Passage*, 75.
[10] Ibid., 76.
[11] Ibid., 75.
[12] Ibid., 93–5.
[13] Ibid., 93.
[14] Ibid., 94.

dressed in white, was marked by the sign of the cross, and permitted communion with honey-water and milk: again, symbols of rebirth, new identity, and acceptance.

This discussion has been lengthy, in order to highlight two things. First, van Gennep stresses the importance of understanding all types of initiation ceremonies as having the same pattern. While all rites in his book are characterized as *rites of passage*—and therefore displaying structural similarities—these initiation rites are for him structurally identical and fall under the same title. Second, one of the most critical ways in which initiation rites are like each other, differing from rites of birth or death, is the importance of the liminal stage. For this reason, a careful understanding of what is "liminal," particularly as applied to people, is necessary. For this we turn to van Gennep's successor, Victor Turner.

Victor Turner's Analysis of the Liminal

In his anthropological studies Turner followed van Gennep, particularly in his understanding of these *rites of passage*. The "liminal" stage of the *rites of passage*, as defined by van Gennep, already included a nebulous sense of being in-between, neither what one was before nor yet what one will become. It is in this stage that the transition and transformation of a person can happen. This stage is closely related to potentiality, therefore, as the person is both pure potential and also functionally invisible and indeterminate. Turner will pick up this nebulous category, expanding upon the sense of "liminality." Two of Turner's essays in particular concern themselves with the subject of liminality.

"Betwixt and Between: The Liminal Period in *Rites de Passage*"

The first of Turner's articles that are important for our purposes is "Betwixt and Between: The Liminal Period in *Rites de Passage*."[15] In this article he seeks to outline some of the "sociocultural properties" of the liminal period as set out by van Gennep.[16] Moreover, Turner specifically examines the prolonged period of liminality involved in many initiation rites.

One of Turner's main points is that, while it is appropriate to use the term "states" (i.e., "a relatively fixed or stable condition"[17]) to describe the periods before and after the *rites of passage*, the liminal period is more appropriately termed as "transitional." Here he refers to something definite: "I prefer to regard transition as a process, a becoming, and in the cases of *rites of passage* even a transformation—here an apt analogy would be water in process of being heated to a boiling point, or a pupa changing from grub to moth."[18] Turner emphasizes the idea that the liminal period enacts a transformation

---

[15] Victor Witter Turner, "Betwixt and Between: The Liminal Period in *Rites de Passage*," in *The Forest of Symbols: Aspects of Ndembu Ritual* (Ithaca: Cornell University Press, 1967), 93–111.
[16] Ibid., 93.
[17] Ibid.
[18] Ibid., 94.

of one's very being. To illustrate this point, particularly as it relates to a people moving through the liminal period, he notes that for the Bemba and Shilluk of the Sudan, "to 'grow' a girl into a woman is to effect an ontological transformation; it is not merely to convey an unchanging substance from one position to another by a quasi-mechanical force."[19] This point cannot be overemphasized: the liminal period represents a period of *ontological transformation*. Furthermore, there are two things that enact this transformation: the ritual itself, and the acquisition of *gnosis* by the initiates. Turner insists:

> the arcane knowledge or "*gnosis*" obtained in the liminal period is felt to change the inmost nature of the neophyte, impressing him, as a seal impresses wax, with the characteristics of his new state. It is not a mere acquisition of knowledge, but a change in being. His apparent passivity is revealed as an absorption of powers which will become active after his social status has been redefined in the aggregation rites.[20]

For Turner, a person undergoing the liminal period is "structurally if not physically, 'invisible.'"[21] Because the person has left her original and stable state, but has not yet entered into her new and desired stable state, she remains in between categories. This observation leads to two related but distinct sets of descriptions: a person is both "no longer" (commonly associated with images of death and nothingness) and "not yet" (with associative imagery of things like gestation and embryos). The descriptive imagery for liminality is hazy, confused, and sometimes contradictory. So, too, the people themselves are nebulous, occupying an unsure position that defies stability and is of necessity difficult to pinpoint. Turner invokes Mary Douglas's foundational work on purity and danger, which underscores the fact that those who are nebulous and difficult to define are often seen as polluting and dangerous. A common response to such people is to separate them from the group, whether for a finite period of "impurity" (menstrual periods or sometimes pregnancies) or decisively and permanently, in the case of essential characteristics. Using these ideas, Turner emphasizes the ways in which many neophytes are physically separated from society at large. Furthermore, it is not merely the imagery or physical separation that highlights this structural invisibility; this extends to other physical markers of society: "a further structurally negative characteristic of transitional beings is that they *have* nothing. They have no status, property, insignia, secular clothing, rank, kinship position, nothing to demarcate them structurally from their fellows."[22] They have been literally stripped of anything that defines them.

This unique place of the neophyte, of being separated from everything that defines him or her, furthermore leads to unique relationships with other neophytes and with their instructor(s). The relationship of neophytes to one another is that of absolute

---

[19] Ibid., 101–2.
[20] Ibid., 102.
[21] Ibid., 95.
[22] Ibid., 98–9.

equality, whatever their status may have been before the period of initiation, and however long the period after the ritual's completion. The relationship of the neophyte to the instructor, on the other hand, is one of absolute submission. This point is developed in greater detail in Turner's second article, "Liminality and *Communitas*," which will be addressed below. For now, it is sufficient to note the structural invisibility of the neophytes that the liminal state creates.

Liminality and *Communitas*

The second of Turner's essays pertaining to our purpose is found in Chapter 3 of *The Ritual Process*, entitled "Liminality and *Communitas*."[23] Taking up many of the same themes as "Betwixt and Between," here Turner is interested in developing some of the thoughts only touched upon in his earlier essay.[24] In particular, he spends the majority of this essay examining and analyzing the unique relationships of neophytes to one another. He begins by making a claim about human interactions. Turner sees two different models at play: one that is fundamentally hierarchical, dividing people up in a way that measures them in a scale from low to high, and one that is fundamentally undifferentiated and unstructured, which he terms *communitas*. He regards the former as the governing model in societies outside the period of the liminal and the latter as particularly representative of the liminal phase. To illustrate the distinction between the properties of liminality and those of a status system, he lists several contrasting pairs, in the format of "*communitas*/status model": "equality/inequality," "absence of property/property," "minimization of sex distinctions/maximization of sex distinctions."[25]

Having noted the diametric opposition of the two models, Turner speculates about the purpose or intent behind the mode of *communitas*. He argues, "[L]iminality implies that the high could not be high unless the low existed, and he who is high must experience what it is like to be low."[26] That is to say, he sees both of these models as deeply imbedded in the psyche of most human societies. The status model is stable; indeed, it is the only one Turner sees as sustainable over an indefinite period of time. However, the *communitas* model, despite its comparative instability, perhaps for this reason shows up in the liminal phase of initiation, a period which itself is finite. Turner is quick to note that this is not the *only* place for the model of *communitas* to emerge,[27] but it is a striking one.

It is also here that Turner takes pains to explicate the parallels to Christianity. His lengthy explanation is notable:

---

[23] Victor Witter Turner, "Liminality and *Communitas*," in *The Ritual Process. Structure and Anti-Structure* (Ithaca: Cornell University Press, 1969), 94–130.
[24] Ibid., 94.
[25] Ibid., 107. The further are a few more key social dyads Turner lists, each of which has application to the Markan conception of the Kingdom of God "transition/state; totality/partiality; absence of rank/distinctions of rank; humility/just pride of position; no distinction of wealth/distinction of wealth; unselfishness/selfishness; total obedience/obedience only to superior rank; suspension of kinship rights and obligations/kinship rights and obligations; foolishness/sagacity."
[26] Ibid., 97.
[27] Ibid., 109.

> The reader will have noticed immediately that many of these properties constitute what we think of as characteristics of the religious life in the Christian tradition… what appears to have happened is that with the increasing specialization of society and culture, with progressive complexity in the social division of labor, what was in tribal society principally a set of transitional qualities "betwixt and between" defined states of culture and society has become itself an institutionalized state. But traces of the *passage* quality of the religious life remain in such formulations as: "the Christian is a stranger to the world, a pilgrim, a traveler, with no place to rest his head." Transition has here become a permanent condition. Nowhere has this institutionalization of liminality been more clearly marked and defined than in the monastic and mendicant states in the great world religions.[28]

Several things in this passage are important. First, Turner overtly recognizes the ways in which liminality influences and describes Christian tradition. Many of my own claims will presuppose the direct connections van Gennep and Turner make with Christianity. Second, Turner expands van Gennep's original concept of the liminal. For van Gennep, the liminal was one phase of the *rites of passage*. Turner begins to use the term "liminal" in a more overarching way that labels general ways of life. He presents the court jester as an example of a liminal figure: one whose state is stable yet whose function allows him, a low-class "fool," to speak with mockery of those of the highest order. The liminal need not *necessarily* be finite. Turner is able to point to metaphors in the Christian tradition that express the sense of *passage*: images of alien status, being disjoined, and so forth. However, these metaphors assume a point of origin from which further growth has occurred. A third point worth noting almost contradicts the second, but not quite: one of the reasons that the entirety of the Christian life looks like the liminal state in *rites of passage* is that Christians have broadly believed the Kingdom of God to be their true home, and that their ontological state of transformation into children of God is being enacted in this life. This third point is particularly relevant to what I will argue about how Mark understands and frames entrance into the Kingdom of God.

Turner makes a related, though not identical, point when he analyzes millenarian movements.[29] Like Christian groups, millenarian groups have many of the same markers as that of the liminal period of transition. Often such groups dispense with property, have radical senses of equality, strive for sexual continence, and insist upon absolute submission to the leader of the group or to the group's creeds. Turner makes two observations about millenarian groups. First, they eventually exhaust themselves and become one more institution (though often more fanatical than normal). He raises this point to highlight the difficulty of a group's maintenance of something essentially unstructured and unstable. But second, and more interesting, he considers the liminal characteristics of the millenarian movements as indicative of the *rites of passage* at work on a metalevel. It is, Turner thinks, generally in periods of great social upheaval

---

[28] Ibid., 107.
[29] Ibid., 111.

that millenarian movements come into being. To him, this speaks to the greater society *itself* passing from one cultural state to another.[30] As such, one would expect to see— and in fact *does* see— markers indicating the standard transitional features of a *rite of passage*: separation, margin, and aggregation. The millenarian movement, therefore, plays its own part in the culture's transition—that of the liminal period.

In this way van Gennep and Turner explicate the idea of the liminal. Van Gennep locates the concept in certain sorts of rituals that he terms *rites of passage*, a consistent series of stages by which a person effects transition from one social state to another. The middle stage is one of ontological remaking: the person is no longer what they were before, and not yet what they will become. This stage is particularly notable in initiation rites, because they are often prolonged in comparison to other rites (e.g., funerary rites). Turner, especially interested in the liminal stage, expands van Gennep's original theory and sets before the reader the various imagery associated with it (*both* death *and* gestation). The liminal stage not only effects transformation—a transformation, he insists, that is on an ontological level—but also creates a particular form of community, or *communitas*, among those within the liminal stage. This form of community is notably similar to that found in early Christian societies, among others.

Mary Douglas

The final anthropologist whose work is important enough to outline in detail is Mary Douglas. In her book *Purity and Danger*,[31] she builds upon the work of Turner and van Gennep, while taking a unique turn. Douglas is most concerned to show that in all cultures, there is a systematic and symbolic relation between dirt and pollution—a relationship that goes far beyond a concern for "hygiene." For her "our pollution behavior is the reaction which condemns any object or idea likely to confuse or contradict cherished classifications."[32] Once again her categories are universal—all cultures, including England or the United States, have understandings of what "dirt" is, how to be clean from it, and even in what contexts one should classify something as "dirty" versus "clean" (e.g., food on the table is considered "clean" in our society, whereas on the floor or on clothing is considered "dirty").[33] Douglas makes the corollary point that each individual body represents the macro culture—and therefore cultural understandings of bodily margins, and excrement therefrom, once again reveal larger cultural systems' perceptions of what is pollutive, what is marginal, what is to be feared. She takes Leviticus as a case study: the prohibitions on what things one should or should not eat are not at their fundamental level hygienic restrictions (e.g., if pigs were forbidden because they might carry specific disease), nor purely arbitrary reasons of separation from other societies. Rather, prohibitions in Leviticus showcases

---

[30] Ibid., 112.
[31] Mary Douglas, *Purity and Danger: An Analysis of Concepts of Pollution and Taboo* (England: Penguin Books, 1970).
[32] Ibid., 48.
[33] Ibid.

where creatures fail to neatly conform to the categories evident in the codes. Thus, her articulation of why eating pig is forbidden is because of its ambiguous situation: it has a cloven hoof but does not chew the cud.[34]

While Douglas's book has innumerable important points and connections, her work on marginal states and marginal beings has the more direct bearing on the topic at hand. Marginal beings are always considered both vulnerable and dangerous, whether or not they have actively done something morally wrong. She gives the example of an unborn child: "Its present position is ambiguous, equally its future. For no one can say what sex it will have or whether it will survive the hazards of infancy."[35] While the child has done nothing wrong, it is both helpless and dangerous—to the mother, to the family, or to the society. Her description of the dangers of *rites of passage* is important enough to quote at length:

> Van Gennep... saw society as a house with rooms and corridors in which passage from one to another is dangerous. Danger lies in transitional states; simply because transition is neither one state nor the next, it is indefinable. The person who must pass from one to another is himself in danger and emanates danger to others. The danger is controlled by ritual which precisely separates him from his old status, segregates him for a time and then publicly declares his entry to his new status. Not only is transition itself dangerous, but also the rituals of segregation are the most dangerous phase of the rites. So often we read that boys die in initiation ceremonies, or that their sisters and mothers are told to fear for their safety, or that they used in the old days to die from hardship or fright, or by supernatural punishment from their misdeeds. Then somewhat tamely come the accounts of the actual ceremonies which are so safe that the threats of danger sound like a hoax. But we can be sure that the trumped-up dangers express something important about marginality. To say that the boys risk their lives says precisely that to go out of the formal structure and to enter the margins is to be exposed to power that is enough to kill them or make their manhood. The theme of death and rebirth, of course, has other symbolic functions: the initiates die to their old life and are reborn to the new. The whole repertoire of ideas concerning pollution and purification are used to mark the gravity of the event and the power of ritual to remake a man—that is straightforward.[36]

This passage is important for many reasons. First, it gives an unusually helpful visual metaphor for van Gennep's tripartite structure found in the *rites of passage*—that of the house with rooms and corridors. Perhaps most helpfully, the idea of the corridors concretizes both the sense of motion and a sense of being in-between. Second, the passage makes the connection between ritual and pollution, between ritual and danger—ritual helps protect, control, and minimize the effects of pollution/danger. Third, it highlights and defines the power found in the margins. That power is not

---

[34] Ibid., 69.
[35] Ibid., 115.
[36] Ibid., 116–17.

always bad: she particularly notes that the power in the margins of initiation rites is that which transforms a boy into a man. However, the power is uncontrolled and therefore dangerous. It is here that the fear for the safety of the boy comes in. Thus, too, the repetition of images of death and resurrection: not only is there the idea of metamorphosis, of discarding the old and emerging anew, but also there is the idea of narrowly escaping death. Here Douglas re-emphasizes, along with Van Gennep, the danger of the separation rites. As we move forward, the importance of Douglas's additions to the insight of van Gennep and Turner will become even more apparent.

I will be utilizing these three anthropologists throughout the rest of this book, arguing that their conceptions of *rites of passage* are useful categories from which to understand Mark and his use of children in Mark 10:13-16. First and foremost, van Gennep, Turner, and Douglas argue that their conceptions of *rites of passage*, and liminality, are categories that spanned a number of cultures and time periods. Each intentionally draws from a variety of peoples—both highly industrialized societies and indigenous ones. Furthermore, each purposefully draws from a variety of eras to illustrate their points. Van Gennep occasionally draws from ancient Greco-Roman practices to bolster his theories.[37] Not only does this prove that his scope of work extends beyond the present but also that he examines on a cursory level the very people and period of interest to the present discussion.

Not only this but also a small yet significant portion of classics scholarship have incorporated the research of van Gennep and Turner. Several collections, including Mark Padilla's *Rites of Passage in Ancient Greece: Literature, Religion, Society*,[38] as well as David Dobb and Christopher Faraone's *Initiation in Ancient Greek Rituals and Narratives*,[39] use the categories of van Gennep and Turner and apply them to Greek literature, narrative, and poetry. Mark McVann, notably, wrote his dissertation incorporating Victor Turner into his analysis of Mark 4:35–5:43,[40] and wrote several other essays exploring Turner in conjunction with the Gospel of Mark.[41] Countless others reference the works of these anthropologists.[42]

---

[37] See Van Gennep, *Rites of Passage*, 38, 66.
[38] Mark Padilla ed., *Rites of Passage in Ancient Greece: Literature, Religion, Society* (Lewisburg: Bucknell University Press, 1999).
[39] David Dobb and Christopher Faraone, eds., *Initiation in Ancient Greek Rituals and Narratives* (London: Routledge, 2003).
[40] Mark Edward McVann, *Dwelling Among the Tombs: Discourse, Discipleship, and the Gospel of Mark 4: 35–5:43* (PhD Dissertation, Emory University, 1984).
[41] For instance, Mark Edward McVann "Baptism, Miracles, and Boundary Jumping in Mark," *Biblical Theology Bulletin* 21.4 (1991): 151–7; "General Introductory Bibliography for Ritual Studies," *Semeia* 67 (1994): 227–32; "One of the Prophets: Matthew's Testing Narrative as a Rite of Passage," *Biblical Theology Bulletin* 23.1 (1993): 14–20; "Reading Mark Ritually: Honor-Shame and the Ritual of Baptism." *Semeia* 67 (1994): 179–98; "Introduction," *Semeia* 67 (1994): 7–12.
[42] Titles are ubiquitous. To give a small sampling: Fanny Dolansky, "Coming of Age in Rome: The History and Social Significance of Assuming the *Toga Virilis*" (Master's diss., University of Victoria, 1999); J. Albert Harrill, "Coming of Age and Putting on Christ: The Toga Virilis Ceremony, Its Paraenesis, and Paul's Interpretation of Baptism in Galatians," *Novum Testamentum* 44.3 (2002): 252–77; Matthew J. Grey, "Becoming as a Little Child: Elements of Ritual Rebirth in Ancient Judaism and Early Christianity," *Studia Antiqua* 1 (2001): 63–85; Beryl Rawson, "Adult-Child Relationships in Roman Society," in *Marriage, Divorce, and Children in Ancient Rome*, 7–30. See below also for adoption of the term *rite of passage* in scholarship on ancient weddings.

68   *The Transformational Role of Discipleship*

In what follows I will argue that ancient Greece and Rome have ceremonies that may be classified as *rites of passage*. Furthermore, I will argue that there are initiation rites, showing how the Greco-Romans conceived of the transition between a boy and a man, a girl and a woman. In the case of the transition between boyhood and manhood, the assumption of the *toga virilis* has been both referenced in passing, and argued at great length, to be a *rite of passage* in the sense of Van Gennep. In the case of the transition between girlhood and womanhood, while there is no separate transitional rite, the wedding ceremony has been both argued and assumed to be a *rite of passage*. I will mostly be focusing on Roman upper-class ceremonies simply because there is a scarcity of material about children in the first place. The *toga virilis* ceremony is as well documented as it is because it involves the burgeoning elite adult male. However, after a survey of the *toga virlis* and the marriage ceremonies, I will briefly address children of lower classes.

The Assumption of the *Toga Virilis* as a Rite of Passage[43]

The *toga virilis* ceremony is an example of a documented, well-established rite-of-passage transition from boyhood to adult male citizen of the Roman Empire. This multipart ceremony follows van Gennep's divisions of separation, liminality, and reincorporation. In what follows I will both summarize the literature attesting the *toga virilis* and (led by Fanny Dolansky's work) attempt to lay out each step of the process.

There are many varied attestations of the ceremony of the *toga virilis*, and Fanny Dolansky attests to the sheer breadth of evidence for it:

> The *toga virilis* ceremony spanned not only several hundred years of Roman history but also occurred on a wide scale geographically… Mention of the *toga virilis* ceremony appears in virtually every genre of Latin literature: poetry, historical writing, biography, didactic, moral and antiquarian works, letters, speeches, even the ancient novel.[44]

Many of these sources reference the event in passing rather than describe it comprehensively. To get a better sense of how the ceremony functioned on a more specific level, the sources have to be overlapped in an attempt to piece together a coherent narrative. However, even the references that give little or no context as to the actual parts of the ceremony are useful: it is clear that the event is momentous, signaling the shift from boy to man. Historians, in particular, are likely to mention the *toga virilis* ceremony as marking the beginning of the public life of the subject in

---

[43] Dolansky, "Coming of Age in Rome," is one of the most useful pieces of research for the topic at hand. Dolansky's thesis aims for a comprehensive treatment of the ceremony of assuming the *toga virilis* in ancient Rome. A specific piece of her thesis is reconstructing what might have occurred, who would have been present, and what distinct steps may have been observed. My analysis here is heavily indebted to her previous work.

[44] Dolansky, "Coming of Age in Rome," 4, 24.

question. Suestonius, for instance, documenting the lives of the Caesars, often uses phrases such as "the principal events of his youth and later life, from the assumption of the gown of manhood to the beginning of his reign, were these,"[45] or "When he assumed the gown of manhood."[46] Tacitus similarly mentions the ceremony as a marker or transition. "Meanwhile, in the beginning of the year, Drusus, one of Germanicus's children, assumed the garb of manhood."[47] In referencing Nero and his assumption of the *toga virilis*, there is stern disapproval in how early there ceremony was performed: "in the consulate of Tiberius Claudius, his fifth term, and of Servius Cornelius, the manly toga was prematurely conferred on Nero, so that he should appear qualified for a political career."[48] There is an obvious sense that Nero is unfit to be called a man, and there is further disapproval in the fact that he is given a consulship "prematurely."[49] Cicero, too, throughout his courtroom defenses mentions the *toga virilis* in passing: "I see the man who in the past year received his toga of manhood from the hand of his father."[50] As implied by Cicero's words, the robes were usually conferred by the boy's father,[51] or a close relative or friend in the case of the father's death.

Beyond the actual assumption of the *toga virilis*, the first step of the ceremony was likely the removal of the *bulla* and/or *toga praetexta*, both symbols of childhood. A boy of noble birth would remove his *bulla*, a gold (or leather)[52] necklace worn since birth, and his *toga praetexta*, a white robe with purple border. A number of sources confirm that these were badges of childhood. So Plutarch in his *Roman Questions* begins by asking, "Why do they adorn their children's necks with amulets which they call *bullae*?"[53] So, too, when talking about the earliest days of the Roman Empire with Romulus, he argues that women are given certain sorts of honor, one of which is that "their children should wear a sort of necklace, the '*bulla*,' so called from its shape [which was that of a bubble], and a robe bordered with purple."[54] Macrobius in his *Saturnalia* spends considerable time describing the *toga praetexta* and *bulla*. He describes them originating with Romulus, granting these two gifts as an honor to the Sabine woman Hersilia, who was the first to bear a "Roman" son.[55] Both of these were signs designed to ward off harm, in particular the gaze of the Evil Eye. Another of the major origin stories of the custom of the *bulla* is attested by Macrobius, Plutarch, and Pliny. Tarquinius Priscus, they say, honored his young son (Macrobius puts him at age fourteen) with the *bulla* for killing a man in battle.[56]

---

[45] Suetonius, *Lives of the Caesars, Book 3: Tiberius*. 320–1 (Rolfe, LCL).
[46] Suetonius, *Lives of the Caesars, Book 7: Galba*. 188–9 (Rolfe, LCL).
[47] Tacitus, *Annals, Book 4*. 8–9 (Jackson, LCL).
[48] Tacitus, *Annals, Book 12*. 372–3 (Jackson, LCL).
[49] Ibid.
[50] Cicero, *Pro Sestio*. 234–5 (Gardner, LCL).
[51] E.g.Cicero, *Letters to Atticus, Volume 3*. 100–1 (Shackleton Bailey, LCL).
[52] There is debate as to whether leather *bullae* were sometimes worn by upper class free boys, or only worn by the lower classes: slaves, freedmen, etc. See Dolansky, "Coming of Age in Rome," 40.
[53] Plutarch, *Moralia. The Roman Questions*. 148–9 (Babbitt, LCL).
[54] Plutarch, *Lives. Romulus*. 152–3 (Perrin, LCL).
[55] Macrobius, *Saturnalia*. 60–3 (Kaster, LCL).
[56] Plutarch, *Moralia. The Roman Questions*. 148–53 (Babbitt, LCL); Pliny the Elder, *Natural History*. 8–9 (Rackham, LCL); Macrobius, *Saturnalia*. 60–3 (Kaster, LCL).

One of the possibilities Plutarch posits while discussing the *bulla* and its potential function in Roman society is that of safeguarding freeborn children—for while "the Romans of early times account it not disreputable nor disgraceful to love male slaves in the flower of youth," he says, "they strictly refrained from boys of free birth; and that they might not be in any uncertainty, even when they encountered them unclad, did the boys wear this badge?"[57] But another of his proposals includes shaming a child into understanding that he is not yet a man: "Or is this a safeguard to insure orderly conduct, a sort of bridle on incontinence, that they may be ashamed to pose as men before they have put off the badge of childhood?"[58] Macrobius expresses a similar sentiment with nearly opposite terminology:

> Some believe that freeborn boys were permitted to wear on their chests the *bulla* with a heart fastened to it, so that they would look upon it and reflect that if and only if they showed exceptional heart could they be truly human; and that they were also given the praetexta so that—consistent with the purple border's blush— they would be guided by the sense of shame proper to free birth.[59]

As discussed in Chapter 2, there is a constant sense of a child's half-formed humanity, of their lack of virtue and reason. It is unclear here whether the sense of being "truly human" is meant literally (viz. "all children are half-formed") or as a cypher for virtue (viz. "all people must strive to be virtuous"). In either case, there is a clear sense of the effort required of the boys, as well as the pessimism involved with it. Furthermore, the *praetexta* (the garment worn by freeborn children both male and female) functions similarly to the previous quote by Plutarch—boys need constant reminder to act well, and the purple border is said to be that reminder.

Once removed, a *bulla* would then be dedicated to the *Lares*, the household gods. This part is less often narrated, but Persius in Satire 5 makes explicit the dedication of the *bulla* to the Hearth gods,[60] and Propertius seems to suggest the same in his *Elegies*.[61]

There is a fairly clear sense of separation, with the removal and dedication of the *toga praetexta* and *bulla*. Some sources reference only one or the other of these signs of a child, but in both cases, it is clear that this moment symbolizes the transition away from childhood. Pairing this with van Gennep's *rites of passage*, this is a clear sense of the first of the three rites, those rites of separation from the past way of being.

Many sources talk about the removal of the *toga praetexta* in conjunction with the assumption of the *toga virilis*. Others reference only the exchange of the *toga virilis* in place of the *toga praetexta*: "strip boyhood's purple from your tender arms and clothe your shoulders in white raiment."[62] In this case the sense of separation from childhood and entrance into adulthood is somewhat conflated—while not simultaneous, one

---

[57] Plutarch, *Moralia. The Roman Questions*. 148–53 (Babbitt, LCL).
[58] Ibid.
[59] Macrobius, *Saturnalia*. 60–3 (Kaster, LCL).
[60] Persius, *The Satires of Persius: Satire 5*. 98–9 (Braund, LCL).
[61] See below for the full translation. Propertius, *Elegies*. 318–21 (Goold, LCL).
[62] Statius, *Silvae*. 320–1 (Bailey, LCL).

follows immediately after the other. Other sources add in details to the ceremony that seem to be consistently incorporated. But the symbolism of transition from childhood to adulthood is most consistently referenced by the exchange of clothing.

However, sources narrated additional pieces of the ceremony. One element is the procession to the Capitol, or forum, or another public place. Servius, for instance, in referencing an ancient tradition, says of the present: "they affirm sensibly that Jupiter attends to growing boys, because when boys have assumed the *toga virilis*, they go to the Capitol."[63] Cicero, specifically mentioning that he has been exiled from Rome, writes that "I gave my son his *toga virilis* at Arpinum in preference to any other place, and my fellow townsmen were gratified at the compliment: though I observed everywhere that both they and others whom I passed in my journey were in low spirits and much dejected."[64] Nicolaus of Damascus writes in his *Life of Augustus* that Octavius "entered the forum, aged about fourteen, to put off the *toga praetextata* and assume the *toga virilis*, this being a token of his becoming registered as a man."[65] Here there is an interesting disagreement between sources about when the *toga virilis* is actually put on. Some sources say that the boy assumes it in his own home. Others insist that the *toga virilis* is put on in the forum itself. In either case, the processional to the forum acts as a clear marker of liminality: there is a physical transition between home and public forum; the child has not finished being celebrated as a man, but no longer is simply a child. If the *toga virilis* is put on in the home, the sense of the public announcement and transition to manhood is heightened: while the boy wears the *toga*, he has not yet "arrived." But the symbolism remains if the boy merely dedicated his *bulla* at home and waits to be clothed at the forum.

At the forum the rites of reincorporation can be seen. The public nature of this event is highlighted; Nicolaus talks about the favorable reception of the crowd, awed by "Caesar's" beauty and nobility, and because of this, they even elevate him to the college of priests (normally reserved for older men). This is a public recognition of a boy's acceptance into society as a man, and it is met with celebration. Nicolaus also mentions that Octavius made sacrifices in celebration of his assumption of the *toga virilis*.[66] The sacrifices are another aspect sometimes attested, but with lessened regularity than some of the other parts of the ceremony. Once again, these sacrifices clearly represent the full incorporation of boys into their new status. Ovid, in this *Fasti*, links the ceremony to Bacchus. Here again there is the sense of the public nature of the affair, and he furthermore links the ceremony to a specific festival:[67]

> It remains for me to discover why the gown of liberty is given to boys, fair Bacchus, on thy day, whether it be because thou seemest ever to be a boy and a youth, and

---

[63] Servius, *Ecl.* 4.49
[64] Cicero, *Letters to Atticus, Volume 3.* 100–1 (Shackleton Bailey, LCL).
[65] Nicolaus of Damascus: *Life of Augustus*, fragment 127:4.8-9 (C.M.Hall). http://www.attalus.org/translate/nicolaus1.html
[66] Ibid.
[67] Dolansky argues strenuously against this being the only day the toga would have been conferred. See Dolansky, "Coming of Age in Rome," 154–5.

thy age is midway between the two; or it may be that, because thou art a father, fathers commend to thy care and divine keeping the pledges that they love, their sons; or it may be that because thou art Liber, the gown of liberty is assumed and a freer (liberior) life is entered upon under thine auspices. Or was it because, in the days when the ancients tilled the fields more diligently, and a senator laboured on his ancestral land, when a consul exchanged the bent plough for the rods and axes of office, and it was no crime to have horny hands, the country folk used to come to the City for the games (but that was an honour paid to the gods, not a concession to popular tastes, the discoverer of the grape held on his own day those games which now he shares with the torch-bearing goddess); and the day therefore seemed not unsuitable for conferring the gown, in order that a crowd might gather round the novice? Thou Father God, hither turn thy horned label, mild and propitious, and to the favouring breezes spread the sails of my poetic art![68]

In this passage there is an interesting identification between Bacchus, himself a liminal figure who does not fit either into childhood nor adulthood or even "youth" but rather melds and blurs the two.

While there are not many detailed descriptions of the *toga virilis* ceremony, the description given by Seneca is exceptionally useful for my purposes. Seneca, in his fourth letter to Lucilius, takes up the theme of death and dying. This is a theme that is prevalent throughout his letters to Lucilius, and in particular he is interested in urging that one turns away from the fear of death, which is so common. In this letter he likens the fear of death to a childish or even infantile fear, one that ought to be beneath grown men. He says:

You remember, of course, what joy you felt when you laid aside the garments of boyhood and donned the man's toga, and were escorted to the forum; nevertheless, you may look for a still greater joy when you have laid aside the mind of boyhood and when wisdom has enrolled you among men. For it is not boyhood that still stays with us, but something worse—boyishness. And this condition is all the more serious because we possess the authority of old age, together with the follies of boyhood, yea, even the follies of infancy. Boys fear trifles, children fear shadows, we fear both.[69]

There are several things important about this passage. First, this passage not only references the *toga virilis* ceremony but also gives the sense of its being a momentous occasion, one that would be clearly marked and remembered by the boy and by those around him. Second, the clear transition between boyhood and manhood is made explicit, and the constituent parts of removing the "garments of boyhood," then putting on the "man's toga," and being escorted to the forum, are all observed. Third, Seneca is carefully taking a known theme, and crafting it to his purposes. He allows

---

[68] Ovid, *Fasti*.176–7 (Frazer, LCL).
[69] Seneca, *Epistles*. 14–15 (Gummere, LCL).

for the distinction between man and boy, but wants furthermore to hold up the idea that one's mind might lag behind the body: "it is not boyhood that still stays with us, but something worse—boyishness." Seneca is furthering his point about fears of death by insisting that fear is one suitable to only the young, the undeveloped, and the immature. Indeed, Seneca clearly looks upon an immature mind as something grave and serious, the combination of the mind of a child in the body of a respectable older man. This is something reprehensible. Thus Seneca, interested in the *toga virilis* ceremony to illustrate a point about fear and childish regression, gives great insight into the feelings and hopes traditionally attributed to the ceremony, as well as the appropriate mental state of a man wearing the toga.

There is a similar state of gravitas associated with a passage from Persius's Satire 5:

> When first as a timid youth I lost the protective purple and my amulet hung as an offering to the girdled Hearth gods; when my indulgent companions and fresh white folds permitted me to cast my eyes over the whole Subura without risk; at the age when the route is unclear and perplexity ignorant of life splits the agitated mind at the branching crossroads, I put myself in your hands. You adopted my tender years in your Socratic embrace, Cornutus. Then your skillful rule was applied unawares and it straightened out my twisted ways, and my mind was overcome by reason and strove to surrender and took on its features, moulded by your thumb.[70]

In this passage from Persius, there is a clear sense of the removal of both the *toga praetexta* and *bulla*, the ceremony that separates the speaker from his childhood. Furthermore, there is the sense that the placement of the "fresh white folds" marks an entrance into a new state of being. The speaker references his newfound freedom because of the "white folds" of the *toga virilis*, freedom that also involves uncertainty. The speaker is capable of virtue, a quality that few if any children are able to actually attain. But the speaker has already been capable of vice, and the new freedom conferred with the donning of the toga also involves increased access to that which is unvirtuous. In fact, it seems that now is the time that real virtue or unfettered vice can develop. Persius speaks of childhood as a state where one is protected and seemingly protected from himself. Now, being potentially free but also unprotected, the narrator agrees to be guided by an older and wiser mentor. This guidance is spoken of as an unmitigated good: it allows the young man to be molded and guided, and his mind is directed into being "overcome by reason."

Statius continues the theme of both the freedom and the danger posed to a young man newly acquainted with the *toga virilis*. In this case the youth in question is bereft of a father to perform the ceremony, which involves clothing him:

> Your father is not by your side; for he died, swallowed by the cruel Fates and leaving two children without a guardian. He did not even strip boyhood's purple from

---

[70] Persius, *The Satires of Persius: Satire 5*. 98–9 (Braund, LCL).

your tender arms and clothe your shoulders in white raiment. Who has not been corrupted by youth uncurbed and the hastened freedom of a new gown, as when a tree ignorant of the pruning hook rears up leaves and exhales its fruit in foliage? But in your young heart were Pierian concerns, and modesty, and character taught to make its own law.[71]

In this case the boy has an uncommon innate ability, and on his own acts with decorum. Usually, Statius notes, a young man recently given the "white raiment" acts like a tree unaware of the necessity of pruning.

In summary, van Gennep's structure of separation, liminality, and reincorporation can be clearly seen through such descriptions of this ceremony. The removal of the childhood objects and dedication acts as clear markers of separation. The journey to the forum/Capitol/public place represents passage through liminality. The dressing in the *toga virilis* and the sacrifices and celebration of the people act as markers of reincorporation.[72] Moreover, sources clearly exhibit the sense of the momentousness of the occasion, of the idea that this ceremony is what marked the transition between childhood and adulthood.

Here is a final note before transitioning to the wedding ceremony. While it is unclear exactly what context Mark is composing his Gospel, it is unlikely that his primary audience is high-class freeborn Roman citizens. There is no known Jewish *rite of passage* for boys in this time period. Why, then, have I emphasized the *toga virilis* ceremony? How, that is, does this ceremony contribute to my understanding of Mark's Gospel?

My reasoning is thus: there is substantial evidence that Greco-Roman society not only sharply distinguished boyhood from manhood but also there was a specific rite that transitioned boys into men. As the dominant force in the known world, and the conquerors of Judea, the Roman Empire's thoughts and practices loomed larger than life, dominating and oppressing. This lends credence to the idea that Mark, and Mark's audience, would have been aware of rites transitioning boys to men, whether the specific *toga virilis* ceremony or even potentially localized customs that we lack documentation for. Mark furthermore is consistently playing with the tropes of the Roman Empire and inverting them, constantly pushing for a countercultural understanding. At a bare minimum I am suggesting Mark likely uses the dominant culture's motifs to contrast with his own vision of what it means to be valuable.

The Wedding Ceremony as a Rite of Passage

A freeborn Roman citizen boy's transition to manhood, then, was celebrated by a series of events surrounding his putting away the *toga praetexta* and putting on the

---

[71] Statius, *Silvae*. 320–1 (Bailey, LCL).
[72] See Dolansky, "Coming of Age in Rome," 128–33, for a full and detailed argument of this very thing.

toga virilis. Was there any similar ceremony for the transition to womanhood, and if so, what was it?

While there was not a separate ceremony celebrating the transition to adulthood for a young girl, for all intents and purposes the wedding ceremony acted as such a *rite of passage*. There are several reasons for this. First, average marriage ages for each of the sexes were quite different from one another. A young Roman girl could be expected to be married by her mid- to late teens; a noble girl could be married even younger. The men, however, were generally married in their mid- to late twenties and early thirties. This meant that for the boys there was a significant length of time between the onset of puberty—the biological marker of transitioning adulthood—and that of marriage. For the girls, however, the onset of puberty was essentially the marker for her readiness for marriage.[73] Furthermore, for men, there was a wealth of public activities for which the distinction between men and boys mattered: admission to the army or to the senatorial or other political bodies, appointment to one of the priesthoods, and inheritance, just to name a few. Each of these was accessible only to adult (free) men, and some of these required further periods of study. In the case of the women, however, the distinction between a girl and woman mattered for the sake of bearing children—an activity tied to marriage (at least, ideally). While in the later Roman periods women had increasing ability to own property, their freedom in the public world was minimal. Entrance into womanhood was tied to entrance into being a faithful wife, a dutiful mother, and a good household administrator.

Just as it is difficult to gain a holistic perspective on the steps surrounding the assumption of the *toga virilis*, so too it is difficult to ascertain what a typical Roman marriage may have looked like. There are many references to weddings and marriages in the primary source literature, but few detail all of the many steps modern scholarship associates with the wedding rituals. Plutarch, for instance, in the section of his *Moralia* called "*Roman Questions*,"[74] gives us many details of the parts of the Roman wedding ceremony that he finds unusual or hard to explain (and goes on to speculate as to the origins of each). He is interested in origins here rather than laying out a comprehensive structure. Similarly, Catullus in several of his poems[75] gives us many flowery details about the wedding ceremony—but here again, these are poems, odes to Hymen, focused on the idealized circumstance where the bridegroom is joyfully expectant, the bride gently fearful.[76] However, there tend to be more detailed references to various parts of the wedding ceremony than to the *toga virilis*, which is usually mentioned in passing, without much explanation.

---

[73] There will be exceptions to this rule, and significant nuance, which will be discussed later.
[74] H. J. Rose, *Roman Questions of Plutarch: A New Translation with Introductory Essays and Running Commentary* (New York: Biblo & Tannen, 1974).
[75] D.F.S Thompson, *Catullus* (Toronto: University of Toronto Press, 1997); Robinson Ellis, *Poems and Fragments of Catullus* (London: Bradbury, Evans and Co, 1871).
[76] There is ongoing debate whether Catullus is describing a primarily Greek mode of weddings, with only one or perhaps two distinctive and unique Roman elements, or essentially a Roman wedding. See Gordon Williams, "Some Aspects of Roman Marriage Ceremonies and Ideals," *JoRS* 48 (1958): 16–29.

Classical scholars generally agree[77] on the basic structure of the Roman wedding, although there is some disagreement on a few of the particulars. First, the bride would dedicate her toys and remove and dedicate her *toga praetexta*. It is unclear whether these were dedicated to the household gods (the *Lares*), Fortuna, or to Venus.[78] In several dedicatory epigrams various objects are being given: "Alcibia dedicated to Hera the holy veil of her hair, when she entered into lawful wedlock."[79] Much like the *toga virilis* ceremony, there is a clear sense here of putting off and putting away the signs of childhood. These acts function as rites of separation.

The young woman would put on a white tunic (*tunic recta*) with an intricate knot around her waist (*cingulum*), symbolizing her chastity. Sometimes her mother would dress her, sometimes her maids. *The Golden Ass* describes a girl being kidnapped on her wedding day. She narrates, "My unhappy mother was holding me in her arms, and clothing me in the wedding-dress for the occasion. She was showering me with honeyed kisses, and murmuring anxious prayers to foster the hope of children to come."[80] In the romance novel *Chaereas and Callirhoe*, the author describes the lovely Callirhoe being dressed for her wedding by her maids, and Callirhoe is in stunned and almost fainting shock, as she has only just been informed that she is to marry, and has yet to be informed who the bridegroom is.[81] Her hair would be styled into six curls, having been divided by a special ceremonial spear (*hasta caelibaris*). In his "Roman Questions" Plutarch discusses parting the bride's hair with a spear, and gives several explanations why this might be so.[82] She would put on a veil, although its color—red

---

[77] See for instance, the similar descriptions of the wedding ceremony in Rose, *Roman Questions*, 101–8; Lynn R. Huber, *Like a Bride Adorned: Reading Metaphor in John's Apocalypse* (New York: T&T Clark, 2007), 128–33; Andrew T. Bierkan, Charles P. Sherman, and Emile Stocquart, "Marriage in Roman Law," *YLJ* 16.5 (1907): 312–14; Jennifer Goodall Powers, "Roman Weddings," SUNY Albany, 1997 https://archive.is/tdsYz; Karen K. Hersch, *The Roman Wedding: Ritual and Meaning in Antiquity* (New York: Cambridge University Press, 2010); Susan Treggiari, *Roman Marriage: Iusti Coniuges from the Time of Cicero to the Time of Ulpian* (Oxford: Oxford University Press, 1993), 161–80; and a much sparser version in Susan Treggiari, "Marriage and Family in Roman Society," in *Marriage and Family in the Biblical World* (ed. Ken M Campbell; Illinois: InterVarsity, 2003), 151–4.

[78] Hersch, *The Roman Wedding*, 65–9.

[79] *The Greek Anthology, Volume I: Book 6.* 370–1 (Paton, LCL). See also "Hippe, the maiden, has put up her abundant curly hair, brushing it from her perfumed temples, for the solemn time when she must wed has come, and I the snood that used to rest there require in my wearer the grace of virginity. But, Artemis, in thy loving-kindness grant to Lycomedes' child, who has bidden farewell to her knucklebones, both a husband and children" (ibid., 446–7). Were these dedications on their wedding day, or merely in preparation for (hoped for?) marriage? The matter remains debated.

[80] Apuleius, *Metamorphoses (The Golden Ass)*. 72–3 (Hanson, LCL).

[81] Chariton, *Callirhoe*. 36–7 (Goold, LCL).

[82] Plutarch, *Moralia. The Roman Questions*. 132–5 (Babbitt, LCL): "Why did they part the hair of brides with the point of a spear? Does this symbolize the marriage of the first Roman wives by violence with attendant war, or do the wives thus learn, now that they are mated to brave and warlike men, to welcome an unaffected, unfeminine, and simple mode of beautification? Comparably, perhaps, Lycurgus, by giving orders to make the doors and roofs of houses with the saw and the axe only, and to use absolutely no other tool, banished all over-refinement and extravagance. Or does this procedure hint at the manner of their—whose? Of bride from her parents?—separation, that with steel alone can their marriage be dissolved? Or is it that most of the marriage customs were connected with Juno? The spear is commonly held to be sacred to Juno, and most of her statues represent her as leaning on a spear, and the goddess herself is surnamed Quiritis. The men of old used to call the spear curis; they further relate that Enyalius is called Quirinus by the Romans." Note here that Plutarch is positing that the hairstyle, as well as the use of the spear in creating it, functions as a rite of separation.

or yellow—is debated.[83] Psyche, in Apuleius's tale, is preparing for both death and marriage, to be sacrificially wed to a "monster" according to the prophecy of Apollo. All of the wedding items take a tragic tone therefore, and "that bride-to-be dried her tears on her very bridal-veil."[84] Plutarch likewise mentions the bridal veil in "Advice to the Bride and Groom." Discussing a peculiarity found in Boeotia, he says that there they give a garland of asparagus (the oddity which he is really interested in) "when they veil the bride."[85] Each of these function as symbols of the bride's liminal status: she has put on special garments that symbolize her status as bride but not yet wife. Next, at her house her parents (if alive) would seek omens, welcome the bridegroom, and the couple's hands would be joined. Callirhoe, still unaware of her bridegroom's identity, waits as Chaereas is brought to her door. Chaereas, in anxiety and love, runs forward to her and kisses her, and Callirhoe recognizes the object of her secret love, and immediately recovers herself as if "a dying lamp once it is replenished with oil."[86] The bride would say something like "Ubi tu Gaius, ego Gaia"—"Where you are Gaius, I am Gaia."[87] Finally, a sacrifice would be made. The next day, a wedding breakfast would be eaten together, presumably still in the bride's family's home. Here there is a notable microcosm: this first day can be viewed as its own *rite of passage*, as a girl transitions from child to bride. The joining of the hands of the bride and groom, the ritual words, and the sacrifice and breakfast all function as a rite of incorporation. And yet within the broader context of the wedding feast, these all are still rites transitioning from rites of separation into rites of liminality.

In the evening, the bride would be ritually torn from her mother's arms,[88] forming one more emotional example of a rite of separation, and a processional, led by young boys with both parents if alive, would lead the bride on foot to the groom's house. This would be amid saucy jokes from those watching.[89] The bridegroom would throw symbolic nuts to the onlookers. The bride would likely have been accompanied both

---

[83] Hersch, *The Roman Wedding*, 94–105. Catullus for instance, describes the wedding veil as a "*flammeum cape.*" Cornish bypasses the issue by translated the phrase as "marriage veil." The passage is nicely phrased in general: "Bind thy brows with the flowers of fragrant marjoram, put on the marriage veil, hither, hither merrily come, wearing on thy snow-white foot the yellow shoe" Catullus, *Poems*. 68–9 (Cornish, LCL).

[84] Apuleius, *Metamorphoses (The Golden Ass)*. 78–9 (Hanson, LCL).

[85] Plutarch, *Advice to the Bride and Groom*, trans. Donald Russel, in *Plutarch's Advice to the Bride and Groom and A Consolation to His Wife: English Translations, Commentary, Interpretive Essays, and Bibliography* (ed. Sarah B. Pomeroy; New York: Oxford University Press, 1999), 5.

[86] Chariton, *Callirhoe*. 36–7 (Goold, LCL).

[87] Treggiari, *Roman Marriage*, 168, says this happens at the threshold of the bridegroom's house; and Hersch, *The Roman Wedding*, 187–90 speaks of the differing primary sources on the matter.

[88] Catullus, has the young maidens accusing Hesperus, the Evening Star, saying, "Hesperus, what more cruel fire than thine moves in the sky? for thou canst endure to tear the daughter from her mother's embrace, from her mother's embrace to tear the close-clinging daughter, and give the chaste maiden to the burning youth. What more cruel than this do enemies when a city falls? Hymen, O Hymenaeus, Hymen, hither, O Hymenaeus!" Catullus, *Poems*, 86–7 (Cornish, LCL). Apuleius plays on irony in *The Golden Ass* when Charite describes how she, dressed for her wedding, is torn from her "mother's trembling arms" not by the bridal procession, but by bandits coming to kidnap her (Apuleius, *Metamorphoses [The Golden Ass]*. 192–3 [Hanson, LCL]).

[89] Plutarch in "The Life of Romulus," spends time arguing that the word "Talasius," which is shouted to the bride and groom on their procession by onlookers, may have its origins in the rape of the Sabine women. Much like in his "Roman Questions" he gives several explanations that he finds possible.

by a torch and by a spindle and distaff. Once again, just as in the *toga virilis*, the sense of motion is apparent, as well as a physical transition between spaces. In both cases this highlights the sense of liminal or transition rites: the bride is no longer at her parents' home, nor has she been safely installed into her bridegroom's house.

Upon arriving at the bridegroom's house, the bride would have rubbed the doorway with oil or fat, and decked it with wool. Plutarch describes this just so in his *Roman Questions*, saying, "when they lead in the bride, they spread a fleece beneath her; she herself brings with her a distaff and her spindle [both were symbols of a wife's purity and chastity, as well as industry, in Greco-Roman as well as Jewish sources][90] and wreaths her husband's door with wool."[91] She either stepped exceedingly carefully over the threshold or was carried. This is a small moment showing the import of the occasion: the bride is in a precarious position that must be crossed with care. Plutarch, for instance, in *The Life of Romulus*, argues: "And it continues to be a custom down to the present time that the bride shall not of herself cross the threshold into her new home, but be lifted up and carried in, because the Sabine women were carried in by force, and did not go in of their own accord."[92] Some scholars assert that the bride touched fire and water upon entering the groom's house.[93] Plutarch references this practice in his *Roman Questions*, and comes up with numerous explanations for why this might be so.[94] There would also be a ceremonial couch for the couple's spirits—the woman's *iunio* and man's *genius*. Finally the bride was escorted to the bedchamber, where the *epithalamia* was sung—a wedding hymn designed to encourage marital consumation. Much of this is recorded in the romantic novel *An Ephesian Tale*:

> There were all-night celebrations and a feast of sacrifices to the god. And when these had been performed, night came (everything seemed too slow for Habrocomes and Anthia); they brought the girl to the bridal chamber with torches, sang the bridal hymn, shouted their good wishes, brought the couple in, and put them on

---

[90] C.f. Miriam Peskowitz, "Domesticity and the Spindle," in Jan Willem van Henten and Athalya Brenner, *Families and Family Relationships as Represented in Early Judaism and Early Christianities: Texts and Fictions* (STAR 2; Leiden: Deo), 118–34.

[91] Plutarch, *Moralia. The Roman Questions*. 54–5 (Babbitt, LCL). In the Life of Romulus, Plutarch furthermore gives a possible origin for the emphasis on spinning: "When the Sabines, after their war against the Romans, were reconciled with them, it was agreed that their women should perform no other tasks for their husbands than those which were connected with spinning. It was customary, therefore, at subsequent marriages, for those who gave the bride away, or escorted her to her new home, or simply looked on, to cry 'Talasius!' merrily, in testimony that the woman was led home for no other task than that of spinning" (Plutarch, *Moralia. Lives, Romulus*. 132–3 [Perrin, LCL]).

[92] Idem., *Moralia. Lives, Romulus*. 132–5 (Perrin, LCL).

[93] Again, Hersch gives a variety of explanations of what may have happened: Hersch, *The Roman Wedding*, 182–7.

[94] "Why do they bid the bride touch fire and water? Is it that of these two, being reckoned as elements or first principles, fire is masculine and water feminine, and fire supplies the beginnings of motion and water the function of the subsistent element or the material? Or is it because fire purifies and water cleanses, and a married woman must remain pure and clean? Or is it that, just as fire without moisture is unsustaining and arid, and water without heat is unproductive and inactive, so also male and female apart from each other are inert, but their union in marriage produces the perfection of their life together? Or is it that they must not desert each other, but must share together every sort of fortune, even if they are destined to have nothing other than fire and water to share with each other?" Plutarch, *Moralia. The Roman Questions*. 6–7 (Babbitt, LCL).

the couch. The chamber had been prepared: a golden couch had been spread with purple sheets, and above it hung an awning with and embroidered Babylonian tapestry.... Under this canopy they brought Anthia to Habrocomes and put her to bed, then shut the doors.[95]

Finally, some scholars argue that the groom would give a present to the bride the next morning. Plutarch briefly mentions this, but it is not widely attested in primary literature.[96] The bride, dressed in new clothes and having redone her hair, would sacrifice to her new household gods for the first time, symbolizing her full incorporation into the groom's household.

To summarize, as in the case of the *toga virilis* ceremony, the wedding ceremony evidences delineated categories of rites of separation, transition, and incorporation according to van Gennep's system. The bride's removal of her *toga praetexta*, her dedication of the garment and her childhood toys, her hair being divided by a spear, and the ritual tearing from her mother's arms are all clear rites of separation. Her journey to the groom's house, surrounded by crowds and guides, the special veil, hairstyle, and clothes, even the vulgar joking and nut throwing, all serve as transitional rites. In this case her physical journey from the home of her parents to her new husband's home is a particularly quintessential marker of transitional rites—both the movement and the specific sense of being in-between clearly illustrate her ambiguous state. Finally, the care by which she must enter her new home, the wreathing of the doorway with fat/oil and wool, her touching the fire and water, and her ceremonial speech—all of these are clear rites of incorporation. Hersch, Treggiari, and Rose among others agree that van Gennep's understanding of *rites of passage* is applicable to the Roman wedding.[97]

From a specifically Jewish perspective, many make the argument that a Jewish wedding looked much like the Greco-Roman counterpart.[98] Josephus, for

---

[95] Bryan P. Reardon, *Collected Ancient Greek Novels* (Berkeley: University of California Press, 1989), 132–3.

[96] Cf. Rose, *Roman Questions*, 102–3; Jennifer Powers, "Roman Weddings."

[97] Rose, *Roman Questions*, 102–8, though specifically on 104; Hersch, *The Roman Wedding*, throughout, though gives a detailed summary from 294–97, Treggiari, *The Roman Marriage*, 180.

[98] Shaye Cohen makes the argument that this was true on a general level: Jewish family life looked very similar to the surrounding Greco-Roman culture. Shaye J. D. Cohen, "Introduction," in *The Jewish Family in Antiquity* (ed. Shaye J. D. Cohen; Atlanta: Scholars, 1993), 2. Micahel Satlow explicitly makes this point: "Palestinian rabbis in the first centuries of this era understood marriage in terms more similar to their Roman and Greek contemporaries than to those of Babylonian rabbis ... *there is nothing essentially Jewish about 'Jewish' marriage in antiquity*" Micahel L. Latlow, *Jewish Marriage in Antiquity* (Princeton: Princeton University Press, 2001), xvi. E. Neufeld in *Ancient Hebrew Marriage Laws: With Special References to General Semitic Laws and Customs* (London: Longmans, Green and Co., 1944) only briefly mentions Greco-Roman practices at all (being more interested in ancient Babylonian/Assyrian practices, which he says have a paucity of information with which to compare to ancient Hebrew practices [150]), but footnotes the similarity between the practice of bathing the bride in Hebrew and Greek literature, 149n6. While Mendell Lewittes does not specifically mention any connection with Greco-Roman practices, his description of the wedding processional is strikingly similar to what has just been described "the bride and groom... were usually escorted from their respective homes by their families and a large following of friends and neighbors through the streets of the town to the wedding site. Wine would be drawn through tubes and roasted kernels of grain and nuts would be thrown in front of the couple as symbols of good luck." Mendell Lewittes, *Jewish Marriage: Rabbinic Law, Legend, and Custom* (London: Jason Aronson Inc, 1994), 86–7.

instance, mentions a bridal procession that is attacked, giving several details of the procession:

> About this time someone came... with the report that the sons of Amaraios were celebrating a wedding and bringing the bride, who was the daughter of one of the distinguished men among the Arabs, from the city of Nabatha, and that the procession accompanying the girl would be a splendid and costly one.... And when they saw them conducting the maid and her bridegroom and a great company of friends, as is usual at a wedding, they sprang out from their ambush and killed them all, and after taking as spoil the ornaments and the rest of the possessions that were then being taken along by these people, turned back. Such, then, was the punishment which they inflicted on the sons of Amaraios for killing their brother John, for these men themselves and the friends who accompanied them, and their wives and children, perished to the number of about four hundred.[99]

Josephus mentions that this particular procession is a costly one; its size may have been unusually large at 400 people. However, he also describes a procession itself, where the bride and groom are processing, and adds in the phrase "as is usual at a wedding." The Mishnah, furthermore, in the context of a specifically virginal bride, talks about a wedding procession, the bride being veiled and having her hair loose, and the distribution of grain during the wedding:

> If there are witnesses that she went out with a hinuma [either a myrtle canopy or a veil which was only used in the wedding ceremony for virgins] and her head uncovered [with her hair on her shoulders, a further indication of being a virgin], her ketubah is two hundred [zuz.]. Rabbi Yohanan ben Beroka says; Also the distribution of [sweet] roasted grain [to the children present at the wedding] is evidence [in his area, this, too, was a custom reserved for virgins].[100]

Later, too, in the Sotah, it talks about wedding practices that were specifically forbidden, and in which time period they were common. This again gives a sense of the similarities between the two, as there was a need for specific delineation of appropriate and inappropriate common traditions:

> During the war with Vespasian, they [the Rabbis] decreed against [the use of] crowns worn by bridegrooms and against [the use of] the drum [at wedding celebrations]. During the war of Titus, they decreed against [the use of] crowns worn by brides and that no one should teach his son Greek. During the final war [in which the Second Temple was destroyed, in which Titus participated], they decreed that a bride should not go out in a palanquin [i.e., a hand held chariot

---

[99] Josephus, *Jewish Antiquities, Volume 5: Book 13*. 236-7 (Marcus, LCL).
[100] M. Ket 2.1 http://www.emishnah.com/Nashim_Vol_1/Ket2.pdf

decorated with gold, to her husband's house] in the midst of the city, but the Sages permitted a bride to go out in a palanquin in the midst of the city.[101]

Jewish fictional literature also portrays similar wedding themes. *Tobit* portrays the wedding of Sarah and Tobias. Sarah has already been given to seven other men, each of whom have been mysteriously killed (by a demon, as it turns out), and so there is a sense of foreboding. After warning Tobias of the danger of marrying his daughter, Sarah's father takes her by the hand, and gives her to Tobias (7:12). A marriage contract is written (7:13), and they feast. Sarah's mother is then instructed to prepare the nuptial room and bring her daughter there, which involves preparing the bed as well as lighting incense (7:16, 8:2). Tobias is then brought to the room separately (8:1). After the night of the wedding (and having checked that Tobias is still living), there is a wedding celebration that lasts for two weeks (8:19–9:6).

In *Joseph and Aseneth*, Aseneth is told by an angel that she will be married to Joseph. She is then instructed to remove her current clothing and "put on your wedding robe, the ancient robe, the first that was stored away in your room, and deck yourself in all your finest jewelry, and adorn yourself as a bride."[102] Later she indeed dresses herself in her finest clothing, jewelry, and puts a veil on her head.[103] She calls for a special dinner to be prepared, then meets Joseph gladly. The next day her father attempts to invite the local lords to celebrate the wedding of Joseph and Aseneth, but, instead, Joseph insists that the Pharaoh himself must approve of and perform the wedding.[104] The encounter with Pharaoh and subsequent wedding is narrated as follows:

> And Joseph got up early in the morning, and he sent away to Pharaoh and told him about Aseneth. And Pharaoh sent and called Pentephres and Aseneth… And Pharaoh took golden crowns and put them on their heads and said, "God Most High will bless you and prosper your family forever." And Pharaoh turned them towards each other, and they kissed each other. And Pharaoh celebrated their wedding with a banquet and much merry-making for seven days; and he invited all the chief men in the land of Egypt. And he issued a proclamation, saying, "Any man who does any work during the seven days of Joseph and Aseneth's wedding shall die." And when the wedding was over and the banquet ended, Joseph had intercourse with Aseneth.[105]

The processional is less clear in this version, although it could be argued that both Joseph and Aseneth indeed process to Pharaoh's court. This particularly rendition

---

[101] M. Sot. 9:14. http://www.emishnah.com/Nashim_Vol_2/Sotah9.pdf
   Michael Satlow notes in his *Jewish Marriage in Antiquity* that "the standard version of the Mishnah reads 'Titus' instead of 'Kitus,' but this latter reading is supported by the manuscripts and makes more sense in this passage. Kitus was a general under Trajan, which would then date the decrees to the Trajianic uprising" (Micahel Satlow, *Jewish Marriage*, 335n55).
[102] *Jos. Asen.* 15.9-10 (Cook).
[103] Ibid., 28.3-7.
[104] Ibid., 20.
[105] Ibid., 21.4-8.

mentions crowns on both the bride and bridegroom, a wedding celebration (this before they consummate the marriage, rather than after), and a public wedding feast.

Two minor concerns must be addressed about treating the wedding ceremony as a *rite of passage*, and specifically a coming-of-age rite of passage, for the young girl. First, while each of these parts can be pieced together from various sources, it is unclear the extent to which all portions were performed in any particular wedding. This is seen as well in the slight differences between Jewish and Roman weddings (notably the hairstyle). Moreover, when examining Roman legal materials on marriage, the bare minimum that was required for a legal marriage was for both bride and groom to be Roman citizens, and for both to consent to the marriage (the father of the bride's consent was needed also, if she was *in patria potestae*, "in patriarchal power").[106] With the Julian marriage laws of 18 BCE and 9 CE, there was a further restriction of who was suitable to marry (not freedmen/women, not actors/actresses, and not adulterers).[107] The Roman world likely saw a diversity of ceremonies—some more lavish, others nearly nonexistent. Treggiari argues that some of the details recorded are only catalogued by "antiquarians," and compares these little rites to the "wassail bowl" of English Christmas traditions.[108] Does this undermine the tenability of overlaying van Gennep's structure on the Roman and Jewish wedding?

The answer here is no, for two reasons. First, van Gennep recognizes patterns in societies that reveal each society's understanding of important social transitions. It goes too far to say that the folklore alone of a particular society demonstrates its underlying structures, independent of actual practices. However, it is *not* going too far to say that the explanation of the most sparse and simplest acts betrays the depth of meaning in an act. That is to say, while a walk from one house to another might not signify much in everyday life, the ritual journey of the bride from her parent's house to her new husband's house is a transitional rite, because it is acknowledged and viewed as such. It does not much matter what specific rites were held for any single wedding: what matters is that the descriptions and explanations of various aspects of the wedding ceremony line up with van Gennep's general tripartite structure. Second, and related to the first: the major components of the wedding, those most likely to be performed by any one individual wedding, involve the ceremony at the parent's house, and the safe journey of the bride from her old house to her new one.[109] Even this simplified and basic version of the ceremony still involves clearly definable moments of separation, transition, and incorporation.

---

[106] Cf. Hersch, *The Roman Wedding*, 19–22.

[107] Ibid.

[108] "We must be careful not to assume that every upper-class wedding incorporated all the small religious rites which are attested, any more than that every individual English family at Christmas clings to all the customs which have clustered around that festival from the Middle Ages to the twentieth century. Wassail bowls and Christmas trees come and go. So may the parting and braiding of a Roman bride's hair or the carrying of a coin in her shoe. Such details are preserved by antiquarians" (Treggiari, *Roman Marriage*, 161).

[109] Treggiari, in summarizing the major literature, says that "a writer who mentions a normal wedding will concentrate on such features as the dinner, the sealing of the dotal tablets by witnesses, the passage of the bride to the bridegroom's house. These were all normal components of an upper-class wedding in the early Principate" (Treggiari, *Roman Marriage*, 161).

The second minor concern that needs to be addressed relates to the age of the girls at marriage. If, as the evidence seems to show, girls were sometimes married at twelve or even before, the likelihood of their having gone through puberty would be extremely low. If this was the case, can we still talk of the wedding ceremony as the "coming of age" ceremony for girls? M. K. Hopkins, in "The Age of Roman Girls at Marriage,"[110] is specifically interested in determining the age of Roman girls at marriage and, even more specifically, cataloguing the evidence for marriages that occurred before the girl turned twelve. He examines a group of 145 funerary inscriptions of young married women, and calculates that 12 of these reveal a marriage age of ten or eleven.[111] He furthermore brings forward literary evidence—discussions of medical professionals like Soranus, lawyers debating legal marriage and age, philosophers like Plutarch, as well as literary-historical records of specific aristocratic marriage that mention the girl's age. Brent Shaw, in his subsequent "The Age of Roman Girls at Marriage: Some Reconsiderations,"[112] using a slightly different method than Hopkins,[113] is more interested in arguing that the average age of Roman girls at marriage was significantly higher than Hopkins argues. However, he does not debate the occasional marriage of very young girls, especially among the Roman elite.[114] It is not important to go into great detail on average Roman marriage ages, but rather to note that there is a high likelihood that a small number of girls were married before the onset of their biological puberty. Again, does this fact undermine the assertion that a wedding in Rome functioned as a coming-of-age ceremony for the Roman girl?

This concern has already been addressed in the brief mention of van Gennep's distinction between social and physiological puberty. The age of Roman girls at marriage was one of his prime examples of a society in which social puberty—the ability to marry—in all likelihood sometimes preceded physiological puberty. This disturbs his system not at all, and indeed, is why he likes the phrase "initiation rites" so much more than "puberty rites."[115] Nor does Hopkins believe that Romans themselves thought of the marriages of girls younger than twelve in a category distinct from those of legal marriage age.[116] Hopkins argues that while there are a very few and

---

[110] Hopkins, "The Age of Roman Girls at Marriage," 309–27.
[111] Ibid., 313.
[112] Brent D. Shaw, "The Age of Roman Girls at Marriage: Some Reconsiderations," *JoRS* 77 (1987): 30–46.
[113] Hopkins uses a collection of funerary inscriptions compiled by Harkness that both give the age of the girl at death and the years she was married. This sample is fairly small. Saller-Shaw instead has studied all inscriptions that give the relationship between the deceased and commemorator. They argue that the point at which the identity of the commemorator shifts from parents to spouses gives a reasonable representation of age at marriage.
[114] Shaw, "The Age of Roman Girls at Marriage," 33.
[115] Van Gennep, *Rites of Passage*, 66.
[116] If we were to be even more precise, the qualification would rather be "before menarche" rather than "before 12." As stated above, Soranus estimates menarche between fourteen to sixteen years old (Soranus, *Gynecology*, 17 [trans. Temkin]). However, the diversity of ages at which menarche was likely to have occurred in any one individual renders this strategy impractical on every scale. This indeed is precisely one of van Gennep's points: the diversity of ages at which the onset of puberty occurs—in males or females—renders the importance of the distinction between physical puberty and social puberty.

vague testimonies to married girls under twelve being untouched sexually until they experienced menarche, there is no reason to believe this was generally the case. Indeed, it is the interest ancient historians showed in these few cases that makes him suspect that they were the exception, rather than the norm.[117] While this idea might make the modern reader squeamish, van Gennep's theories clearly adhere to Roman cultural practices. Thus, while the onset of biological puberty may not have corresponded to the Roman girl's wedding, it still seems clear that the Roman wedding acted as a *rite of passage* transitioning a girl to womanhood.

Summary and Conclusion

This chapter has built upon the idea, introduced in the previous chapter, that a child was seen in the ancient world as an unformed, unfinished being, but one with the unique potential to be transformed and become a complete and finished product: an adult. The primary purpose of this chapter, then, has been twofold. First, I have introduced van Gennep's understanding of the *rites of passage*: rites that specifically aid a safe transition from one state of being to another, and which follow a predictable sequence of events. Of particular note as well was the subcategory of *rites of passage* that he terms "initiation rites." Second, I have demonstrated that van Gennep's basic schema correlates with two ceremonies common in the Greco-Roman world: that of the *toga virilis*, where a boy formally became a man, and that of the marriage ceremony, where a girl formally became a woman via the role of wife. In each case, I have demonstrated that these ceremonies follow exactly the pattern of ritual separation, transition, and incorporation. I will be utilizing both of these objectives when arguing for understanding Mark 10:14-15 within the framework of a *rite of passage*. When Mark's Jesus says that one must receive the Kingdom of God like a child, I will argue that he is both reminding the reader of the fundamental difference conceived between adults and children and emphasizing the specific process of transformation needed to convert one to the other.

These two main points have been further strengthened by the arguments of anthropologists Turner and Douglas. Turner highlights the fundamental transformation that happens through *rites of passage*, and particularly rites of initiation, which, in turn, emphasizes both the radical alteration that happens throughout the process and the sense of community cemented within the group of initiates. Douglas adds her own contribution by way of her emphasis on the danger understood to be inherent in these rituals—in the process of fundamental transformation, the initiate is particularly susceptible and vulnerable. Douglas will be particularly useful when examining Mark, particularly his narrative which shows the disciples in a decidedly unflattering light at times, and which even shows Jesus as one who relentlessly marches on toward his known suffering and death. A fundamental theme of Mark is that of the difference between the things valued in the Kingdom of God and those valued by the world. In

---

[117] Hopkins, "The Age of Roman Girls at Marriage," 316.

fact, to enter the Kingdom of God, radical transformation is needed. Moreover, there is a consistent sense of the perils and dangers of such a transformation. As we turn to an examination of Mark, and in particular Mark's understanding of entrance into the Kingdom of God, it will be crucial to keep in mind van Gennep's schema of *rites of passage*. As I will argue, it is possible to see not only this schema in Mark but also Mark's demonstration of a sort of inversion of the *rites of passage*, at least according to the social values of his day. That is to say, Mark's understanding of the finished product, the person *post* ritual transformation, is, in fact, more closely allied with that of the ancient world's conception of a child: that is, exactly what constitutes an individual *prior to* society's expected transformation.

4

Rites of Passage and Entrance into the Kingdom of God

In the previous chapter, I examined a group of anthropologists who define and explore a group of rites they term *rites of passage*. A *rite of passage* serves to guide and transform one from a previous state of being into a new, different state via a tripartite process. Initiation rites, a subcategory of *rites of passage*, encompass both ceremonies of coming of age and ceremonies of induction to a religion. I have argued that the ancient Greco-Roman world had clear examples of *rites of passage* whereby children become adults: in the case of boys, the *toga virilis* ceremony, and in the case of girls, the marriage ceremony, serve as their entrance into adulthood. In both cases, these ceremonies clearly follow the tripartite structure of separation, liminality, and reincorporation. Finally, I argued that this ceremony helped guide a person from one distinct state of being to another different state of being, and the word "transformation" was a decidedly appropriate term for this transition. I suggested in my conclusion that these *rites of passage* could be a useful lens by which to examine Mark 10:13-16, particularly the enigmatic statement that one must enter the Kingdom of God "as a child."

In this chapter, I will examine the gospel of Mark, showing that language of the Kingdom of God is always accompanied by images of transformation, a transformation that involves putting aside one's old life, a middle process of indeterminacy, and a final entrance once the change has been completed. Of primary interest will be Mark 10's use of the "Kingdom of God" in both the pericopes where Jesus welcomes and blesses children (Mark 10:13-16) and converses with a rich man (Mark 10:17-31).

Mark 10:13-16

Καὶ προσέφερον αὐτῷ παιδία ἵνα αὐτῶν ἅψηται οἱ δὲ μαθηταὶ ἐπετίμησαν αὐτοῖς. ἰδὼν δὲ ὁ Ἰησοῦς ἠγανάκτησεν καὶ εἶπεν αὐτοῖς· ἄφετε τὰ παιδία ἔρχεσθαι πρός με, μὴ κωλύετε αὐτά, τῶν γὰρ τοιούτων ἐστὶν ἡ βασιλεία τοῦ θεοῦ. ἀμὴν λέγω ὑμῖν, ὃς ἂν μὴ δέξηται τὴν βασιλείαν τοῦ θεοῦ ὡς παιδίον, οὐ μὴ εἰσέλθῃ εἰς αὐτήν. καὶ ἐναγκαλισάμενος αὐτὰ κατευλόγει τιθεὶς τὰς χεῖρας ἐπ᾽ αὐτά.

And they were bringing children to him so that he could touch them, but the disciples scolded them. But when Jesus saw this, he was indignant and said, "Let the children come to me; do not stop them, for the Kingdom of God is of such as these. Truly I say to you, whoever does not accept the Kingdom of God as a child will never enter into it." And wrapping them into his arms, he laid his hands on them and blessed them.

The passage is at once powerful, and unclear. Judith Gundry notes that this story is of particular interest when studying children in Mark, as it combines "Jesus' *teaching about* little children and the Kingdom of God and Jesus' *ministry to* children and shows the relationship between them."[1] While the narrative showing Jesus's actions to children is fairly clear, his teachings about children and their relationship to the Kingdom of God are remarkably opaque. Beginning with the more straightforward piece of the pericope, Jesus is seen to bless children despite the attempts of the disciples to bar their way. Children, as we have seen repeatedly in the ancient world, might be individually loved by their parents, but as a group did not command respect or admiration. "They" were bringing children to Jesus to bless them. One presumes this was a group of parents, but "they" begin as unnamed characters, and recede even further into the background as the story continues. The disciples attempt to rebuke "them." The intended antecedent is certainly the adults, but it easily could include the children as well. The disciples' motivations for barring their entry are not explicit, nor does the audience have insight into what words the disciples used to scold those gathered before Jesus. But the reality of children as insignificant and unimportant is fairly clearly at hand—the disciples think Jesus has better things to do. The disciples arguably view themselves as Jesus's gatekeepers: it is up to them to keep the less important from Jesus so he can focus on the more important.[2] Jesus, however, confronts the disciples, as he does so often. Stressing the value he feels for the children, he scolds the disciples for their presumption, while simultaneously encouraging the children to come forward. As the children come up, he wraps them into his arms, places his hands on them, and blesses them. Judith Gundry has rightly stressed the aspect of "hugging"[3] going on here: Jesus is not only formally blessing these children but ἐναγκαλίζομαι implies a physical embrace that is visually potent. Gundry also notes that ἐναγκαλίζομαι is removed from both Luke and Matthew's recensions of the story, and speculates that this warm and cuddly Jesus may not have fit well with a later portrait of Jesus.[4] ἐναγκαλίζομαι is used rarely in the Septuagint[5] but appears in

---

[1] Judith Gundry-Volf, "Children in the Gospel of Mark, with Special Attention to Jesus's Blessing of the Children (Mark 10: 13-16) and the Purpose of Mark," in *The Child in the Bible* (eds. Marcia J. Bunge, Terence E. Fretheim, and Beverly Roberts Gaventa; Eerdmans, 2008), 149.

[2] See, for instance, Adela Yarbro Collins's argument that disciples act in a similar function as Elisha's servant Gehazi in 2 Kings 4:8-37, and Rabbi Akiva's disciples, both barring the way of "unimportant" people. Her summary is "the attendant(s) of the charismatic figure assume(s) the role of gate-keeper, allowing or denying access to him, and presumes(s) to know his wishes" (Adela Yarbro Collins, *Mark: A Commentary* [Hermenia; Minneapolis: Fortress, 2007], 472). In all three cases, they are wrong about their master's wishes. See also R. Alan Culpepper, *Mark* (Smyth & Helwys Bible Commentary; Macon, Geor.: Smyth & Helwys, 2007), 333, who instead characterizes this as "brokers, protecting Jesus from unworthy clients."

[3] See Gundry-Volf, "Children in the Gospel of Mark," 150, 154–8.

[4] Gundry-Volf, "Children in the Gospel of Mark," 150, f. 27.

[5] The only pair of instances are in the parallel Proverbs 6:10 and 24:33, used for clasping hands together: ὀλίγον μὲν ὑπνοῖς ὀλίγον δὲ κάθησαι μικρὸν δὲ νυστάζεις ὀλίγον δὲ ἐναγκαλίζῃ χερσὶν στήθη (Proverbs 6:10 BGT); ὀλίγον νυστάζω ὀλίγον δὲ καθυπνῶ ὀλίγον δὲ ἐναγκαλίζομαι χερσὶν στήθη (Pro 24:33).

several instances where children are taken lovingly into the arms of adults who are not their parents.⁶ It is possible the word was simply perceived to be superfluous to Matthew and Luke, but Mark's expanded description certainly adds an emotive layer to the scene. Jesus demonstrates on a physical level the acceptance of children into his kingdom.

The further layers of Jesus's words about children, however, are much more complex. Jesus insists that τοιούτων ἐστὶν ἡ βασιλεία τοῦ θεοῦ. The phrase is a simple genitive indicating possession, and translations indicate this. However, while the translation is fairly straightforward, the meaning is much more difficult to decipher. In what way is the Kingdom of God of "such as these ones"?

In a similar manner, the next phase ὃς ἂν μὴ δέξηται τὴν βασιλείαν τοῦ θεοῦ ὡς παιδίον, οὐ μὴ εἰσέλθῃ εἰς αὐτήν has a straightforward translation, but a much more difficult intention. The neuter παιδίον in the phrase ὡς παιδίον, "as a child," can be taken as nominative case—the kingdom should be received as a child would receive it—or accusative—the kingdom should be received as one would receive a child. There are proponents of both positions.⁷ I argue that the more straightforward translation understands παιδίον as nominative. This more straightforward translation, however, leads to difficulty in discerning *in what way* a child would receive the kingdom.

The emotional impact on the disciples, and likely the ancient readers of the text, is striking: this is a stunning thing for Jesus to say, one that the disciples do not expect. The disciples often serve as a foil for Jesus throughout Mark—thus, Jesus issues a cryptic warning about the "yeast" of the Pharisees and Herod, while the disciples are confused that Jesus is reprimanding them for forgetting to buy loaves of bread for

---

⁶ See for instance, Plutarch *Lives, Camillus*. 104, speaking of Mater Matuta "ταύτην ἄν τις ἀπὸ τῶν δρωμένων ἱερῶν μάλιστα Λευκοθέαν νομίσειεν εἶναι. καὶ γὰρ θεράπαιναν εἰς τὸν σηκὸν εἰσάγουσαι ῥαπίζουσιν, εἶτ' ἐξελαύνουσι καὶ τὰ τῶν ἀδελφῶν τέκνα πρὸ τῶν ἰδίων ἐναγκαλίζονται, καὶ δρῶσι περὶ τὴν θυσίαν ἃ ταῖς Διονύσου τροφαῖς καὶ τοῖς διὰ τὴν παλλακὴν πάθεσι τῆς Ἰνοῦς προσέοικε." See also Diodorus Siculus, *The Library of History* 270: ἐνταῦθα τῷ παιδίῳ κατά τινα θείαν πρόνοιαν τάς τε παρδάλεις καί τινα τῶν ἄλλων τῶν ἀλκῇ διαφερόντων θηρίων παρέχεσθαι τὴν θηλὴν καὶ διατρέφειν, γύναια δέ τινα περὶ τὸν τόπον ποιμαίνοντα κατιδεῖν τὸ γινόμενον, καὶ θαυμάσαντα τὴν περιπέτειαν ἀνελέσθαι τὸ βρέφος, καὶ προσαγορεῦσαι Κυβέλην ἀπὸ τοῦ τόπου. αὐξομένην δὲ τὴν παῖδα τῷ τε κάλλει καὶ σωφροσύνῃ διενεγκεῖν, ἔτι δὲ συνέσει γενέσθαι θαυμαστήν· τήν τε γὰρ πολυκάλαμον σύριγγα πρώτην ἐπινοῆσαι καὶ πρὸς τὰς παιδιὰς καὶ χορείας εὑρεῖν κύμβαλα καὶ τύμπανα, πρὸς δὲ τούτοις καθαρμοὺς τῶν νοσούντων κτηνῶν τε καὶ νηπίων παίδων εἰσηγήσασθαι· διὸ καὶ τῶν βρεφῶν ταῖς ἐπῳδαῖς σῳζομένων καὶ τῶν πλείστων ὑπ' αὐτῆς ἐναγκαλιζομένων, διὰ τὴν εἰς ταῦτα σπουδὴν καὶ φιλοστοργίαν ὑπὸ πάντων αὐτὴν ὀρείαν μητέρα προσαγορευθῆναι. συναστρέφεσθαι δ' αὐτῇ καὶ φιλίαν ἔχειν ἐπὶ πλέον φασὶ Μαρσύαν τὸν Φρύγα, θαυμαζόμενον ἐπὶ συνέσει καὶ σωφροσύνῃ. Plutarch narrates the same event in similar wording in Plutarch *Moralia, On Brotherly Love* 324: "ἣ τε Λευκοθέα τῆς ἀδελφῆς ἀποθανούσης ἔθρεψε τὸ βρέφος καὶ συνεξεθείασεν· ὅθεν αἱ Ῥωμαίων γυναῖκες ἐν ταῖς τῆς Λευκοθέας ἑορταῖς, ἣν Ματοῦταν ὀνομάζουσιν, οὐ τοὺς ἑαυτῶν παῖδας ἀλλὰ τοὺς τῶν ἀδελφῶν ἐναγκαλίζονται καὶ τιμῶσιν.

⁷ Proponents of understanding παιδίον as nominative include Judith Gundry-Volf, "To Such as These Belongs the Reign of God: Jesus and Children," *TheoT* 56 (1999): 472n5; Sharon Betsworth, *Children in Early Christian Narratives* (London: Bloomsbury, 2015), 68–9; C. Clifton Black, *Mark* (Abingdon New Testament Commentary; Abingdon Press, 2011), 224. Proponents for understanding παιδίον as accusative include P. Spitaler, "Welcoming a Child as a Metaphor for Welcoming God's Kingdom: A Close Reading of Mark 10.13-16," *JSNT* 31.4 (2009), 425; Larry L. Eubanks, "Mark 10:13-16," *Review & Expositor* 91.3 (1994), 403. James Bailey, "Experiencing the Kingdom as a Little Child: A Rereading of Mark 10:13-16," *WW* 15.1 (1995), 61–2, exhibits insights from reading the text in both ways.

their journey in the boat (Mark 8:14-21). Indeed, in Jesus's greater discussion about both metaphorical and physical bread, the disciples seem to only become even more bewildered. The disciples' continued failure to understand how Jesus expects them to act, or what Jesus means when he speaks obliquely, allows Mark's Gospel to often stress again, even more clearly, what Jesus desires. But even these direct statements can confound the reader, much like the disciples in the narrative.[8] What does Jesus intend when he says one must receive the kingdom "as a child" if one wants to enter it at all?

Beginning with patristic authors, several theories have been proposed for the way in which a child is a model recipient of the kingdom. Clement of Alexandria holds up innocence and lack of guile as the fundamental quality of a child,[9] whereas Augustine, committed as he is to original sin, focuses more intently on physical weakness and dependence.[10] In recent scholarship Ernest Best argues for a child's basic trust in the ability of his or her parent to provide.[11] R. Alan Culpepper argues for a sense of delight, humility, or gladness.[12] Lately many have begun to settle on the child's dependent status. Clifton Black,[13] Joel Marcus,[14] Judith Gundry,[15] and W. A. Strange[16] all argue in some way for this understanding. There is something of merit in this latter suggestion, and this project takes seriously the idea of the child as a socially marginalized, dependent creature. However, it seems that there is more than mere dependence or even social marginalization at the heart of this passage.

It is Dan Via's interpretation that aligns most closely with what I am arguing. Via's use of Carl Jung employs many of the same images and metaphors as anthropology's *rites of passages* uses, but from a psychological rather than socially developmental perspective. Via, in his *Ethics of Mark's Gospel*, argues that Mark 10:15 is, in fact, implying a transformation. To accept the kingdom as a child "obviously involves a change, from adult to child. Thus the adult is being told to *become* like a child."[17] He argues that Matthew states this explicitly as well, but that this is also intended in Mark. Dissatisfied with modern scholarship's multitude of attempts to explicate what "become like a child" might mean, he argues that rather than look for the "*particular* meaning of

---

[8] While in class one day, Dr. C. Clifton Black memorably said the same about Mark 8:21: "Jesus says 'Do you not understand yet?' and our only reply is 'No, we don't!'"

[9] Clement of Alexandria, *Paedagogus* 1.5 (Wilson): "Rightly, then, are those called children who know Him who is God alone as their Father, who are simple, and infants, and guileless, who are lovers of the horns of the unicorns." Later, 1.5: "The child [(νήπιος)] is therefore gentle [(ἤπιος],), and therefore more tender, delicate, and simple, guileless, and destitute of hypocrisy, straightforward and upright, which is the basis of simplicity and truth." In *Clement of Alexandria* (trans. William Wilson; Edinburg: T&T Clark 1867), 125–7.

[10] "It was the low stature then of childhood which Thou our King didst commend as an emblem of lowliness, when Thou saidst, Of such is the kingdom of heaven" (Augustine, *Confessions*. 21 (Pusey)).

[11] Ernest Best, *Following Jesus: Discipleship in the Gospel of Mark* (Sheffield: JSOT Press, 1981), 108.

[12] R. Alan Culpepper, *Mark* (Smyth & Helwys Bible Commentary; Macon: Smyth & Helwys, 2007), 357–8.

[13] Black, *Mark*, 224–5, 227–9.

[14] Joel Marcus, *Mark 8–16* (New Haven: Yale University Press, 2009), 718.

[15] Gundry-Volf, "To Such as These Belongs the Reign of God," 473.

[16] W. A. Strange, *Children in the Early Church: Children in the Ancient World, the New Testament, and the Early Church* (Cumbria: Paternoster Press, 1996), 51.

[17] Dan Via, *The Ethics of Mark's Gospel: In the Middle of Time* (Eugene: Wipf & Stock, 2005), 129.

childlikeness"[18] that Mark fails to make clear, "let us ask about the *most formal* meaning of the image, one from which all particular meanings must derive."[19] For this he draws on Jungian theory of archetype. Jung is interested in examining the subconscious, allowing the self to notice and differentiate from conscious and subconscious elements. One of the ways Jung went about this was examining archetypes and assigning meaning to them. The "child archetype" is one of many of these archetypes, and in two essays ("The Psychology of the Child Archetype"[20] and "The Special Phenomenology of the Child Archetype"[21]) he examines why the "child" shows up so often in dreams, fairytales, and other mythologies. Via, summarizing Jung, says that "one of the essential features of the child archetype is its futurity. By that Jung means that the child is potential future. The appearance of this image is the anticipation of future developments even though at first sight it may seem like a retrospective configuration."[22] However, Via explains that the child is constantly moving toward independence in a future where there is a separation from origins.[23] This separation is not without its hazards, however. Jung, referencing the injunction in the Gospels to become like children, notes that "this refers to a development and transaction that is difficult and dangerous."[24] In fact, Via employs death as a fitting metaphor: "the very terminology of the loss of life expresses the radicalness of this move."[25]

In summary, it is Via's ideas that most strongly correspond to the argument I have been crafting about what is meant by this passage in Mark 10. It will be useful to look at direct synoptic parallels to this pericope, as well as one in John that have some family resemblance.

Mark 10:13-16 Parallels

Matthew 19:13-15

Τότε προσηνέχθησαν αὐτῷ παιδία ἵνα τὰς χεῖρας ἐπιθῇ αὐτοῖς καὶ προσεύξηται· οἱ δὲ μαθηταὶ ἐπετίμησαν αὐτοῖς. ὁ δὲ Ἰησοῦς εἶπεν· ἄφετε τὰ παιδία καὶ μὴ κωλύετε αὐτὰ ἐλθεῖν πρός με, τῶν γὰρ τοιούτων ἐστὶν ἡ βασιλεία τῶν οὐρανῶν. καὶ ἐπιθεὶς τὰς χεῖρας αὐτοῖς ἐπορεύθη ἐκεῖθεν.

Then children were brought to him so that he might lay hands on them and pray, but the disciples scolded them. But Jesus said, "Let the children come to me and

---

[18] Ibid.
[19] Ibid.
[20] C. G. Jung, "The Psychology of the Child Archetype," in *Psyche & Symbol: A Selection from the Writings of C.G. Jung* (ed. Violet S. deLaszlo; New York: Doubleday Anchor, 1958), 113–31.
[21] C. G. Jung, "The Special Phenomenology of the Child Archetype," in *Psyche & Symbol: A Selection from the Writings of C.G. Jung* (ed. Violet S. deLaszlo; New York: Doubleday Anchor, 1958), 132–47.
[22] Via, *Ethics of Mark's Gospel*, 130.
[23] Ibid.
[24] Ibid. Here Via is referencing Jung, "The Special Phenomenology of the Child Archetype," 133–4.
[25] Via, *Ethics of Mark's Gospel*, 130.

don't stop them, for the kingdom of heaven is of such as these." And after laying his hands on them, he departed from there.

Much of this passage in Matthew nearly duplicates Mark's version. The most notable change is the omission of Mark 10:15: "Truly I say to you, whoever does not accept the Kingdom of God as a child will never enter into it." (Matthew rewords this phrase and relocates to 18:3). Matthew is more specific in 19:13 about what the supplicants want Jesus to do for the children—lay hands on them and pray (instead of Mark's "touch them"), although in Matthew 19:15 the description is much shorter and without mention of either Jesus blessing or he gathering them into his arms.[26] But the actions of the disciples in trying to prevent the children and Jesus's rebuke are repeated nearly word for word: Matthew uses "kingdom of heaven" instead of Mark's "Kingdom of God," and he uses the aorist active infinitive for ἔρχομαι instead of the present middle infinitive used in Mark. In displacing Mark 10:15, Matthew focuses solely on the importance of children in the Kingdom of Heaven. The story becomes one of acceptance and attention toward the children, without the added step of the adult disciples needing to become as children themselves. This point will be made more fully in Matthew 18:1-15, to which we turn next.

Matthew 18:1-5

Ἐν ἐκείνῃ τῇ ὥρᾳ προσῆλθον οἱ μαθηταὶ τῷ Ἰησοῦ λέγοντες· τίς ἄρα μείζων ἐστὶν ἐν τῇ βασιλείᾳ τῶν οὐρανῶν; καὶ προσκαλεσάμενος παιδίον ἔστησεν αὐτὸ ἐν μέσῳ αὐτῶν καὶ εἶπεν· ἀμὴν λέγω ὑμῖν, ἐὰν μὴ στραφῆτε καὶ γένησθε ὡς τὰ παιδία, οὐ μὴ εἰσέλθητε εἰς τὴν βασιλείαν τῶν οὐρανῶν. ὅστις οὖν ταπεινώσει ἑαυτὸν ὡς τὸ παιδίον τοῦτο, οὗτός ἐστιν ὁ μείζων ἐν τῇ βασιλείᾳ τῶν οὐρανῶν. καὶ ὃς ἐὰν δέξηται ἓν παιδίον τοιοῦτο ἐπὶ τῷ ὀνόματί μου, ἐμὲ δέχεται.

At that time the disciples came to Jesus saying, "Who would you say is the greatest in the kingdom of heaven?" And he called a child whom he set in the middle of them and he said, "Truly I say to you, if you don't change and become as children, you will never enter into the kingdom of heaven. Therefore, whoever humbles himself as this child, that one is the greatest in the kingdom of heaven. And whoever receives a child such as this in my name receives me."

Matthew combines Mark 10:15 and Mark 9:33-37. Matthew 18:6-10 goes on to parallel Mark 9:42-48, and Matthew explicitly connects these verses, strongly implying the connection between παιδίον and μικρῶν τούτων, whereas there is debate in Mark's version as to whom μικρῶν refers.[27] Matthew's reworked version of Mark does several things. First, like Mark 9:33-37, Jesus uses children as an example of

---

[26] As Judith Gundry notes, as referenced above. Judith Gundry-Volf, "Children in the Gospel of Mark," 150, f. 27.

[27] Joel Marcus, for instance, argues that the intervening verses strongly point to identifying the "little ones" of Mark 9:42 as the Christian community (Marcus, *Mark 8–16*, 689).

the reversal of greatness in God's kingdom, and asserts that receiving children acts as receiving Jesus himself. In Matthew, however, there is the addition of the phrase ὅστις οὖν ταπεινώσει ἑαυτὸν ὡς τὸ παιδίον τοῦτο in verse 4, specifically connecting the idea of children with the trait of "humility." It is in this way that one becomes the greatest in the kingdom. This necessarily informs the intent behind verse 3, when adults are told to στραφῆτε καὶ γένησθε ὡς τὰ παιδία. στρέφω can mean "turn around" in a metaphorical sense ("change one's mind"), but there are better words to use if he intended "transform." However, Matthew seems to push for some sort of alteration with the further strengthening of γίνομαι. While Matthew does not seem to envision Jesus as urging his followers to physically become children (his use of "ὡς" in the phrase "ὡς τὰ παιδία" signals a metaphorical, rather than a literal, command), he does seem to be saying something jarring here. One must change to become like a child to enter the kingdom of heaven. Adela Yarbro Collins agrees: "The Matthean Jesus calls for a personal transformation involving 'becoming like children' and defines that as 'humbling oneself.'"[28] Placing 18:3 in the context of the question of greatness in 18:1, and the specific reply that one must be humble like a child (as well as receive children), strongly points to Matthew's understanding this injunction to be primarily about the humility of children.

Luke 18:15-17

Προσέφερον δὲ αὐτῷ καὶ τὰ βρέφη ἵνα αὐτῶν ἅπτηται· ἰδόντες δὲ οἱ μαθηταὶ ἐπετίμων αὐτοῖς. ὁ δὲ Ἰησοῦς προσεκαλέσατο αὐτὰ λέγων· ἄφετε τὰ παιδία ἔρχεσθαι πρός με καὶ μὴ κωλύετε αὐτά, τῶν γὰρ τοιούτων ἐστὶν ἡ βασιλεία τοῦ θεοῦ. ἀμὴν λέγω ὑμῖν, ὃς ἂν μὴ δέξηται τὴν βασιλείαν τοῦ θεοῦ ὡς παιδίον, οὐ μὴ εἰσέλθῃ εἰς αὐτήν.

And they were also bringing to him babies so that he could touch them, but when the disciples saw, they scolded them. But Jesus called for them, saying, "Let the children come to me and do not stop them, for the Kingdom of God is of such as these. Truly I say to you, whoever does not accept the Kingdom of God as a child will never enter into it."

Luke's version is even more notably closer to Mark's than Matthew's is. Luke changes the scene so that it is specifically βρέφη, "babies," instead of the more ambiguous παιδία found in Mark and Matthew. Luke sets the scene slightly differently by having the disciples notice what is happening before scolding the people. One gets the sense that the disciples are interrupting Jesus in Luke's version, whereas they may well be attempting a preemptive blockade in Mark. Luke omits Mark's ἠγανάκτησεν

---

[28] Collins, *Mark*, 473. In her estimation, however, the Matthean version "goes beyond the implications of the Markan form of the saying," with which I disagree. I would rather frame it that Mark's version is not as explicit about its implications, but that the intent *to do what?* is still there. Collins goes on to briefly mention the *Gospel of Thomas*'s version of the saying, arguing, "The *Gospel of Thomas* (22) interprets the saying (probably the Matthean version) as calling for the abolition of dichotomies, for example, that of male and female."

and instead replaces it with the more congenial προσεκαλέσατο. But the rest of Luke 18:16-17 is identical to Mark 10:14-15, including the reappearance of παιδία. Luke's version finishes with these verses and omits Mark 10:16, leaving the reader unclear as to whether Jesus goes back to the children, or whether he has finished with them.

Because Luke duplicates Mark's story almost identically, there is very little to go on when trying to get a sense of how Luke interprets Mark's intent. Substituting "babies" for "children" potentially narrows the age range Jesus means when he argues for children as model recipients of the Kingdom, which in turn potentially narrows the characteristics of children intended in the passage. But he follows Mark by using the more generic "children" when Jesus actually speaks of the kingdom and how to accept it. In Luke's version there is a sense of a more serene Jesus: he neither gets as angry at the disciples' behavior nor appears as warm toward the children themselves. But in terms of unraveling the mystery of what Mark 10:14-15 intends, Luke offers very little help.

John 3:3-10

ἀπεκρίθη Ἰησοῦς καὶ εἶπεν αὐτῷ· ἀμὴν ἀμὴν λέγω σοι, ἐὰν μή τις γεννηθῇ ἄνωθεν, οὐ δύναται ἰδεῖν τὴν βασιλείαν τοῦ θεοῦ. λέγει πρὸς αὐτὸν [ὁ] Νικόδημος· πῶς δύναται ἄνθρωπος γεννηθῆναι γέρων ὤν; μὴ δύναται εἰς τὴν κοιλίαν τῆς μητρὸς αὐτοῦ δεύτερον εἰσελθεῖν καὶ γεννηθῆναι; ἀπεκρίθη Ἰησοῦς· ἀμὴν ἀμὴν λέγω σοι, ἐὰν μή τις γεννηθῇ ἐξ ὕδατος καὶ πνεύματος, οὐ δύναται εἰσελθεῖν εἰς τὴν βασιλείαν τοῦ θεοῦ. τὸ γεγεννημένον ἐκ τῆς σαρκὸς σάρξ ἐστιν, καὶ τὸ γεγεννημένον ἐκ τοῦ πνεύματος πνεῦμά ἐστιν. μὴ θαυμάσῃς ὅτι εἶπόν σοι· δεῖ ὑμᾶς γεννηθῆναι ἄνωθεν. τὸ πνεῦμα ὅπου θέλει πνεῖ καὶ τὴν φωνὴν αὐτοῦ ἀκούεις, ἀλλ' οὐκ οἶδας πόθεν ἔρχεται καὶ ποῦ ὑπάγει· οὕτως ἐστὶν πᾶς ὁ γεγεννημένος ἐκ τοῦ πνεύματος. ἀπεκρίθη Νικόδημος καὶ εἶπεν αὐτῷ· πῶς δύναται ταῦτα γενέσθαι; ἀπεκρίθη Ἰησοῦς καὶ εἶπεν αὐτῷ· σὺ εἶ ὁ διδάσκαλος τοῦ Ἰσραὴλ καὶ ταῦτα οὐ γινώσκεις;

Jesus answered him, "Truly truly I tell you, unless a person is born again/from above, (s)he cannot see the Kingdom of God." Nicodemus said to him, "How is it possible that a person be born after being old? (S)he can't climb into the mother's womb a second time and be born, can (s)he?" Jesus answered, "Truly truly I tell you, unless a person is born from water and the spirit, (s)he cannot enter the Kingdom of God. That which is born from the flesh is flesh, and that which is born from the spirit is spirit. Don't be astonished when I say to you, 'You must be born again/from above.' The wind/sprit blows where it wills, and you hear its sound/voice, but you do not know where it came from or where it goes: so it is with everyone born of the Spirit." Nicodemus answered him saying, "How can these things be?" And Jesus responded, "You are a teacher of Israel and you do not understand these things?"

Another useful passage toward gleaning the meaning of Mark 10:14-15 is the discussion between Jesus and Nicodemus in John 3. Aloysius Ambrozic, in his *The Hidden Kingdom*, mentions as an aside the similarities between Mark 10:14-15 and

John 3:3-5.[29] He argues that the Aramaic word that was probably behind Mark 10:15's παιδίον was probably בר. He says, "[I]f this suggestion is correct, it may be easier to explain the divergence between Mk 10:15 and its probable Johannine variant in 3:3, 5. 'Son' brings the thought of birth and rebirth more readily to mind than does 'child.'"[30] While the interest of this study lies far outside redaction criticism, the link between the basic concepts of John 3 and Mark 10:15 is of value in arguing for what I am proposing. John 3 involves perception of and entrance into the Kingdom of God. John 3, moreover, involves Jesus instructing a person who both desires instruction and also is surprisingly obtuse. Finally, John 3 involves imagery entirely in keeping with the sorts of metamorphosis needed for entrance and, like Mark 10:15, uses the example of a child to signal this transformation. In John, however, this transformation is explicit. Jesus states that "no one can see the Kingdom of God without being born again/from above." Nicodemus, bewildered by Jesus's assertions, asks, "How is it possible for a person to be born again once he is an old man? Can one enter into the mother's womb a second time and be born?" Jesus answers that only through water and the spirit can one enter the kingdom. In this passage the mystery of the kingdom is explicitly referenced, as is the necessity of God's active work to transform a person. Jesus, in a clever wordplay, uses the word ἄνωθεν, meaning both "born again" and "born from above." Hence the language implies both the heavenly agency but also imagery of birth and rebirth. One must become a baby, and be birthed again. Nicodemus gets at the fundamental impossibility of what Jesus is saying, and Jesus in reply does not deny the impossibility from a human's perspective. Utter transformation is needed. A person must become as a newborn, entering via a loving mother's labors. This metaphor of being "born again" has become a key metaphor for the Evangelical church, and yet as the metaphor has been adopted, it has also lost the startling quality associated with it. A person, to see God's kingdom, must both repeat and also invert a *rite of passage* both ubiquitous and momentous. And in John 3 as well, the danger of the process can easily feature in the background: infant mortality was particularly high and birth dangerous both to mother and to baby. While Mark 10:15 moves quickly connecting entrance into the kingdom and being "as a child," I would argue that the thematic similarities between it and John 3 strengthen my case that a radical transformation is plausibly intended in the passage.

Complementary Passages in Mark

Several passages in Mark describe various aspects of the Kingdom of God. These serve as useful companions to Mark 10:13-16, particularly those that hint at some sort of reversal and transformation.

---

[29] Marcus also makes this connection, although he describes it as "the apparently independent forms of this wandering logion in John 3:3, 5" (Marcus, *Mark 8-16*, 716).
[30] Aloysius M. Ambrozic, *The Hidden Kingdom: A Redaction-Critical Study of the References to the Kingdom of God in Mark's Gospel* (Washington: Catholic Biblical Association of America, 1972), 152.

---

that Mark, when adding the detail about Jesus's love for the rich man, is highlighting the fact that the "radical demand that follows flows from Jesus' love" and does not act as an arbitrary test.[35] Collins explicitly connects Jesus's proclamation about the camel in 10:25 to that of 10:15: "the threat 'shall surely not enter into it' in 10:15 foreshadows the saying of v. 25, 'it is easier for a camel to pass through the eye of a needle than for a rich man to enter into the Kingdom of God.' This link suggests that receiving the kingdom as a child means receiving it without being held back by wealth and possessions."[36]

Jesus's warning about the high cost of entrance into the kingdom is mirrored by the disciples' incredulity. Their former way of life must be drastically severed, and a radical transformation is necessary before entrance can be accomplished. This transformation is impossible, according to Jesus, save by the power of God. It is through God that all things are possible. This motif calls to mind John 3, as well as the parables of Mark 4: whatever the content and readiness of the soil, it is the sower who transforms potential into actuality.[37]

---

[33] While Jesus says nearly the same thing this second time, he specifically calls the disciples τέκνα, and instead of talking about how hard it will be in the future for the rich specifically to enter the kingdom, he seems to broaden the statement, saying that it is hard here in the present for anyone to enter. Notable later manuscripts, in fact, add τοὺς πεποιθότας ἐπὶ χρήμασιν. (sc, rp tg, A, D, 1141).
[34] Drury, for instance, cites and disparages this idea: "The little parable about the *camel and the needle's eye* at 10.25 is not in the least obscure, but it is deliberately absurd in a way which has attracted efforts to make it realistic for a very long time: e.g., by suggesting that there was a gate in Jerusalem through which camels could just squeeze" (John Drury, *The Parables in the Gospels* [New York: Crossroad, 1985], 64). See also Ched Myers, *Binding the Strong Man: A Political Reading of Mark's Story of Jesus* (Mary Knoll: Orbis Books, 1988), 275; Black, *Mark*, 227; Marcus, *Mark 8-16*, 730-1.
[35] Culpepper, *Mark*, 336-7.
[36] Collins, *Mark*, 473.
[37] While I have not addressed the seed parables in Mark 4, they too imagine God's kingdom in ways that fit with the tripartite structure of *rites of passage* in sowing, growing, and harvesting. Seeds and children are often connected in ancient literature, where the harvest represents adulthood. The seed parables emphasize not only how God's kingdom might start as a small, overlookable seeds but also the difficulty of producing a harvest of truly worthy kingdom members. Both of these images fit quite well with the need for transformation, a transformation that is unexpected, and that is possible only by God.

Mark 9:33-37

Mark 9:33-37 serves as an example of the symbolism of children employed by Mark in his Gospel. As the disciples are arguing over who is the greatest, Jesus has them sit and says, "Whoever wishes to be first ought to be last and a servant of all." This proclamation is followed by Jesus taking a child (παιδίον) and setting the child in the midst of the disciples. Then, as if this placement were not emphatic enough, Jesus ἐναγκαλισάμενος, "wraps [the child] in his arms." Jesus then continues by saying, "Whoever receives one such as these children in my name receives me, and whoever receives me receives not me, but the one who sent me."

The parallels between Mark 9:33-37 and Mark 10:13-16 are striking both on a linguistic and thematic level. Thematically, Jesus is stressing the importance of children, and of his close connection with children. He emphasizes this connection by making physical contact with them, a contact that is tender and loving.[31] Linguistically, several words and phrases are in common: Mark uses his preferred term for child, παιδίον, but he also uses ἐναγκαλισάμενος, which is mirrored in 10:16, as well as δέχομαι and τοιούτων in conjunction with a person's need to accept Jesus or the Kingdom of God. In the Mark 9 passage, Jesus is implying a connection between children and those who are last, but he is explicitly articulating the necessity of welcoming children, and those like children. In this specific part of Mark 9, Jesus does not invoke the Kingdom of God by name, but employs the phrase later (9:47). But Jesus does equate himself powerfully and directly with "the one who sent me," and, by transitive logic, those who welcome children welcome God.

While there is much to be gathered from the connection between the two passages, the Mark 9 passage fails to be explicit about the way in which children represent the "last," or possibly, "servants" (διάκονοι). What *is* made explicit is that in Jesus's economy, one must utterly reverse one's societally conditioned impulses. To be first, one must be last, and serve. To welcome God, one must welcome children, and those like them. In a hierarchical culture where men vied for status and those who were not men were not worth mentioning, Jesus is radically shifting and even reversing the conversation, introducing a profound sense of equality and *communitas*. Even in this short pericope, Jesus insists that children have a place at his side, and an important one, and that those

Peter, ever ready to blurt out whatever he is thinking, pleads and boasts in equal measures: "See, we have left everything and followed you" (v. 29). Jesus responds by saying that anyone who leaves family or possessions behind "for my sake and the gospel's" will receive a hundredfold of those things in this age, along with persecutions, and eternal life in the age to come (v. 30). He finishes by saying that "many who are first will be last, and last first." The formulation is telling on a number of levels. At the beginning of Jesus's reply, it looks like Jesus is offering a Job-like replacement by way of upgrade: give up a few worldly things and family members,[38] and I'll give you many times as many in return.[39] But Jesus abruptly turns the "bigger and better" game into a serious one, as he adds "with persecutions" to the list of promised items for this age. It is only in the age to come that unambiguously good rewards are promised: eternal life.

Mark 10:17-22 also displays resonances with the tripartite structure of separation, liminality, and reincorporation found in *rites of passage*, which is significant in a passage about entering the Kingdom of God. First, Jesus tells the man to go away and sell his possessions. There is a strong sense throughout Mark that entrance into the Kingdom of God requires separation from wealth, and more generally, from a former life.[40] Second, Jesus says to give what he has to the poor: here the focus is partially on removing his wealth but also on reversing the status of the rich and the poor, resulting in the topsy-turvy hierarchy so common to the liminal period, and so important to Mark's Gospel. The rich man will lose all he has, but simultaneously gain treasure in heaven. Third and finally, Jesus tells him to return, and follow him—rejoining the followers with a new status and new identity as true follower. There is tension here: the instructions are simple and clear, but the difficulty of obedience is staggeringly high, indeed, too high for the rich man to oblige. There is a tension as well in 10:23-31, when the disciples query their own status with Jesus: he both praises them for their actions but also leaves the sense of two distinct periods of reward—now, and in the age to come. While the tripartite structure appears in this passage, there is *also* the sense that following Jesus acts more broadly as a liminal period of instruction before the full and final entrance into the Kingdom of God is possible, because the Kingdom of God has not been fully and finally revealed. So Jesus proclaims, "the Kingdom of God has drawn near" (Mark 1:15): it is on the threshold.[41]

---

[38] C. Clifton Black notes that "fathers" are notably absent from this list, a startling omission in a world where the *paterfamilias* was the most important member of the family. He argues that this omission signals that in the new family, "there is no such figure, because there is no place for such 'great ones' who 'are tyrants over' others (10:42-43a)" (Black, *Mark*, 228–9). I would suggest that the motif of God as Father looms large throughout Mark—while one may acquire multiple sets of siblings and even mothers, there will be only one Father. This may, however, unnecessarily limit God's gender.

[39] Myers interprets these promises as "the miracle of multiplication through sharing implied in the wilderness feedings is thus enacted in the new economic practice of the community. The reference to homes (in which the discipleship community has taken refuge throughout its journeys) and lands (that singularly priceless foundation of life in traditional societies) can only signify the gathered assets of the community of faith" (Myers, *Binding the Strong Man*, 276).

[40] As seen enacted by the disciples in Mark 1:16-20; 2:13-14.

[41] Contra C. H. Dodd, "The Kingdom of God," in *The Parables of the Kingdom* (New York: Charles Scribner's Sons, 1961), 29.

Victor Turner and his specific sense of liminality and *communitas* are useful here. Jesus is setting up a protracted sense of the liminal stage: the age to come will bring the final entrance into the Kingdom, but for now, one must learn how to be a true follower of Jesus through separation *from* a past life. Social class, wealth, gender, and age can all be stripped away, and there is a stark role reversal as the rich are stripped of their wealth and the poor stripped of their poverty. Turner suggests "a further structurally negative characteristic of transitional beings is that they *have* nothing. They have no status, property, insignia, secular clothing, rank, kinship position, nothing to demarcate them structurally from their fellows."[42] He goes on to explicitly say that "their condition is indeed the very prototype of sacred poverty."[43] This stripping away of things also has positive qualities: Turner is emphatic that in initiation rites there is a strong sense of *communitas* among the initiates. Liminality is the great equalizer, the time when new and different kinship bonds are formed. One is reminded of the pericope in Mark 3:31-35, where Jesus declares that his true family is his followers, rather than his biological kin.

Many commentators connect this passage with the earlier sections in Mark, particularly Jesus's blessing the children. C. Clifton Black, for instance, finds many parallels, from the rich man's assertion that he has kept the commandments "since his youth." Black argues this is "a vague intimation that he just might qualify as a child who receives the kingdom."[44] Black furthermore argues that the love Jesus feels mirrors his affectionate response to the children in 10:13-16. When Jesus talks to his disciples later, explaining his interaction with the rich man, he calls them "children," τέκνα,[45] which again Black sees as a reference to Mark 10:13-16.[46] All of these parallels cause Black to assert that "what the child lacks that the rich have is the power to make things happen. In the economy of God's kingdom, the advantage a child enjoys is the helplessness to do what only God can do for him or her (10:27)."[47] He goes on to clarify that "only the helpless can enter eternal life, because things divine and not human propel *God's* kingdom... Grace is an impossible possibility."[48] Black's general assertion of dependence and helplessness is widely agreed with, and I certainly think this is a central piece of what is being argued throughout Mark. Black hits on an important

---

[42] Victor Witter Turner, "Betwixt and Between: The Liminal Period in *Rites de Passage*," in *The Forest of Symbols: Aspects of Ndembu Ritual* (Ithaca: Cornell University Press, 1967), 98–9.
[43] Ibid., 99.
[44] Black, *Mark*, 226.
[45] It should be noted that nearly every time Mark uses τέκνον instead of παιδίον, he either is addressing a grown person or people or is concerned with the family relation between parents and children, without specifying age. Nearly every time he uses παιδίον he has in mind nonadults. The exception may be Mark 7:24-30. In 7:27, Jesus uses τέκνον in his parables about feeding the children, and in 7:28 the woman replies using παιδίον. It is possible the woman is humanizing Jesus's own argument: Jesus is thinking grand thoughts about Israel and those outside, she is thinking about her sick daughter (later I will address Sharon Betsworth's version of this argument when I address the Syrophoenician women). Black notes the shift in word choice for "child," but associates παιδίον etymologically with servanthood (Black, *Mark*, 180).
[46] Ibid., 227.
[47] Ibid.
[48] Ibid.

comparison that ought to be highlighted more: both 10:25 and 10:15 ask something impossible save for God's power. But Black does not seem to take the instructions in 10:15 as literally as that of 10:25: in both cases Jesus is asking for an imaginative mental image that presents a physical impossibility, save for a dramatic transformation.

In each of the Markan pericopes examined so far, the idea of "children" seems to fit well with low status, and the accompanying insufficiencies associated with it (wealth, power, position). In God's kingdom, those used to being first in society will find themselves last, and only those serving others will be first.

Summary and Conclusion

In this chapter, I have used the anthropological understanding of *rites of passage* to examine the way the Kingdom of God, and entrance into it, is described throughout the Gospel of Mark. I have argued that the key passage, Mark 10:13-16, not only speaks of children as worthy of attention and care as such but also uses them metaphorically to describe the transformation needed to enter the Kingdom of God, which both mirrors *rites of passage* in the structure of separation, liminality, and reincorporation but also *inverts* the traditional statuses of "before" and "after." Generally, a child goes through a *rite of passage* to become an adult and attain the social standing and inward characteristics associated with it. Here, however, child is shown as model: an adult must remove social expectations and inward characteristics to become like a child instead. This is a shocking sentiment, and displays radical differences between the way the Kingdom of God functions and the way the contemporaneous society did.

In Chapter 5, I pick up the idea of the longevity of the liminal middle stage of transformation. I turn from the process of transformation via the *rites of passage* to the ways in which ideal kingdom members are described. I look at the disciples, who fail to represent an ideal kingdom member, and they fail in particular ways, ways that highlight how different the kingdom's moral and social makeup really is from the surrounding culture, and ways that highlight the difficulty of the liminal period of transition. I furthermore look at Jesus, who *does* represent an ideal kingdom member, and who notably is identified as a "son," a child—whether the "Son of Man" or the "Son of God." Throughout Mark, Jesus walks the road to the cross, a road marked by separation and liminality. Jesus begins with power, prestige, family connections, and a perceived wisdom, all of which are stripped of from him as he nears his crucifixion. In Gethsemane he is represented in particularly childlike terms—fearful, alone, and begging for mercy from his Father. The crucifixion seems to strip him even of his connection to God as he cries out that God has abandoned him (15:34). In each of these things the importance of the child as a model kingdom member is apparent.

5

To Become Like a Child: Children and Childish Characters in Mark

In the last chapter, I have mapped the revelation of the Kingdom of God, and entrance into it, onto the anthropologist's tripartite structure of separation, liminality, and reincorporation. These passages in Mark exhibit a notably protracted sense of development—the Kingdom might have come, but it has not come in its fullness; one might desire to follow Jesus, but that does not mean the person succeeds in entering the kingdom. The followers of Jesus in Mark occupy a similarly indeterminate status to that of the kingdom—a status that looks like liminality.

This chapter moves from the transition *to* discipleship and entering *into* the kingdom, to what a disciple and member of the kingdom looks like. When searching for a more fully formed "model recipient" of the kingdom in Mark, one comes up surprisingly and yet notoriously short. Some scholars, like Mary Ann Tolbert and Elizabeth Struthers Malbon, hold up minor characters as models of true faith. Both Malbon and Tolbert highlight some of the healing narratives as key examples of people who respond with faith. I will start by examining the three healing narratives that involve children, highlighting another aspect of Mark's portrayal of children, as well as Mark's portrayal of the parent-child relationship. Taken together, the healing narratives that involve children fail consistently model "great faith" on the part of the parents (only the Syrophoenician mother is portrayed as relentlessly faithful). While not exhibiting great faith, the parents *do* all exhibit a sense that their children are loved and treasured. When it comes to the children themselves, the narratives consistently show the children as in grave danger because of, and resulting in, their liminality.

Next, I will move on to examining Mark's characterization of the disciples as well as Mark's characterization of Jesus. Markan scholarship has puzzled over the portrayal of both the disciples and Jesus in Mark. When it comes to the disciples, the other three Gospels portray the disciples as a mixture of good and bad. However, when they are confronted with the resurrected Christ, they receive him with joy and faith.[1] Mark's

---

[1] Obviously, there are exceptions to this rule: Matthew 28:16-20 narrates the eleven disciples going to Galilee as instructed. Matthew 28:17 says that "when they saw him, they worshipped him, but some wavered." The word for "wavered, doubted" is διστάζω, which Jesus uses to describe Peter in Matthew 14:31 when Peter begins to sink after walking on the water. "Doubting Thomas," found in John 20:24-29, is the exception that proves the rule: while he doubts the other disciples' account of seeing Jesus, once he comes into contact with the risen Christ his response is, "My Lord and my God!" (John 20:28).

disciples have a higher proportion of negative portrayals, and because Mark omits an appearance of the resurrected Christ,[2] he also omits a scene of the reconciliation between the disciples and Jesus. The disciples in Mark, therefore, have both successes and failures, but seem to be portrayed with increasing failures, culminating in their scattering at Jesus's arrest and Peter's denial. While many scholars have debated the intention behind such a presentation, I propose a new reading lens to help make sense of the disciples' portrayal in Mark, reading them in light of stereotypical negative associations of children in the ancient world. In doing so, Mark shows the difficulty of the task of following Jesus:[3] the disciples continuously cling to their previous way of seeing the world and Jesus, such that they seem as though they are children in their incomprehension. Mark, therefore, subtly uses the image of childhood in two intertwining and opposite ways: he consistently has Jesus point to actual children as the sort of person followers of Christ should aspire to be, but he also uses the commonly held negative associations of childhood connected with the disciples as a way to underscore the humiliation and difficulty the disciples go through in attempting to follow Christ. The disciples become like children as they strive to follow: they succeed sometimes, and fail miserably other times. Jesus patiently and consistently instructs them as a parent instructs children on the journey, and their frailty is apparent throughout. This message applies to the implied readers of Mark as well: the readers are led to both scoff at the failures and stumbling of the disciples but also sympathize with them, for what Jesus is demanding is almost unimaginably hard and thoroughly incomprehensible. The readers, too, find assumptions, values, and societal norms stripped away one by one.

Yet it is not merely the disciple can be viewed through the lens of childhood. This complicated use of childhood applies to Jesus as well. Markan scholars equally attempt to explain why Jesus seems to be so powerful and perform so many miracles in the first half of Mark, but in the latter half Jesus is increasingly focused on the cross and suffering. I argue that for Mark, it is Jesus, and not the disciples, who models true discipleship. On the one hand, the disciples act as Jesus's foil in many of Mark's stories. Most often Jesus appears wise, competent, and calm in the face of the disciples' incomprehension, incompetence, and fear. This in many ways is expected: the disciples act as children where Jesus acts as the adult, as more than an adult, as God incarnate. But on the other hand, Jesus, far from simply typifying the ideal adult male, himself is connected to children and childhood in two interlacing ways. First, in Jesus's consistent preaching message, he insists on the way in which following requires a radical shift in thinking. He persistently emphasizes outsiders, who are to be granted a seat at the table—the sinners and tax collectors, women and children. They are given not just a seat but a prime seat: the first will be last and the last first. Jesus is constantly arguing that discipleship means stripping of—removing wealth, status, family connections, and even dignity and power. The Kingdom of God is a road of suffering and persecutions. And while anyone

---

[2] Here I follow the general scholarly consensus that has Mark ending at 16:8.
[3] As argued by Elizabeth Struthers Malbon in her book *In the Company of Jesus* and others like her. See below, particularly page 113–5.

may follow Christ, there is a long and protracted sense of growing and changing that is involved, fraught with danger. Jesus's teachings underscore the need for the tripartite separation and liminality before entrance into God's kingdom is possible: one must become like a child. Second, the categories and associations with childhood can be overlaid on Jesus himself, and his narrative journey in Mark. Jesus, as God's child, himself shows childlike qualities both traditionally seen as positive and traditionally seen as negative, and the negative qualities dominate the further into Mark's Gospel it gets. Jesus is seen consistently displaying dependence on God, humility, and filial piety toward God. Jesus honors God as a parent, and obeys God's commands as a good child ought. But as he approaches the cross, Jesus is increasingly scorned and shamed by the powerful. He becomes fearful in Gethsemane, pleading like a child to be protected instead of facing his death with manly courage. He fails to be rhetorically persuasive at his trial, and ultimately shows physical vulnerability and weakness at his death, even expressing abandonment even by his Parent. Jesus himself regresses toward childhood, stripping of those characteristics associated with adults, until he is separated ultimately from his former adult life via death. And Mark is remarkably reticent in his ending, failing to show us what the resurrected and transformed Christ looks like. While Mark leaves his readers with hope, he also leaves them in a liminal state of ambiguity.

Healing Narratives with Children: Children as Vulnerable, Liminal, and Cherished

Throughout Mark, Jesus encounters a broad range of people who request of him miraculous care. These stories serve to show Jesus's compassion, as well as his extraordinary power. He is able to cast out demons, restore sight to the blind, make the lame to walk, and even raise the dead. In three of these stories, children are the recipients of Jesus's ministrations. In these stories, while the children are helpless to petition for themselves, the parents act on their behalf. While many, including Malbon and Tolbert, have argued for these stories to be signs of exemplary faith, the reality is more complicated, featuring dialogue between the parent and Jesus that brings to light confusion and despair, and sometimes even exposes indecision and narrowmindedness in Jesus himself. What is also apparent through these stories is that the children are vulnerable to both physical maladies and spiritual oppression. They occupy a societally marginal space by virtue of their status as nonadults, but these healing stories also show them as occupying a liminal space via their nearness to death and nearness to spirit possession. Through these stories they are obviously valued and cherished, both by their parents, who go to extraordinary lengths to help their children, as well as the ministrations of Jesus, who takes time (sometimes hesitantly) to heal them.

The Healing of Jairus's Daughter: Mark 5:21-43

Children are the subjects of several healing episodes throughout Mark. The earliest of these, and perhaps the most famous, is the healing of Jairus's daughter found in

Mark 5:21-43. This story is rich in meaning, symbolism, irony, poignancy, and hope. It is also a Markan intercalation, a literary technique Mark employs several times throughout his Gospel where one story (A_1) is interrupted by another story (B), before the original story is completed (A_2). In this case, the story begins with a Jewish leader, Jairus, coming to Jesus to beg of him healing for his little daughter, who is on the point of death. This story is interrupted by the story of another "daughter" being healed, this one of an illness lasting as long as Jairus's child has been alive. Jesus heals the woman who was bold and proactive in her belief, pausing to acknowledge and affirm her action. Meanwhile, however, Jairus receives word that it is too late, that his child is already dead and that Jesus should not be bothered anymore. Jesus responds with his typical Markan taciturn, cryptic optimism: "fear not, only believe." Continuing on their way, they arrive at the house, where people are mourning the daughter's death, wailing and weeping loudly, to excess. In fact, Jesus beholds an uproar. Baffling those who surround him, Jesus asserts that they need not mourn: the girl is not dead, but asleep. The crowd responds with nervous or derisive laughter—surely this joke is in rather poor taste—and Jesus throws the crowd outside, leaving only the bereaved parents and three chosen disciples. Taking the girl by the hand, he commands her to get up. What is death in the face of Jesus? She obeys, immediately, and walks about the room. Jesus orders the family to keep silent about what happened. They should also give the poor girl something to eat—as she is firmly back in the living, she again has physical needs to attend to.[4]

There are many things to touch upon in this passage, and scholars have noted almost everything imaginable about this passage. However, a few things are important for our purposes. First, referring back to Plutarch's *Consolation to His Wife*, we see the frenzy of mourners common in the ancient world and also the nearly identical derisive language about them—both use the word ἀλαλάζω "loud wailing," or, as Donald Russell translates it in his version of Plutarch's letter, "shrieking."[5] Each pairs this response with a synonym (ὀλοφύρμαι in *Consolation*, κλαίω in Mark). The mourners are doing what is socially acceptable and, indeed, may earnestly be trying to help. However, both the *Consolation* and Mark's Gospel communicate a sense of excess. In each case the writer is communicating disdain, but for slightly different reasons: Plutarch worries that the frenzy of these mourners can only exacerbate and harm, as "fire heaped upon fire," or as scratching a festering sore. Mark is certainly interested in this as well, but he is most interested in contrasting the power of Jesus with the power of the frantic crowd.

This brings us to the second important thing about this passage. The passage is resplendent in layers of irony: Jesus, a single person, is able to expel the frantic crowds as easily as he has earlier expelled the demon army "Legion" into the swine; Jesus gives an

---

[4] C.f. Luke 24:41-43. Mark McVann, on the other hand, argues that the imagery reminds one of the Eucharist, and argues for the scene being read through the lens of baptismal practices (Mark McVann, *Dwelling Among the Tombs: Discourse, Discipleship, and the Gospel of Mark 4:35–5:43* [PhD diss., Emory University, 1984], 179–81).

[5] Plutarch, *A Consolation to His Wife*, trans. Donald Russel, in *Plutarch's Advice to the Bride and Groom and A Consolation to His Wife: English Translations, Commentary, Interpretive Essays, and Bibliography* (ed. Sarah B. Pomeroy; New York: Oxford University Press, 1999), 61.

"alternate fact" about the daughter's condition, which turns out to be true (depending on one's perspective in each case); Jesus, who appears rather unsympathetic and rude (both in his delays on the way to Jairus's house and to the crowd he finds there), enacts the deepest compassion; and finally Jesus, who performs a miracle on the highest scale (reversing death itself), asks that they should not talk about it.

A third notable aspect of the passage is the danger the girl herself is in, a danger that can be seen both within a context of childhood mortality in general and of her precarious perch on the cusp of womanhood. We have seen before that the ancient child's mortality rate was exceptionally high. Saller estimates that about half of children died before the age of ten, with the vast majority of those dying in infancy.[6] The possibility of death loomed over children constantly, and this was a danger and vulnerability that all parents in the ancient world would have been aware of. It is interesting to note that the girl is identified as a child rather than a young woman, and several designations are ascribed to her that emphasize this point. She is affectionately called τὸ θυγάτριόν μου, "my little daughter," by her father as she is introduced into the narrative. Both the narrator and Jesus speak of her most often as παιδίον, the more neutral and common word for "child" or "infant." Later, Jesus uses the Aramaic אֲחָיִלְעַ, "girl, little girl," which the narrator likewise translates into Greek κοράσιον: "girl." Stylistically Mark favors diminutives across a variety of subject matters;[7] however, it is striking just how often and what variety of words is used to describe her. I agree with Betsworth here that the constant identification of the girl's youth highlights her importance in the story. Betsworth furthermore rightly points out that "Jairus's daughter is the emotional focus of the story, even though she never speaks and does not even act until 5:42."[8]

The narrative consistently identifies Jairus's daughter as a child, thus highlighting the danger she is in by virtue of her youth. But the narrative also mentions that she is specifically twelve years old. Saller notes that about half of children who made it to age ten could be expected to reach age fifty,[9] which are some of the more stable and promising numbers in the ancient world's mortality figures. Jairus's daughter has made it past the most perilous years as far as mortality goes, and therefore Betsworth is right to note that "she is not among the very young who so frequently died before reaching maturity."[10] In fact, twelve years old, as we have seen earlier, is around the time that many girls would be given in marriage or formally betrothed. She is on the eve of adulthood, and not merely a child. This, however, raises a different kind of danger and vulnerability. As we have seen, any transitions of such a state render a person vulnerable. In the process of changing into something or someone fundamentally different, there is a particular sort of danger. Therefore, the narrative successfully heightens both kinds of tension at her tenuous grasp on life: she is in danger on all levels, whether she is classified as a child or as a young woman. And true to this dangerous liminality on

---

[6] Saller, *Patriarchy, Property and Death in the Roman Family* (Cambridge: Cambridge University Press, 1994), kindle location 357.
[7] e.g. Mark 3:9, 7:27, 8:7, 14:47.
[8] Sharon Betsworth, *The Reign of God* (New York: T&T Clark, 2010), 110.
[9] Saller, *Patriarchy, Property, and Death in the Roman Family*, location 357.
[10] Betsworth, *The Reign of God*, 111.

a social level, she exhibits liminality on a physical level: she hovers with one foot in the grave for the majority of the story, briefly passes over into death, and is pulled back again firmly to the side of the living. The narrative also makes vitally clear that Jesus has power over death itself. Only by his merciful power is the daughter able to be drawn back over the threshold to life, and he demonstrates care to her and to her parents not only via the miraculous (in her resurrection and restoration) but also via the mundane (in his concern that she be fed).

The Healing of the Syrophoenician Woman's Daughter: Mark 7:24-30

A second story about a young girl being healed is found in Mark 7. In this story, like that of Jairus's daughter, it is the parent who comes to Jesus, begging for his help. Neither story has the daughter physically present in the beginning.[11] However, while Jairus is described as a leader of the synagogue, the mother in Mark 7:26 is described as a Gentile, and a Syrophoenician by birth. This description shapes the trajectory of this story over against that of Jairus's daughter: whereas Jesus is immediately willing to follow Jairus,[12] Jesus initially rejects the Syrophoenician mother's request. In a racial slur that attracts much scholarly interest,[13] Jesus says that dogs should not be fed the children's food. In essence, he is saying that he has come for the Jews first, not the Gentiles. The mother replies with humility, strength, and witty wordplay: "even the dogs beneath the table eat from the children's scraps." Using Jesus's own humiliating metaphor against him, she presses her petition. Betsworth puts it nicely: "in her retort, the woman hijacks Jesus' metaphorical insult, turning it to her daughter's advantage."[14] Betsworth notices further that while Jesus uses in his metaphorical wordplay τέκνων,

---

[11] Cf. Betsworth, *The Reign of God*, 128.

[12] Technically the text says "καὶ παρακαλεῖ αὐτὸν πολλά": "begged him repeatedly," which could imply a sense of delay or even hesitation on Jesus's part. Furthermore, when Jesus takes time to find and talk to the woman who has just been healed of her hemorrhaging, there is ambiguity in the narrative as to whether this delay results in Jairus's daughter dying.

[13] See for instance T. Alec Burkill, "The Historical Development of the Story of the Syrophoenician Woman (Mark vii: 24-31)," *NovT* 9.3 (1967): 161–77. He spends pages 169–74 devoted solely to explicating this phrase, as well as detailing several scholars who want to soften the force of the phrase to "puppies." He himself will argue that the term refers to house dogs rather than scavenger dogs, but in graphic language emphasizes that this does not diminish the insult: "as in English, so in other languages, to call a woman 'a little bitch' is no less abusive than to call her 'a bitch' without qualification. In the parable the dogs may not be street scavengers, but the fact remains that they are not truly members of the household" (ibid., 173). David Rhodes similarly attempts to both soften the insult while also admitting that it is indeed an insult: he says that Jesus is being "playful" in his language, while also admitting that Jesus is rejecting the request to heal a little child with insults (David Rhoads, "Jesus and the Syrophoenician Woman in Mark: A Narrative-Critical Study," *JAAR* 62.2 [1994]: 356–7). Wendy Cotter, in *The Christ of the Miracle Stores* (Grand Rapids: Baker Academic, 2010), 148–54, similarly covers the range of options, and argues that Jesus insults the woman to show a "very conservative Jewish perspective," a perspective that implied readers might themselves hold (ibid., 151–2). Sharon Betsworth herself makes an interesting argument: she argues that the use of the diminutive doesn't make Jesus's words any less biting, but rather is a literary choice by Mark to maintain the use of diminutives to heighten the focus on the child (Betsworth, *The Reign of God is Such as These*, 12, 130–1n105). Rhodes makes a similar point (Rhoads "Jesus and the Syrophoenician Woman," 357).

[14] Betsworth, *The Reign of God Is Such as These*, 131.

the Syrophoenician woman replaces τέκνων with παιδίον, subtly bringing to the front of the metaphor the concrete reality of her own daughter, her sick daughter, who deserves to be fed.[15] Jesus acknowledges her victory, saying that because of her reply (διὰ τοῦτον λόγον) she may go, and that the demon has gone out of her daughter. The mother finds it just as Jesus says: having gone home, she finds her daughter on the bed, and the demon gone.

Much like Jairus's daughter's healing, the Syrophoenician woman's daughter does not appear on the scene until almost the very end. She is given almost no narrative spotlight at all: Jesus is not physically present for her healing, nor does Mark narrate the moment of her healing. Rather, the story is finished from the vantage of the mother herself: her discovery of her daughter's recovery. Unlike Jairus's daughter, we know neither the Syrophoenician daughter's age nor is there a sense of her renewed activity and vibrant life[16] post-healing: it is unclear whether she is even awake for her one narrative scene. She is described as perfectly passive. She is, however, the driving emotional force behind the story.[17] Her mother, who is both present and speaks, displays great resources of energy, intelligence, persistence, and love. She has found the secret place where Jesus attempts and fails to hide. She will not be turned away, evincing willingness to endure insults to save her daughter. She accepts the title of "least" or "last"[18] while simultaneously asserting her existence and reiterating her request. In the wordplay between Jesus and the mother, the first indeed becomes the last, and the last first. All this she does out of concern for her daughter, whom she wishes to save. Like Jairus, her every word and action broadcast her connection to her daughter, and concern for her fate.

The Healing of the Spirit-Possessed Boy: Mark 9:14-29

Mark 9:14-29 again features Jesus healing a child—a boy this time. Ironically, it is nearly at the very end of the narrative before we are able to conclude that he, in fact, is a child, rather than a grown-up son. In Mark 9:17 the father introduces the boy as τὸν υἱόν μου, giving his relationship to the boy but also masking his age, and the narrative consistently refers to the son in the generic αὐτός. While the adverb παιδιόθεν is used in 9:21, even this is intended to give a sense of the longevity of the boy's condition; it is therefore just as plausible that the father's son is now an adult, having suffered for a decade or more from the spirit. It is not until 9:24 that the word παιδίον is used for the boy, the singular time the word is used in the entire story.

Like the story of the Syrophoenician woman, the boy is possessed by a spirit. However, while the spirit in the story of the Syrophoenician woman is first called

---

[15] Ibid.
[16] By this I mean that Jairus's daughter is described as getting up and walking around, and the scene ends with Jesus instructing people to get her food. None of these details are present with the Syrophenician woman's daughter.
[17] Betsworth agrees, and puts it this way "although the daughter does not have an active role, she is nevertheless the emotional focus of the story… even though the woman is the protagonist in the narrative, her focus throughout is on her daughter." Betsworth, *The Reign of God is Such as These*, 130.
[18] C.f. Mark 9:33-37; 10:43-45.

an "unclean spirit" (πνεῦμα ἀκάθαρτον, 7:25), and later referred to consistently as a δαιμόνιον, the story in Mark 9 consistently uses the word πνεῦμα, modifying it only once with ἀκαθάρτῳ (9:25) and twice describing it by how it manifests in the boy: the father describes his son as ἔχοντα πνεῦμα ἄλαλον, "having a spirit making him mute," and Jesus himself addresses the spirit in 9:25 as τὸ ἄλαλον καὶ κωφὸν πνεῦμα, "spirit of deafness and muteness." The actions of the spirit are furthermore described in verses 18 and 22: it has the ability to make the boy rigid or roll around, throw him to the ground, and make him foam at the mouth and gnash his teeth. Finally, the father of the boy describes the spirit as being able to throw the boy into the fire or water, and in these cases the father describes that this spirit is having malicious intent: it does so ἵνα ἀπολέσῃ αὐτόν, "intending to destroy him." While the Syrophoenician woman's daughter is not present for the healing, the boy with the spirit is both present and active—although the actions are nearly all self-destructive, attributed to the demon's work.

The story is furthermore notable for Jesus's interaction with the boy's father and the father's startling honesty. The father, wanting his son to be healed, has helplessly watched the disciples fail to exorcise the demon. His emotion and near hysteria are plain, and he pleads with Jesus in verse 22: "but if you are able to do anything, have pity on us and help us!" Jesus reacts to this saying, "'If you are able?' Everything is possible for the one who believes." Jesus's reaction feels unsympathetic and grating. That feeling is exacerbated when paired with the disciples' previous inability to exorcise the demon in the prelude to the story, as well as Jesus's explanation of their inability to cast out the demon at the end of the story. This kind of demon, he says, is impossible to cast out except by prayer (9:29).[19] Despite this reception, the father of the spirit-possessed boy, much like the Syrophoenician woman earlier, "took the shoddy reproof and touched it into immortality."[20] The father immediately cries out,[21] "I believe; help my unbelief!"

Jesus is able to call the demon out of the boy, but the exorcism is so dramatic that the boy is again convulsed and ἐγένετο ὡσεὶ νεκρός, "becomes like a corpse," so much so that people declare the boy dead. Jesus, however, takes the boy by his hand and lifts him up, and the boy gets up. The word play here is subtle and interesting, and mirrors the narration of Jesus raising Jairus's daughter. In both cases, Jesus takes them by the hand in nearly identical wording: καὶ κρατήσας τῆς χειρὸς τοῦ παιδίου in 5:41, compared to κρατήσας τῆς χειρὸς αὐτοῦ in 9:27. Moreover, the boy is said to ἀνέστη, which is the same word used for Jairus's daughter in 5:42, just after being raised from the dead. The near impossibility of the boy's exorcism is highlighted through this

---

[19] Sharyn Echols Dowd notes the scholarly debate as to whom Jesus is insisting have faith. I have here assumed that Jesus is demanding the father have faith, but Dowd notes that commentators like Lohmeyer, Schniedwind, Gnilka, Ebeling, and Achtemeier instead argue that Jesus is saying that "his own ability to exorcise the boy comes from his faith." See Dowd, *Prayer, Power and the Problem of Suffering: Mark 11: 22-25 in the Context of Markan Theology* (Atlanta: Scholars Press, 1988), 110 n67. The narrative as it stands strongly points to Jesus's asking the father to have faith, or at least this is how the father in the story seems to interpret Jesus's exclamation, given his reply, as indeed Dowd points out. Dowd thinks that the question is intentionally ambiguous, such that "Jesus has faith and he calls the father to have faith" (ibid., 111).

[20] E.M. Forster, *A Room with a View* (Norfolk: New Directions, 1922), 254.

[21] Several variants include "with tears" (sc 1141, rp, A^b, D), and while these are fairly certainly not original to the text, they heighten the deeply emotional context of the father.

description: the spirit intends the death of the child countless times throughout his life, and in its last moments exiting it seems to have finally succeeded in its goals. This also serves to emphasize Jesus's power: the disciples are unable to cast the spirit out, and even Jesus first appears as though he fails. But the raising of Jairus's daughter gives the reader comfort: even if this boy has, in fact, been killed by the exorcism, we already know that Jesus is able to raise the dead. Both children are at the threshold of death: Jesus rescues a boy from the very brink, and the girl is called back from the other side.

Mark's own view of children, as seen through the healing narratives, is a heightened sense of their vulnerability. Two of the three children have been oppressed by evil spirits, and neither they nor their parents are able to do anything to drive them away. Jairus's daughter is not said to be afflicted by an evil spirit, but she is sick and succumbs to death. Each of these three children is influenced by unseen forces. In this way too, they function as liminal figures—neither fully in one plane of existence nor in the other. The boy possessed by a spirit particularly exemplifies this: he is not only passively vulnerable but an active danger to himself because of his liminal status. These three healing narratives also show how the children are cherished. In each case their parents serve as the emissaries to Jesus, begging for his attention and his help. There is an implied sense of attention and care for their children: each parent is willing to go to great and desperate lengths to find a cure for what seems to be incurable. In both the raising of Jairus's daughter and the exorcism of the boy with the unclean spirit, Jesus is able to perform a miracle that the parents only dimly believe is possible. It is only the Syrophoenician woman who seems both confident in Jesus's power and undismayed by his initial refusal. Jesus's power is extraordinary, and he is shown to heal these children, giving them new life, and reuniting them with their parents.

Jesus's Teachings about Discipleship

Jesus, in modeling a true disciple's characteristics, consistently turns societal expectations on their head. He constantly both teaches and exemplifies through action the new community he is building. This community reverses and rebuilds family and social ties, and Jesus, instead of prioritizing the high and mighty of society, prioritizes the socially marginal and outcast.

From almost the beginning in Mark, Jesus, rather than seeking out the elite, powerful, and well-connected, picks more unassuming followers. Mark 1 narrates two stories of Jesus calling the disciples: Simon and Andrew, James and John. In both cases the sets of brothers are fishermen. Jesus uses clever wordplay, saying, "Follow me, and I will make you fish for people." The scene also shows Jesus choosing low-class workers[22]

---

[22] See for instance, K. C. Hanson, "The Galilean Fishing Economy and the Jesus Tradition," *Biblical Theology Bulletin* 27 (1997): 99–111. This article is helpful for many reasons, not the least of which "Diagram 1" where she charts "The Political Economy of Galilean Fishing." C. Clifton Black puts it nicely: "In a setting where poverty was prevalent, James and John's precipitate departure from their business would jeopardize their family's livelihood and risk dissolution of the household" (C. Clifton Black, *Mark* [Abingdon New Testament Commentaries; Nashville: Abingdon Press, 2011], 70). His latter point about the dissolution of family ties is an important one, and will be picked up later.

as his intimate followers. Fishermen go to the dangerous[23] spaces, contending with the capricious sea. Simon and Andrew moreover seem to be of lower class than James and John, the latter brothers who are said to leave their father "and hired hands" (1:20), implying that James and John's family had a small degree of wealth.

In Mark 2:14 Levi the tax collector is called to follow Jesus. In the next verse Jesus is dining "ἐν τῇ οἰκίᾳ αὐτοῦ." Although the antecedent of αὐτοῦ is unclear, it is plausible that Levi is intended. Even if it is not Levi's house specifically, Jesus is said to be there with "many tax collector and sinners."[24] This grouping informs the reader of a tax collector's standing, and is repeated three times in the span of two verses. Jesus has deliberately called a tax collector to follow him, and now is eating in the midst of them. Lest the visual clues to Jesus's strategy of seeking out and welcoming the marginal be lost, the scribes of the Pharisees question the disciples as to Jesus's meaning and intent. Jesus overhears, and states explicitly, οὐ χρείαν ἔχουσιν οἱ ἰσχύοντες ἰατροῦ ἀλλ᾽ οἱ κακῶς ἔχοντες·οὐκ ἦλθον καλέσαι δικαίους ἀλλὰ ἁμαρτωλούς ("The healthy have no need of a physician but rather the sick; I have not come to call the righteous but the sinners"). In a set of analogies, one metaphorical and one literal, Jesus is declaring his purpose and intent. He is not embarrassed by his company, nor does he find himself in their company by happenstance. He is seeking out those who are marginalized with the intent to transform them. This set of analogies also implies that the opposite is true as well: those who are "well" or "righteous" have no need of Jesus, and therefore do not seek him out. They often go further, actively distancing themselves from him. It is not only the outsiders become insiders but also the insiders become outsiders.

In Mark 3:20-1; 31-35 there is again a scene where Jesus turns away from cultural norms and structural expectations, and redefines what a true disciple means. This section represents the A_1 and A_2 sections of one of the Markan sandwiches, interrupted by the B section found in 22–30. This Markan sandwich is particularly opaque: the text uses the phrase οἱ παρ᾽ αὐτοῦ in verse 21 to describe the main actors against Jesus, but to whom it refers is debated.[25] Whoever the reference is, they are both tied to Jesus in some intimate way, and reacting to rumors of his being mentally incapacitated. They attempt to restrain him, but the narration either trails off or is abruptly cut off: a dispute suddenly arises about whether Jesus casts out demons because he is possessed by Beelzebub. After Jesus successfully outmaneuvers the scribes with rabbinic logic, the narrative started in 21 presumably resumes. Jesus's family—his mother and siblings—arrive. They stay outside the house, sending word for him to come to them. Whether

---

[23] Importing anthropological terms, the sea would count as a "marginal" space.
[24] On the association of Jesus with "sinners," as well as the cultural assumptions that went with the epitaph "sinner," see Greg Carey, *Sinners: Jesus and His Earliest Followers* (Waco: Baylor University Press, 2009), in particular chapter two, where he analyzes this very scene. See also Black, *Mark*, 90–3, who teases out the link between tax collectors and sinners: "both groups evoked among their fellow Jews the suspicion of 'professional sinfulness,' perhaps even political betrayal" (ibid., 92).
[25] Most scholars argue that the phrase intends Jesus's family (who are explicitly named in v. 31); this is borne out by the NRSV's decision to translate the phrase "his family." Other suggestions include the scribes (which is present in ancient manuscript traditions like D and W), or the more generic crowd around him. See brief discussions in Black, *Mark*, 108–10, and Joel Marcus, *Mark 1-8* (Anchor Bible 27; London: Doubleday, 2000), 270–1.

or not they are the same people as represented in verse 21 helps contextualize their intentions: if they are attempting to "restrain" Jesus for fear of his insanity, that is one thing; if they whimsically want his attention, that is another thing altogether. Either way there is an assumption that Jesus will acquiesce to their request. The crowd relays their message to Jesus. Instead of doing as his family hopes and as society expects, Jesus both verbally and physically demonstrates his allegiance. Staying where he is, Jesus responds by saying, "Who are my mother and siblings?"[26] Looking around at those seated with him, Jesus says, "Here are my mother and my siblings." Going one step further, he clarifies: "whoever does God's will, that one is my brother and sister and mother." In this scene, Jesus is not simply implying that the ones seated around him are equal to his biological kin but, rather, arguing that they are greater than his biological kin. Sharon Betsworth puts it this way: "Jesus makes it clear that kinship is no longer based upon biology or ethnicity; rather, those who do the will of God are part of the family of God. The fundamental unit of the 'new social world,' of the Reign of God, will be the new family of Jesus."[27]

That scene with Jesus's family informs the story in Mark 6:1-6, when Jesus teaches in the synagogue of his hometown. Jesus preaches, and preaches with wisdom (6:2). Those who hear him simultaneously recognize his wisdom, as well as his ability to do miracles, yet also take offense at him. They stumble over him (ἐσκανδαλίζοντο) because of their knowledge of his upbringing: they know his profession and his family by name (6:3). This offense is later understood by Jesus as unbelief (6:6), and linked to Jesus's failure to do "deeds of power" there (6:5).[28] Jesus gives commentary on the encounter: "a prophet is not without honor except in his own home town, and among his own relatives, and in his house." It is not just the people of the town or region he is criticizing; he narrows his critique to his relatives, and then to his specific household. His critique of his family in 6:4 and the resulting lack of power in 6:5 help inform his rejection of them in 3:31-35. Because Mark 3:21 is ambiguous, the family's request in 3:31-32 might be reasonable, and Jesus's response could therefore be conceived as rude. But 6:4-5 gives the sense that there is mutual distrust. Moreover, the negative portrayal of Jesus's relatives and family in 6:4-5 supports the argument that οἱ παρ' αὐτοῦ in 3:21 indeed intends a reference to his family. If so, there is an interesting echo between the two passages: while his family intends to restrain him physically in 3:21 for fear of his insanity, but fail to do so, his family members (along with the town) succeed in restraining him in 6:5, preventing him from doing deeds of power due to their unbelief.

The ancient world particularly valued and expected children to honor their parents. Each part of the family reflected on the others: a shameful wife reflected on

---

[26] The noun used for siblings is οἱ ἀδελφοί. Technically this could mean either "brothers" or a group with brothers and sisters. Since the text does not give clues as to what it means, I stick with a generic English translation to preserve the ambiguity.

[27] Betsworth, *The Reign of God*, 99.

[28] Mary Ann Tolbert describes this passage as indicative that "miracles in the Gospel are not signs to induce faith in unbelievers; they are, instead, the fruits of faith" (Tolbert, *Sowing the Gospel: Mark's Work in Literary-Historical Perspective* [Minneapolis: Augsburg Fortress, 1996], 180).

her husband, and sons young or old were expected to hold their father and mother with the utmost respect, both in the way they treated their parents and also in the way they conducted themselves in public. Jesus throughout Mark seems to disregard his biological earthly family, but strongly identifies himself as Son—the Son of Man. Others throughout Mark also identify Jesus as "Son," but use the more explicit phrase "Son of God."[29] Jesus's deference and obedience to God models the societal norm of a child's allegiance to his or her father, but he reconstructs what "family" means. True family is made up of those whom God has brought together.

The Disciples and Jesus: The Struggle to Understand True Discipleship

Scholarly Overview: The Difficulty of the Portrayal of the Disciples in Mark

Much critical scholarship has taken up the conundrum of the portrayal of the disciples in Mark. Far from being the powerful apostles the church would come to revere, or even the bumbling yet ultimately redeemed followers found in Matthew, Luke, or John, Mark portrays a bleaker picture. The disciples begin with some measure of success, yet as the narrative progresses, they increasingly react with misunderstanding and fear, culminating in their scattering and Peter's denial at Jesus's arrest. Perhaps most difficult of all, Mark lacks a scene of restoration between the disciples and the Risen Christ. Mark's ending is infamous in its ambiguity: Jesus is declared to be raised from the dead by a man clothed in white garments at the tomb. The young man tells the women who have arrived there to go tell Peter and the disciples to meet Jesus in Galilee. But instead, the book ends in 16:8 with the women fleeing in terror and amazement, and not saying anything to anyone because of their fear. The book ends without Jesus physically appearing on the scene, it ends without the assurance that the disciples were in fact given the message, and it certainly ends without any narrated reconciliation of the disciples with Jesus or indication that they intend to act differently in the future. In Luke-Acts, by contrast, Peter transforms from a bumbling but lovable fool to a powerful preacher, leader, and miracle worker.

Mark's severe treatment of the disciples along with his ambiguous ending has led to multiple attempts from multiple types of biblical criticism to account for the reasoning behind Mark's portrayal of the disciples. Some, like Johannes Schreiber,[30] Joseph Tyson,[31] Theodore Weeden,[32] and Werner Kelber,[33] argue from a particular

---

[29] See below for a discussion of the instances where this title is given to Jesus.

[30] Johannes Schreiber, "Die Christologie des Markusevangeliums," *Zeitschrift für Theologie und Kirche* 58 (1961): 175–83.

[31] Joseph B. Tyson, "The Blindness of the Disciples in Mark," *JBL* 80.3 (1961): 261–8.

[32] Theodore J. Weeden, "Heresy that Necessitated Mark's Gospel," *Zeitschrift Für Die Neutestamentliche Wissenschaft Und Die Kunde Der Älteren Kirche* 59.3–4 (1968): 145–58.

[33] W. H. Kelber, "Mark 14: 32-42: Gethsemane; Passion Christology and Discipleship Failure," *Zeitschrift Für Die Neutestamentliche Wissenschaft Und Die Kunde Der Älteren Kirche* 63.3–4 (1972): 166–87. See also W. H. Kelber, *The Kingdom in Mark: A New Place and a New Time* (Philadelphia: Fortress Press, 1974).

reconstruction of the historical setting of the readership of Mark. Mark uses the negative characterization of the disciples as an intentional polemic against various factions of the contemporaneous community, who have followed what Mark considers to be heretical doctrine. This heretical doctrine is represented by the disciples, or at least a contingent of them in the community contemporaneous to the writing of Mark.[34] Mark portrays the disciples in his Gospel in such a way that they are viewed negatively, highlighting the disciples' failure to grasp the true message of Jesus. In each of these authors' cases, the subject of Mark's polemic attack differs, whether Christological (Weeden, Schreiber, Tyson) or eschatological (Kelber). In all of these cases, however, these scholars take seriously and at face value Mark's negative portrayal of the disciples: they are portrayed negatively by intention, as they are not to be followed or admired.

Mary Ann Tolbert's book *Sowing the Gospel*[35] uses literary-historical criticism to argue that the best way to view the disciples in Mark is through the lens of Mark 4's Parable of the Sower, or as she calls it, "the Parable of the Types of Soil." She argues that throughout Mark the disciples act as the rocky soil—where the word is at first received with joy but withers under heat. Mark references Simon's nickname "Peter," "the Rock"; unlike Matthew, where this name is clearly linked to positive characteristics,[36] Tolbert argues that this nickname mirrors and highlights his function as rocky soil.[37] The disciples' actions throughout exemplify reactions of fear instead of faith. Their characterization is therefore complicated but ultimately negative.

Other scholars, using narrative criticism, analyze Peter and the disciples as literary characters, and generally find that they are portrayed in a way designed to elicit a certain sort of response from the implied reader.[38] John Donahue identifies a subsection of these authors, like Robert Tannehill, Elizabeth Struthers Malbon, and Joanna Dewey, who argue for the "positive function of the negative role of the disciples in Mark."[39] That is to say, the disciples play a negative role in Mark's Gospel so that the implied reader can in some way be edified and learn to do differently than the disciples. Tannehill puts it this way: "The composition of Mark strongly suggests that the author, by the way in which he tells the disciples' story, intended to awaken his readers to their failures as disciples and call them to repentance."[40]

---

[34] Theodore J. Weeden Sr., *Mark Traditions in Conflict* (Philadelphia: Fortress Press, 1971), 26.
[35] Mary Ann Tolbert, *Sowing the Gospel: Mark's Work in Literary-Historical Perspective* (Minneapolis: Augsburg Fortress, 1996).
[36] C.f. Matthew 16:18-19.
[37] Tolbert, *Sowing the Gospel*, 145-7.
[38] Literary critics, wary of arguments (such as those employed by Weeden, et al.), based on theoretical knowledge of the author and or context of the reader, instead use the terms "implied author/reader" as a way to specify the sorts of data one can extrapolate from within the text about what sort of person the author or readers could be. Malbon explains in her first chapter of *In the Company of Jesus* what "implied reader" means "recent literary criticism has taught us to conceive of the author and the reader not as isolated entities but as poles of a continuum of communication. A real author writes a text for a real reader. An implied author, a creation of the real author that is implied in his or her text, presents a narrative to an implied reader, a parallel creation of the real author that is embedded in the text" (Malbon, *In the Company of Jesus*, 7).
[39] John R. Donahue, *The Theology and Setting of Discipleship in the Gospel of Mark* (Milwaukee: Marquette University Press, 1983), 27.
[40] Robert C. Tannehill, "The Disciples in Mark: The Function of a Narrative Role," in *The Shape of the Gospel: New Testament Essays* (Eugene: Cascade Books, 2007), 144.

Much of the scholarship once again concentrates upon the Gospel's ending as the key to understanding the entire trajectory of the disciples' story arc, but even in this subsection of scholarship, there is variation of exactly how this gets explicated. Elizabeth Struthers Malbon, for instance, argues that Mark consistently portrays "fallible followers"[41] in order "to communicate clearly and powerfully to the reader a twofold message: anyone can be a follower, no one finds it easy."[42] She uses Mark's ending to drive home the idea that the women followers are fallible just as the disciples are. Furthermore, Malbon argues that the ending is significant "in the outward movement of the text from author to reader."[43] Although the ending is bleak from within the story, she argues that it is clear that the story does not end there: the author, for instance, must have heard about the resurrection from somebody! Not only does this allow her to argue that the reader is to assume that the women did tell the disciples, who, in turn, reconciled with Jesus, but the ending is ambiguous to form a call on the reader to break the silence with their own speech.

Ernest Best attributes the disciples' weakness and failures to Mark's desire to show that God's strength is what true disciples need to rely on.[44] In explicating 16:7, he argues that "though it does not recount the actual restoration of Peter and the disciples, surely implies it."[45] Citing several instances where the conclusion to the story is clear, but not spelled out (e.g., it is not narrated that Jesus, in fact, overcomes Satan in the temptations),[46] the disciples are ultimately redeemed, thinks Best, through the promise in 16:7 and through the knowledge that Mark's readers would have of the disciples great faith after Mark's Gospel ends.[47]

Robert Tannehill's article "The Disciples in Mark: The Function of a Narrative Role"[48] similarly argues for the importance of the disciples' story arc as a mode of communicating with the reader, calling the audience to conviction. His argument is more neutral on the fate of the disciples than Malbon and Best. The disciples are

---

[41] She uses followers/followership in intentional distinction from "disciples/discipleship" as she sees the former pair of terms as a broader category, which includes the women followers of Jesus.

[42] Elizabeth Struthers Malbon, "Fallible Followers: Women and Men in the Gospel of Mark," *Semeia* 28 (1983): 29.

[43] Elizabeth Struthers Malbon, *In the Company of Jesus: Characters in Mark's Gospel* (Louisville, Ken.: Westminster John Knox 2000), 65.

[44] Ernest Best, *Mark: The Gospel as Story* (Edinburgh: T&T Clark, 1984), 47.

[45] Ernest Best, *Disciples and Discipleship: Studies in the Gospel According to Mark* (Edinburgh: T&T Clark, 1986), 130.

[46] Ibid.

[47] Best, *Mark: The Gospel as Story*, 47-8. In focusing on the role of Peter specifically, Best argues that Peter is something of a "spokesman" for the group. Where Peter succeeds, he does so as the representative of the disciples. More important, however: where Peter fails, he fails along with the disciples. This likewise holds true in Best's estimation of 16:7. By specifically naming Peter, Best believes it clear that this is "to show special favor on the Lord's part towards him, presumably to balance the unfavorable impression created by the denial." (Best, *Disciples and Discipleship*, 173). It is Peter, the most clearly fallible of the disciples, the one whose last words are narrated as bringing down curses upon himself in denying association with Christ, who alone is mentioned by name in 16:7.

[48] Robert C. Tannehill, "The Disciples in Mark: The Function of a Narrative Role," *The Journal of Religion* 57.4 (1977).

portrayed positively at first to gain the implied readers' appreciation and trust, as they would have been familiar with the positive role of the disciples in the life of the church. Later, as the disciples are portrayed increasingly negatively, the reader identifies with yet wants to be different from the disciples in their failure. The ambiguous ending, therefore, acts as a "possibility" for reconciliation. This word choice is important for Tannehill, as in his estimation the renewal "is not a simple and automatic affair,"[49] nor are we certainly told that "the disciples have changed their ways and become true followers."[50] This has importance for the reader, in pressing for and emphasizing the need for change and action in following Jesus.

Paul Danove comes to similar conclusions. Through an analysis of neutral, sophisticating, and deconstructive rhetorical devices, he concludes that the disciples are construed in a way that both agrees with and also complicates the preconceptions of the "real audience." Mark's ending at 16:8 is of critical importance to Danove. While up until this ending most of the rhetorical devices had been neutral or sophisticating, the abrupt ending forces the audience to conclude that the disciples "never really understood, continued to fear, and never proclaimed the gospel."[51] This produces a "crisis of interpretation," one which firmly thrusts the audience into the role of actor:

> At this point, the real audience may recognize the operation of a rhetorical strategy that transforms a story about Jesus into an invitation for a response of understanding, fearlessness, and proclamation of the gospel. If this occurs, the real audience experiences a call to become a faithful disciple; and the Gospel becomes gospel.[52]

For Danove, therefore, the disciples function as failures, but failures that goad the audience into attempting to succeed where the disciples have failed.

Most of these authors, therefore, place great importance on the role of 16:7-8 in interpreting Mark's final evaluation of the disciples. According to these authors, if the implication of 16:8 is that disciples never got the message, the final evaluation is negative. If the implication of 16:8 is intentionally ambiguous, the disciples remain ambiguous. If, however, the implication is that the disciples would one day receive the message, the role of the disciples ends hopefully.

Viewing the Disciples and Jesus through the Lens of Childhood

I would like to follow in the vein of the narrative theologians just explicated, taking a slightly different approach to the "positive use of the negative portrayal of the disciples in Mark." I propose that a helpful way to understand Mark's purpose in this portrayal

---

[49] Tannehill, "The Disciples in Mark," 404.
[50] Ibid.
[51] Paul Danove, "The Narrative Rhetoric of Mark's Ambiguous Characterization of the Disciples," *JSNT* 70 (1998): 36–7.
[52] Ibid.

is to overlay some of the generally negative assumptions the ancient world held about children onto the actions of the disciples. There is a striking resonance between the two. As seen in Chapter 2, Philo sums up neatly the common association of children with vice. "For when the life of man begins, from the very cradle till the time when the age of maturity brings the great change and quenches the fiery furnace of the passions, folly, incontinence, injustice, fear, cowardice, and all the kindred maladies of soul are his inseparable companions."[53] The disciples are consistently portrayed as cowardly and fearful, representing moral incompetence. They are persistently unable to understand Jesus's sayings and intentions, showing intellectual inferiority. They are physically weak, unable to control their bodies by staying awake. This in itself is not very surprising: children were spoken of as morally weak and mentally inferior, but they only represented a small portion of those who also were considered "morally weak and mentally inferior."[54] To read the disciples as specifically *childlike* and not merely "generally inferior," however, adds an important interpretive layer when puzzling over the question of the portrayal of the disciples in Mark.

I argue that Mark portrays the disciples in terms similar to children for three reasons. First, the disciples act as literary foils to Jesus. Jesus, as the teacher or the rabbi, needs to have students or learners along with him. In the same way children needed adults via education to mold and shape them into "proper" adults, the disciples act as children because they are young in their path of radical transformation, and Jesus to teach them. They are slowly being stripped of their preconceived understandings of how the world works to make room for Jesus's message of the way the Kingdom of God works. They cannot make sense of Jesus's revelation of his own path of suffering, death, and resurrection because it is counterintuitive to their own sense of thinking. Good students must put aside their childish ways to become educated, refined adults. And yet the disciples, far from improving under Jesus's teaching, instead are portrayed as regressing. They become more and more childish as Jesus dismantles their own conception of reality, a reality that they are consistently unable to grasp. If the disciples are portrayed as childish to make Jesus a visibly effective teacher, why does Mark have them continually regress? I argue this leads to the second major reason the disciples are portrayed as children.

Second, the disciples are presented as children because the implied reader, too, must understand the humiliation and radical transformation needed to follow Jesus. This point essentially agrees with Malbon and others, but adds a significant piece: the disciples are not merely shown to be "followers," communicating the successes and failures of being a follower; they are intentionally shown in a humiliating way to deconstruct the preconceptions of the implied readers. Jesus communicates to the disciples twice that they need to become like children from within the Gospel.[55] This idea would have been radical in the ancient world for both the characters inside the

---

[53] Philo, *On the Birth of Abel and the Sacrifices Offered by Him and Cain*.102–3 (Colson & Whitaker, LCL).

[54] As we saw in Chapter 2, these categories applied to women, slaves, children, and even to non-virtuous or low-class adult males.

[55] Mark 9:33-36, Mark 10:13-16.

narrative and the implied readers. Nonetheless, one could imagine the implied readers nodding along, shaking their heads that the disciples could be so obtuse. But as the implied readers finish the story, their own assumptions about how the disciples' story would finish are rattled. The disciples, while given the hope of reconciliation, show no final scene of competence, faith, and transformation. This disorientation of the implied reader mirrors the disorientation of the disciples in response to Jesus through the narrative. An expert craftsman, Mark leaves his implied readers as confused as the disciples, and puts them at a crisis point. The readers stumble as the disciples stumble.[56] There is no guarantee the implied reader can do better than the disciples, and I argue that the narrative attempts to make this obvious to the reader.

Finally, the disciples are shown as children to show a resonance between the faithfulness of God to Jesus, his Beloved Son, and the faithfulness of both God and Jesus to these disciples, the adopted children.[57] While children in the ancient world were known to be weak and unmanly in all aspects of life, individual children were loved and protected by their parents. Throughout their stumbling, Jesus remains absolutely faithful to the disciples. Even predicting their greatest abandonment, Jesus equally predicts their reconciliation with himself in Galilee. The narrative works to assure both disciples and the implied readers that despite their failings, God is faithful.[58] This third strand weaves expertly with the other two: the students may not be teachable, but Jesus is faithful in continuing to try to teach, just as we the readers may be hopelessly confused but not without hope.

The Sea Voyages: Incompetence and Anxiety versus Mastery and Peace

Three of the accounts of the disciples' acting with fear or ignorance occur on the sea. The sea represented the great cosmic force—untamable, unruly.[59] That God was Lord over even the sea is a constant refrain in the Old Testament, and in particular comes up in Wisdom Literature.[60] Mark consistently shows Jesus to be Master of the Sea as well, truly God's child.

---

[56] Don Juel makes a similar point about the implied reader's perspective on parable of the sower, in light of Mark 16:8." "No guarantee is given that even readers can have him, no reason for confidence that anyone will perform in such a way as to ensure his coming." Don Juel, *A Master of Surprise: Mark Interpreted* (Minneapolis: Augsburg Fortress, 2002), 62.

[57] Cf Mark 10:24.

[58] Again, Don Juel makes a similar point: "whatever promise must be at the expense of any confidence in human ability to bring on the harvest. Hope is at hand only because 'for God all things are possible' (10:27)." Juel, *Master of Surprise*, 63.

[59] For a brief summary on the sea as unruly, see Jindřich Mánek, "Fishers of Men," *Novum Testamentum* 2.2 (1957): 138–41.

[60] For instance, Job 9:8; 26:10; 38:8-11, 16-18; Proverbs 8:28. The Psalms, too, communicate God's mastery over the sea. Marcus Borg, *Rereading the Bible Again for the First Time* (San Francisco: Harper, 2002), 208, compares these sea voyages of the disciples with Psalm 107:23-32, a reference that was recognized as far back as the patristics (for instance St. Augustine's exposition on Psalm 107; see Augustine, *Expositions on the Psalms 99–120* [ed. Boniface Ramsey, trans. Maria Boulding; Hyde Park: New City Press, 2003]).

The disciples consistently display fearful and cowardly behavior throughout the narrative of Mark. As John R. Donahue puts it, "The response of those who come in contact with Jesus in Mark is most often that of fear, wonder, or surprise."[61] In Mark 4:35-41, the disciples are crossing the sea, and a storm comes upon the boat. The narrator sets the scene with conflicting messages: on the one hand, the storm is described as a "great windstorm," strong enough that waves were filling the boat with water. On the other hand, Jesus is in the stern of the ship, asleep on the pillow, presenting an image of a peacefully rocking boat that functions as Jesus's cradle. The disciples are in a panic and wake Jesus from his restful nap, crying out, "Teacher, don't you care that we are perishing?" Jesus immediately is able to calm the storm but reproaches the disciples with the rhetorical query, τί δειλοί ἐστε; οὔπω ἔχετε πίστιν; "why are you so cowardly? Have you still no faith?" Here the narrator reveals the purpose behind the ambiguous setting: there is both an emphasis on the miracle Jesus has done, calming a raging storm with a word, and yet also an emphasis on the cowardly response of the disciples. Jesus is powerful, competent, and peaceful, in contrast with the disciples' weakness, incompetence, and fearfulness. Jesus further uses this moment to instruct the disciples like a good teacher to put away fear, and have faith.

A second story, found in Mark 6:45-52, has the disciples reacting with fear and terror, as well as incomprehension. Jesus, having just fed 5,000 men, sends the disciples across the water while Jesus dismisses the crowd. Jesus prays on the mountain alone and sees the disciples straining to make progress on the sea, as the wind is against them. Jesus comes toward them, walking on the sea. Here the narrative signals the causality of the process: Jesus is coming toward them *because* he has perceived their distress. And yet the same sentence also reports that he intends to pass them by. Before he is able to do so, the disciples panic: seeing Jesus, they think he is a ghost, and cry out in fear. Jesus immediately gets into the boat, tells them not to fear, and asks them to take courage. As Jesus does this, the great wind stops. Jesus again is portrayed as having supernatural powers, but also tender concern. He worries about their distress, both making the decision to come to the disciples and getting into the boat, comforting them once their fear of the ghostly apparition becomes greater than their struggle against the sea. The disciples, however, in response are described as λίαν [ἐκ περισσοῦ] ἐν ἑαυτοῖς ἐξίσταντο οὐ γὰρ συνῆκαν ἐπὶ τοῖς ἄρτοις, ἀλλ᾽ ἦν αὐτῶν ἡ καρδία πεπωρωμένη—"utterly stupefied, because they did not understand about the loaves, but their hearts were hardened." This last verb, πωρόω, carries meanings like "dull" or "obtuse" or "blind": all of these translations function well here. The story mirrors that of 4:25-41 in the fear and terror of the disciples. They are frightened easily, and their imaginations immediately jump to an extreme. In both stories, too, Jesus shows mastery over the elements—proving his power, but also implying that the disciples should know enough to trust him. This leads to a second point: in 6:45-52, unlike 4:35-41, the disciples are not only fearful but are described as uncomprehending, with a range of descriptors to emphasize this point. The verb συνῆκαν (6:52) conveys an array of meanings; when used metaphorically its meanings range from "perceive/observe" to "understand/comprehend." When used in a different setting, it can also mean "band

---

[61] Donahue, *Theology and Setting of Discipleship*, 4.

together" often in a hostile sense (e.g., band together *against* something). The verb conveys, therefore, the sense that the disciples *ought* to have been able to recognize or understand something, but fail to. The verb πωρόω, on the other hand, is generally not used in the metaphorical sense at all outside the Testaments. Its meaning suggests "petrification" or, in the passive, "to become thickened, hardened." Paul, John, and Mark, however, use the word in conjunction with the heart or mind, to convey the heart's being "hardened" or eyes being "blinded." The word conveys missing important observations (like συνῆκαν), but also more strongly implies a moral quality: they are *refusing* to understand, or they are *culpable* in their lack of perception.[62] Where Jesus is portrayed as reacting with compassion to their fear, the disciples add to their cowardliness close-minded ignorance. This same turn of phrase will be used in yet another nautical voyage in Mark 8, and again will refer to the loaves of bread.

The disciples are represented this way in Mark 8:13-21 in nearly identical wording. Jesus has just finished feeding the 4,000, and the Pharisees attempt to pressure Jesus to show a sign, which he declines to do. Jesus is shown to do miraculous things in response to true need, but not in response to idle curiosity or bold-faced skepticism. Jesus then gets back into a boat with his disciples. Jesus cautions against the "yeast" of the Pharisees and Herod. However, in a literary aside, the narrator informs the reader that the disciples had forgotten to bring bread and have only one loaf with them in the boat. The disciples reason with each other that Jesus's comment must be because they have no bread (8:16). Jesus, realizing this, is seemingly dumbfounded. He says to them, "why are you discussing that you have no bread? Don't you yet perceive or understand? Are your hearts hardened?" Jesus's word choice mimics the description of the disciples in 6:52:

οὐ γὰρ συνῆκαν ἐπὶ τοῖς ἄρτοις, ἀλλ᾽ ἦν αὐτῶν ἡ καρδία πεπωρωμένη. (Mark 6:52)
οὔπω νοεῖτε οὐδὲ συνίετε; πεπωρωμένην ἔχετε τὴν καρδίαν ὑμῶν; (Mark 8:17)

In so carefully mirroring 6:52, Mark is mirroring the same flaws in the disciples. This time, their flaws are not just noted by the narrator but spoken aloud by Jesus: Jesus acts as a reflection for the disciples so that they can perceive *themselves*. They are both intellectually and morally deficient: they are unable to comprehend things they should be able to comprehend, and they are unable to do so because their hearts are hardened.

Jesus continues to drive these separate points home through his additional questions in 8:18: "Don't you have eyes, and yet you fail to see, and don't you have ears, yet fail to hear? And do you not remember?"[63] Mark 8:17 mirrors the wording

---

[62] The interplay between God and an individual hardening the individual's heart is a long-standing trope in the Bible. Most notably in Exodus Pharaoh's heart is described as being hardened: several times by Pharaoh himself (Exodus 8:32, 9:34), and several times by God (9:12; 10:1, 20, 27; 11:10; 14:8). Several more times Pharaoh's heart is described as "being hardened" in the passive (7:13, 14, 22; 8:19; 9:35); these times agency seems to be ascribed to Pharaoh. It seems, however, that whoever the agent is, nonetheless blame falls squarely on Pharaoh. This seems unfair at a personal level, but there is still the sense of human culpability even while the divine will may be acting for God's own purposes.

[63] Ernest Best, in *Mark: the Gospel as Story*, notes, "Some of his harshest statements about their failure to understand relate to their failure to understand the miracles. Both 6.52 and 8.14-21 come from Mark's hand and stress the hardness of heart and the blindness of mind of the disciples in the face of Jesus' feeding the five thousand" (Best, *Mark: The Gospel as Story*, 46).

of 6:52; Mark 8:18 has strong resonances with Mark 4:12, when Jesus is explaining to the disciples the purpose of the parables. The ironic connection between these verses has been often noted: in 4:12 Jesus is explaining how the disciples (and potentially "those around") are given the mystery of the kingdom, but "those outside" are given parables *so that* they will neither see nor hear nor perceive. In 8:18, however, it is the same disciples who are *supposed to* see and hear that fail to do so.[64] Some of this irony is already obvious in 4:13 as well. Jesus finishes talking about those outside, and then promptly reproves his own disciples: "Don't you understand this parable? Then how will you understand all parables?" Jesus goes on to explain the meaning of the parable in Mark 4. In Mark 8, however, the rhetoric is amplified: they do not merely miss the point of one parable but are acting as those who are outside and can never understand the parables. Jesus here functions as a teacher painfully drilling his most unpromising pupils. Having scolded them for their obtuseness, he asks them basic, nonrhetorical, arithmetic questions about his miraculous feedings. "When I broke five loaves for the 5,000, how many baskets full of broken pieces did you collect?" "Twelve," they reply. Again, Jesus asks them, "And the seven among 4,000, how many baskets full of broken pieces did you collect?" Again, they dully reply, "Seven." Jesus replies to them, "Do you not yet understand?" This last question is again a famous one: many scholars confess that their own answer to the question is "No, I don't understand."[65] The topic of bread is consistent throughout the story, but the basic connective thought is not as clear. What *is* clear is that both the narrator and Jesus show the disciples to be incompetent and uncomprehending. They act in the stereotypical way contemporaneous authors talk of children. Contemporaneous authors would also agree with Jesus's next step: a child's deficiencies are to be remedied through reproof and education. In this last sea voyage, Jesus does not merely respond with kindness and gentle chiding but questions them about their past experiences, showing Jesus's questions to have a pedagogical purpose, even if that purpose is thwarted.

In each of these three sea voyages, the disciples are represented as fearful, unintelligent, and obtuse. Each of these general sorts of descriptors are used of children in ancient literature: they are exceptionally fearful, and unable to grasp obvious concepts. Each of these settings serves to contrast Jesus to the disciples. Jesus is courageous, compassionate, and insightful. He not only is Master of the Sea, showing his filial connection to God and divine power, but also uses his power to calm the sea and the fears of his disciples. When they show themselves childish in their responses, Jesus is the father[66] or the teacher, responding with protection as well as instruction.

---

[64] Cf. Donahue, *The Theology and Setting of Discipleship*, 23.

[65] Black, *Mark*, 187; Ched Myers, *Binding the Strong Man: A Political Reading of Mark's Story of Jesus* (New York: Orbis Books, 2008), 225–9; Marcus, *Mark 1–8*, 512–13. Marcus emphasizes that the word οὔπω should be translated "not yet" as opposed to "still not," implying the disciples will someday understand (Marcus, *Mark 1–8*, 508).

[66] Here I use "father" because in the ancient world this particular form of teaching a reproof would lie squarely within the purviews of the father's domain. In a modern context, "parent" is an appropriate substitute.

The Transfiguration: Bewilderment versus Revelation

The juxtaposition between Jesus's peace and understanding and the disciples' fear and bewilderment is also modeled in the transfiguration. Directly after Jesus's first prediction of his passion and resurrection (to be discussed below), Jesus brings three of his disciples up onto a mountain. He is transfigured, his clothing becomes unnaturally and inhumanly white, and Moses and Elijah appear and converse with Jesus.

Peter steps in and speaks up: this is a good place, and we should make three dwellings, one for each of you (9:5). The narrator steps in to help explain Peter's words: "he did not know how to respond [lit., 'what to answer'], for they were terrified." Once again, a representative group of the disciples responds with fear to a revelation of Jesus's supernatural qualities. They are unable to grasp what they are seeing, and are terrified by this. Peter furthermore appears absurd, but absurd in a particular way: while he seems earnest to do good, his efforts do not match the intention. His offer to build dwellings for Jesus and his companions seem genuine, but it seems absurd to think of containing or normalizing this event. This is particularly a childish way of acting. Specifically, Peter's actions are reminiscent of the sentiment of childish naiveté—that of a mind unable to grasp the world around it, while being equally unaware of one's own ignorance. Epictetus references such naiveté in children and adults, arguing that one should at times refrain from correcting their viewpoint, but rather respond with patronizing forbearance.[67]

Indeed, neither Jesus nor Moses nor Elijah seeks to engage or correct Peter. However, a voice from the clouds interposes, silencing Peter[68] and instructing the disciples to listen to the "Beloved Son" (9:7).[69] Jesus then further silences them: he orders them to refrain from disclosing what they have seen, until he has risen from the dead (9:9). Mark 9:10 continues by saying καὶ τὸν λόγον ἐκράτησαν πρὸς ἑαυτούς, συζητοῦντες τί ἐστιν τὸ ἐκ νεκρῶν ἀναστῆναι. The most usual translation of the first half of the verse is something like "they kept the matter to themselves."[70] However, an alternate translation would be "And they seized upon the saying."[71] The former implies that the disciples are actively acquiescing to Jesus's command, while the latter implies that the disciples, still in the throes of confusion, latch onto a new conundrum around which to spin their wheels: "what the rising of the dead could mean." The text is ambiguous, but I am inclined toward the latter translation: the disciples are still in a muddle about the transfiguration and are further bewildered by Jesus's reference to his own resurrection. Whether or not the first part of the verse further portrays the disciples as obedient or bewildered, the second half of the verse clearly shows their incomprehension. Jesus has clearly referenced the Son of Man's rising from the dead (9:9), and yet they are

---

[67] See Chapter 2, pp. 64–5; Epictetus, *Discourses*. 190–1 (Oldfather, LCL).
[68] To be fair, the narrative is unclear whether the voice interrupts Peter as he continues to babble. However, the instructions to "listen" is clearly juxtaposed to Peter's speaking out through his fear.
[69] It is at this point also that, just as suddenly as they appeared, Moses and Elijah disappear, and only Jesus remains.
[70] See the NRSV, KJV, NIV and others.
[71] The NAS for instance, translates the phrase, "And they seized upon that statement."

unable to receive the idea. The disciples, furthermore, act as a foil to Jesus, just as in the sea voyages. Jesus is shown to be special through his physical appearance: he is μετεμορφώθη before the disciples—literally transformed. This is potentially a glimpse of how Mark imagines the resurrected Christ. His clothing shows a transformation as well: the language stumbles as it tries to describe how no human could ever make them as white as they become. Jesus is furthermore flanked by some of the mightiest figures of the Hebrew Scripture. Finally, a voice from the clouds specifically claims Jesus as the "Beloved Son." Jesus is not just a special person but claimed by God as in a unique relationship with Godself: God's child.[72]

The book of Mark ascribes to Jesus the title of "the Son of God." Mark makes this clear from the very first verse: Jesus is the Christ, the Son of God.[73] This is not just a statement of fact, but is "good news." The scene of God speaking about Jesus at the transfiguration is the second time where God the Creator speaks directly (the first is at Jesus's baptism). The language between the two resonates with each other: in both cases, God is described as "a voice from the heavens" (1:11) and "a voice from the cloud" (9:7). The language of Mark 9:7 mirrors the language of Mark 1:11 in what God says of Jesus: at the baptism, God speaks directly to Jesus, saying, σὺ εἶ ὁ υἱός μου ὁ ἀγαπητός, ἐν σοὶ εὐδόκησα, and in Mark 9:7 God speaks about Jesus to the disciples, saying, οὗτός ἐστιν ὁ υἱός μου ὁ ἀγαπητός, ἀκούετε αὐτοῦ. In each case, God announces God's relationship with Jesus: Jesus is God's son, and specifically God's beloved son. Unclean spirits, or demons, proclaim Jesus's identity as God's child as well: Mark 3:11 narrates that "whenever unclean spirits saw him, they would fall down before him and cry out 'you are the Son of God'." The verse does not seem to describe one particular healing; rather, it seems to narrate how spirits often and repeatedly would address Jesus with this title. In Mark 5:7 also, as Jesus is casting out Legion from the Gerasene demoniac, Legion cries out to Jesus, pleading with him not to torment him and calling him "Son of the Most High God." Finally, in 15:39 the centurion standing guard at the cross watches Jesus die, and exclaims, "truly this man was the Son of God." In each of these instances Jesus's particular closeness to God is emphasized, connoting both power and status, but the words used also bring to the forefront Jesus's role as son, as child. I believe Mark will do two things with this concept: on the one hand, Mark's insistence that Jesus is God's beloved child allows people both within the narrative and reading it to understand Jesus's status relative to the rest of humanity: Jesus is akin to God in a way others are not. When compared to the disciples, Jesus is godlike in his wisdom, power, and authority. On the other hand, Jesus himself will show childlike and even childish qualities in Mark, again confounding the implied reader: Jesus is not the manly man one might expect a hero to be. This becomes increasingly apparent as Jesus draws closer to the cross.

---

[72] C.f. 1:9-11.

[73] The textual history of this phrase is particularly tricky. While many important manuscripts contain the phrase "son of God" (sc, rp, A, 1141), and others have variations on it, a few key texts (most notably ℵ) omit the phrase entirely, making its originality suspect. See for instance, Marcus, *Mark 1-8*, 141, for a short summary of the textual variations and his argument that "son of God" was an addition, rather than original to the text.

The Passion Predictions: Glorification versus Humiliation

The disciples respond with a lack of understanding not only in voyages across the sea, or in reaction to the transfiguration, but also in response to Jesus's three formal predictions of his passion and resurrection. In each of these, the disciples are bewildered by what Jesus is saying, continuing their portrayal of failing to understand, despite Jesus's relatively clear articulations of what will happen to him. The disciples fail to grow and change; however, there is a noticeable shift in the portrayal of Jesus through these passion predictions. While Jesus still appears calm and knowledgeable compared to the disciples, the emphasis is no longer on his dramatic powers. Rather, the passion predictions serve to highlight Jesus's understanding and acceptance of the cost of discipleship, along with its countercultural reversals of social expectation. The disciples' incomprehension and bewilderment, rather than simply functioning to show their incompetence, now adds a new dimension—to highlight just how difficult a journey discipleship is. Each passion prediction is surrounded by the disciples' desire for their own glorification and elevation, along with Jesus's consistent teaching of the role reversals necessary to be a true follower, of the transformation necessary to enter the kingdom, and the new hierarchy there.

The First Passion Prediction

The first of these formal passion predictions, Mark 8:27-38, is particularly suited to demonstrate the theme that discipleship requires an intense reversal of societal norms, which Jesus models, and the disciples fail to grasp.

Jesus begins by asking his disciples who others say he is. The disciples respond with various impressive figures: John the Baptist, Elijah, one of the prophets. Jesus then turns the question to the disciple's own opinion: "but who do *you* say that I am?" (8:29). Peter responds with one of his most insightful comments in Mark's Gospel: "You are the Messiah." Peter is bold as well as correct. Jesus acknowledges Peter's answer in a rather strange way: he ἐπετίμησεν the disciples to not tell anyone about him. Despite the fact that Jesus is the one who asked the question, he acts almost as if Peter has said something in error. Mark will use ἐπιτιμάω twice more in this passage, and in both cases the word has a sense of "rebuke" or "censure." Here the more traditional translation is "warn." But even if one grants the less caustic translation, there seems to be a misfit between Peter's answer and Jesus's reaction. Matthew evidently agrees: in his Gospel Peter is given flowery language of praise, and he is promised the keys to heaven.[74] It is possible, however, that Mark crafts Jesus's response in conjunction with Peter's upcoming blunder, to which we now turn.

Jesus proceeds to describe the future that awaits him—suffering, trials, death, and resurrection. Ernest Best points out that not only does Jesus shift the discussion to his actions but he also substitutes the title "Son of Man" for "Messiah."[75] In Mark's narrative, *others* speak of Jesus, using the term "Son of God," but when Jesus speaks of

---

[74] Matthew 16:17ff.
[75] Best, *Mark: The Gospel as Story*, 80.

himself, his consistent appellation is "Son of Man," and occasionally "the Son."[76] It is also a term that, like the "Son of God," uses the language of sonship.

Peter, who has just proclaimed the Messiah, turns about and takes Jesus aside to ἐπιτιμᾶν αὐτῷ (8:32). The action comes off as reactionary and brash, both common characteristics of Peter throughout the Gospel. Peter's motive is not made explicit, nor does Jesus explain what "human things" Peter is intent upon, but scholars generally agree that Peter's understanding of what a "Messiah" is or should be precludes suffering and death.[77] Peter not only fails to grasp the word Jesus is saying but also acts rashly, presuming his superiority to Jesus and attempting to exert control and power over Jesus's speech. The narrator describes Jesus as mirroring the word ἐπιτιμάω back at Peter: Jesus ἐπετίμησεν Πέτρῳ (8:33) saying, "Get behind me Satan, for you espouse not the things of God but of humans."

Jesus then calls both the crowd and the disciples together, and explicitly relates his own path of suffering to that of true followers: they must deny themselves, and take up their crosses and follow (8:34). Jesus argues for a direct reversal of general beliefs and desires: "whoever wishes to save his life will lose it, but whoever loses his life because of me and the gospel will save it." Mark's Jesus is, of course, speaking both literally and metaphorically here: he himself will actually bear a cross, and his followers might be required to as well. On the other hand, the language of denial and suffering also serves as a metaphor to reverse social expectations of promoting one's honor and having a meaningful life. Jesus, in Mark's narrative, is setting up the idea that there are things more important than staying alive, and indeed, by striving after life, one is actually losing it, rather than gaining it. In both cases this language of denial and death resonates with the *rites of passage* (as we have seen in Chapters 3 and 4), which both encompass funerary rites and incorporate the language of death and denial in the liminal stage, where participants are separating from a former way of life and (hopefully!) entering safely into a new one. The language of danger once again serves to highlight what a radical shift is required of initiates. Jesus here clearly emphasizes a similar thing.

Plutarch, in his *Consolation*, is making a similar sort of appeal to his wife as Jesus is making to the disciples. Each is, of course, speaking in a different context for divergent purposes. Plutarch is speaking in the context of the untimely death of his daughter. As we have seen in Chapter 2, children were constantly on the brink of death. Funerary inscriptions mention and model the fact that children may lose out on and miss all the important rites and accomplishments that go with being an adult. Their parents bemoan their untimely demise, and wish that they had grown up to become more. But Plutarch, when offering consolation to his wife over their daughter's death, urges his wife not to mourn the things that the little girl will never do. Rather, since her

---

[76] See 2:10, 2:28, 8:31, 8:38, 9:9, 9:12, 9:31, 10:33, 10:45, 13:26, and 14:62.
[77] See for instance, Larry W. Hurtado, who says that "in 8:32-33 Peter recoils from Jesus' prediction of his approaching violent death, and Jesus rebukes Peter for his purely human reaction" (Larry W. Hurtado, "Following Jesus in the Gospel of Mark—and Beyond," in *Patterns of Discipleship in the New Testament* [Grand Rapids: Eerdmans, 1996], 12). See also Black, *Mark*, 194–7; Meyers, *Binding the Strong Man*, 241–9; R. Alan Culpepper, *Mark* (Smyths & Helwys Bible Commentary; Georgia: Smyth & Helwys, 2007), 269–79. B. A. E. Osborne, "Peter: Stumbling-Block and Satan," *NovT* 15 (1973): 187–90, further argues that the link between Peter's name references the idea of the stumbling block, and that both are associated with Satan, and the evil impulse which pits itself again the good impulse.

soul is now free of the body, it can "leap up towards its natural home."[78] While their daughter has died, she is, as it were, "in a better place." Plutarch is offering comfort for a death that could not be avoided, but does not go so far as to promote seeking death voluntarily. Jesus, while making a similar argument as Plutarch, goes one step further: those who lose their lives will actually gain them. Both emphasize the opposite as well. Jesus argues, "For what does it profit a person to gain the whole world but forfeit her soul? Indeed, what shall a person give in exchange for her soul?" A constant theme throughout Mark is the theme of suffering and death for the sake of the gospel. Disciples, like children, live constantly in the shadow of death. Jesus, on the other hand, preaches just the opposite. Those who suffer persecutions and death do not "miss out" on the important aspects of life, but they, in fact, *gain* life in a new and unique way. Plutarch's remarks about his daughter's death follow a similar pattern: because she died so young, she did not become used to the "cage" that the body represents, such that her soul resisted leaving the body.[79] Despite some similarities where both seek to persuade the listener that death is not the worst evil, Jesus and Plutarch have different motivations for their admonitions, and different basic understandings of the afterlife. Jesus is arguing for death and denial to be seen as an appropriate lens by which to view life and human relationships. But Plutarch is attempting to soften the pain of an untimely death, without glorifying it as a good to be sought after.

Again, in Jesus's preaching one can see a blend of literal and metaphorical. Jesus's preaching about being ready to lose one's life has the potential of being metaphorical: he does not seem to imagine that *every* disciple will suffer death.[80] However, his descriptions of his own suffering and death are literally true, even if misunderstood by the disciples around him. Jesus walks the road to the cross, a road he is both aware of and insistent upon communicating to his followers.

The Second Passion Prediction

The second time Jesus predicts his death, in Mark 9:30-32, he and his disciples are passing through Galilee. He again gives specifics about his death and resurrection, and again adopts the title of "Son of Man." In this iteration the disciples are said to "not understand what he said, and were afraid to ask him" (9:32). The encounter comes across as yet another failure of the disciples. Jesus is describing in perfect and clear detail what will actually happen to him, and the disciples are incapable of even understanding this. The theme of completely missing Jesus's teaching is augmented as the story transitions into the disciples' argument over which of them is the greatest (9:33-37). This story, as detailed in Chapter 4 of my book, gives Jesus the platform to reframe the question by pointing to a child as model. Once again, he insists that those who want to be first must be last (9:35). Jesus furthermore creates equivalence

---

[78] Plutarch, *A Consolation to His Wife*, 62.
[79] See above, Chapter 2, pp. 52–5 for in-depth discussion of Plutarch's *Consolation to His Wife*.
[80] It is quite possible that the narrative in Mark does, however, envision some combination of persecution and/or death as an inevitable part of discipleship. There doesn't seem to be the caveat of a long and happy life that John 21 seems to provide for the "beloved disciple" at the least, although John 21:18-19 suggests that Peter in contrast, will be dragged away where he wouldn't want to go.

in 9:36 between welcoming "one such child," himself, and "the one who sent me." The thrust of his argument is, of course, to emphasize the importance of welcoming "one such child." Furthermore, by pairing these three statements together, he proclaims his own special relationship to and with God as well as his own special relationship to and with children. Jesus can and does welcome "children" whether they are actually not adults, those who are least (and therefore are metaphorically related to children), and perhaps even those who act like children unwittingly. Jesus willingly gives up status by associating with and even serving those "beneath" him or those considered "shameful," instead of associating only with his equals or betters. The disciples, on the other hand, vie for superiority. Jesus teaches the disciples that in acting this way, they still fail to grasp the society of the kingdom, where lowliness, not grappling for power, counts as truly high status. Furthermore, Jesus, as God's Son, models the will of God in obedience, bringing God honor. What God considers "honorable," however, again reverses the societal norms: God's will for God's child is suffering and death, reaching those outside, and welcoming the children.

The Third Passion Prediction

Jesus's third prediction of his death and resurrection comes directly after his teaching on how hard the rich find it to enter the Kingdom of God.[81] The disciples are assured that everything they have given up will be returned to them, and more, including persecutions (10:30). This is a rare moment of approbation for them, yet even this set of praise and promises is mixed with promises of suffering. Jesus finishes this section by saying, "many who are first will be last, and last first" (10:31). As they turn to Jerusalem, Mark narrates that the disciples are amazed, and "those following" Jesus are afraid.[82] Jesus then takes aside the Twelve and again tells them for a third time what is going to happen to him: the "Son of Man" will be handed over to the chief priests and scribes, who will condemn him to death. Then they will hand him over to the Gentiles, who will both verbally and physically abuse him, and ultimately kill him, and after three days he will rise again. The gravity and comprehensiveness of his prediction is at its highest. He not only tells the disciples what will happen in the greatest detail of all the predictions but also communicates the imminence of the event: they are walking ever nearer to Jerusalem, where all this will happen.

The third time Jesus predicts his death and resurrection, the disciples seem to ignore it completely. Rather than express bewilderment, fear, sadness, or trust, the scene moves to James and John, who come asking for seats next to Jesus "in his glory" (10:37). Jesus tells them they do not know what they are asking (10:38) and attempts to humble them with a rhetorical question about their ability to imitate him: "Are you

---

[81] Furthermore, as Jesus teaches his disciples about the near impossibility for the rich to enter the kingdom, he calls them "children" (τέκνα).

[82] Scholars debate as to whether both the disciples and those following are both amazed and afraid, but the majority of scholarship agrees that the Greek grammar points toward connecting amazement specifically with the disciples, and fear specifically with those following. See Marcus, *Mark 8-16*, 741–5.

able to drink the cup I drink or to be baptized with the baptism I am baptized with?" Blowing through the rhetorical cues, they instead insist that they will be able to do exactly what Jesus asks. Jesus, surprisingly, agrees with them: they will, in fact, drink the cup he will drink and be baptized with the baptism with which he is baptized. However, he cannot grant their request: to sit at his right and left hands is only for those whom it has been prepared (10:40). James and John show a selfishness and self-absorption that ignores Jesus's direct predictions and his subtler allusions in 10:38, while focusing on their own elevation.

The other disciples react to this exchange fairly predictably: they are angry with James and John. Jesus takes this opportunity to echo 9:33-37, this time using the metaphor of servant/slave: "whoever desires to become great among you must be your servant, and whoever wants to be first among you must be a slave of all" (10:43-44). Jesus reverses the social norms, citing the way the Gentiles do things (10:42), and insisting that his way is the opposite. Once again, we see that those traits associated with maturity and adulthood are disregarded in favor of those traits associated with childhood, and slavery. He himself models this countercultural viewpoint: "likewise the Son of Man did not come to be served, but to serve, and to give his life a ransom on behalf of many." In doing so, he insists not only that he has come to serve but that his own life will be a part of this service, bringing the discussion full circle back to his impending death. The precise way in which the giving of his life functions is also made clear: it is a λύτρον ἀντὶ πολλῶν.

The Final Portrayal: Desertion versus Obedient Degradation

The final narrative portrayal of the disciples before Jesus is arrested and ultimately crucified is perhaps most stunning of all. In Mark 14:18 during the Passover meal, Jesus announces that one of them will betray him. They are all distressed and sadly ask him, "Surely not I?" (14:19). Jesus answers rather vaguely, "It is one of the twelve, the one who dipped with me in the bowl," without specifying who he means, and moves on to imbue new meaning into the bread and the cup. Once they arrive at the Mount of Olives, Jesus again picks up the refrain, modifying it slightly: "All of you will fall away, as it is written: 'Strike down the shepherd, and the sheep will be scattered.' But after I have been raised up, I will go before you to Galilee" (14:27-28). The word for "fall away" is the future passive form of σκανδαλίζω, littered throughout Mark,[83] and notably in the Parable of the Sower, when Jesus talks about why those sown on the "rocky soil" fall away. Mary Ann Tolbert uses this verbal connection as yet another proof that the disciples as a whole represent this second type of seed in Mark.[84] However, contra Tolbert, Jesus joins the stark realism about the disciple's future actions with hope of reconciliation: Jesus will προάξω ὑμᾶς in Galilee, signaling his intention to meet them. The disciples may act like children, but they are not rejected or cast out by Jesus, but rather continuously corrected and promised reconciliation.

---

[83] 4:17, 6:3, and four times throughout 9:42-47.
[84] Tolbert, *Sowing the Gospel*, 154–5. She goes on to describe how Paul's letters support this analysis, characterizing Peter as fickle in Galatians 2.

Ever willing to speak up, Peter declares that he for one will not fall away, even if everyone else does (14:29). Jesus replies that Peter will deny him three times, that very night, before the rooster crows twice (14:30). Jesus reveals to Peter not just his future failure to triumph over the other disciple's behavior but also his particular surplus failure. Instead of heeding the warning, Peter redoubles his protests, insisting, "Even if I have to die with you, I will never deny you" (14:31). The others are described as saying the same things as well. They would rather contradict Jesus than be instructed by him.

In a microcosm of the future events, they arrive in Gethsemane, and Jesus asks his disciples to sit while he prays. He then takes Peter, James, and John and, while feeling intense distress, articulates this intimate emotional turmoil to them: "My spirit is deeply grieved, to the point of death; remain here and be watchful" (14:34). He both feels agitation and reaches out to his friends for solidarity.

Proceeding a bit further, Jesus prays to God. He throws himself at God in a position of humility, calling God αββα ὁ πατήρ (14:36). Jesus not just is humble but places himself firmly in the position of child. He begs that the "hour might pass from him" (14:35) and that God might "remove the cup" from him. Jesus proclaims his knowledge that God is able to do all things (14:36). Yet he ends by saying, "Not what I desire, but what you do." Jesus positions himself as the obedient child, fearful and afraid, begging to be protected and rescued, and also submitting himself to his father's will. Once again, this contrasts starkly with the expectations of mature adults. Respect of one's parents and obedience toward them both were considered virtues (in fact, the virtue was specifically *pietas* in Latin— "familial piety"), but there was a different sort of respect expected from an adult son than from a boy: temperate, deferential, courteous, but also self-controlled and full of manly courage. Honoring one's parents went hand in hand with not bringing them shame. In this scene, there is an interesting mixture going on of both admirable and shameful portrayals of Jesus. On the one hand, Jesus is portrayed as ultimately submitting to his father's will, which would be seen as admirable. On the other hand, he is shown begging and pleading with his parent in a way that would have been shameful, as would his implied fears of death itself.

In contrast to Jesus's soulful prayer, he returns to his friends, but finds them sleeping.[85] Jesus asks Peter in amazement, "Are you sleeping? Couldn't you keep watch for one hour? Keep watch and pray, so that you won't come into temptation: the spirit may be willing, but the flesh is weak" (14:37-8). Jesus here specifies that this present predicament is a failure of "the flesh," not of the inner willingness of his disciples. Nonetheless, the former has true consequences: a failure of the flesh now puts the whole person in danger of temptation.

The second time Jesus goes to pray, "he spoke the same words" (14:39). Jesus's desire to avoid the coming event is not a momentary failure of nerves but a true climactic moment. Likewise, the second time he returns to the sleeping disciples, "for their eyes were heavy" (14:39-40). Again, the physical frailty of the disciples is used as an explanation, and "they did not know how to answer him." The scene repeats a third time. This last time Jesus announces that the hour has come, and his betrayer is at

---

[85] The narrative is unclear whether this represents the three, or the eleven, but there is a particular focus on Peter and the three in their failure.

hand (14:41-42). As Jesus is arrested, there is a brief, feeble attempt to defend him: "one of those standing near him" draws his sword and cuts off the ear of the slave of the chief priest (14:47). This seems to get no reaction at all from the crowds, from Jesus, or from the victim himself. But as Jesus submits to the arrest, announcing that the "scriptures need to be fulfilled" (14:49), they all panic: "all of them abandoned him and fled" (14:50). One unnamed young man even is said to have fled naked, wiggling out of his linen cloth as he is caught (14:51-52). Jesus's prediction that they will "scatter" is literally true, and once again, their fear and lack of understanding get the better of them. Jesus is taken away to the high priest to be judged.

Peter, on the other hand, follows Jesus "from afar." It is unclear whether he initially flees, and doubles back, or whether he makes himself inconspicuous in the chaos. However, he follows "right into the courtyard of the high priest" (14:54). Three times Peter is accused of being one of the people with Jesus (14:67, 14:69, 14:70), and all three times he denies it (14:68, 14:70, 14:71), the last time bolstering his claims by cursing and swearing an oath. In Mark's Gospel the cock crows once after the first denial, and a second time after the third, heightening the sense that there is both agency and inevitability in Peter's actions. Peter notices the rooster's second crow, remembers Jesus's words, and, "throwing himself down, he wept" (14:72).

Therefore, in the final narrative moments, the disciples fail utterly. They prove themselves cowardly, scattering instead of standing by Jesus. Peter himself is a liar twice over: he unwittingly lies to Jesus about his intentions to stand by him even unto death, and he intentionally lies three times about his association with Jesus. The others, likewise, have proven by their actions that their words of commitment to Jesus were empty boasts. They may have believed they were speaking the truth, but just like Peter, they unwittingly lie. Their fear overcomes their faithfulness. Once again, these are key negative characteristics associated with children: culpable naivety combined cowardliness.

Jesus meanwhile shows himself to model characteristics of a child. While the collection of chief priests, scribes, elders, and high priest are "seeking testimony against Jesus to put him to death" (14:55), they are unable to find any. Instead of Jesus dazzling everyone with his elocution and rhetoric—key characteristics of an educated man—Jesus is silent. He only answers one question: "Are you the Messiah, the son of the Blessed One?" to which he replies that he is, and again substitutes his chosen appellation τὸν υἱὸν τοῦ ἀνθρώπου—"the Son of Man"—for the high priest's ὁ χριστὸς ὁ υἱὸς τοῦ εὐλογητοῦ. He goes on to allude to both Daniel 7:13 and Psalm 110:1. In each case there is both truth and irony to his allusion: Daniel 7:13 pictures the triumph of the Son of Man over the beasts of the world, of the heavenly kingdom overcoming the earthly one. The Ancient of Days in Daniel 7 grants kingship to the Son of Man, and all nations will serve him, and his kingship will never end (Daniel 7:13, 14). Likewise Psalm 110 pictures the LORD granting power to "my lord"—allowing him to sit as his right hand, crushing the enemies before him, and granting him priesthood in the line of Melchizedek. In each case there is absolute triumph and glory: God ordains and approves in a climactic way. By narrating Jesus as alluding to these two passages, Mark communicates to the implied reader the truth of his statements: Jesus is indeed the triumphal king, the holy priest, the Son of Man. And yet the mechanism by which all this will happen is the perfect opposite of these allusions. Jesus proclaims his kinship to God at just a moment in which it will enrage and justify his accusers, assuring his death; Jesus proclaims his power at just a time in which he is most powerless; Jesus proclaims his exaltation at the moment of his humiliation. Jesus instead is portrayed in the opposite way that a well-educated man would portray himself: he is instead a bumbling child who is unable to sway the court. And yet, even while he is portrayed as inarticulate, this is also in service to his obedience to God. Jesus is also, therefore, portrayed as the obedient child.

Jesus is then condemned, mocked, spit upon, and struck (14:63-65). He is sent to Pilate, where again he is silent, save one reply obliquely affirming Pilate's query over whether Jesus is the king of the Jews (15:2-5). The crowd, which followed Jesus with wonder throughout Mark, is now stirred up to abandon him and call for his crucifixion. Jesus has lost his freedom and the favor of the masses. He is again mocked, struck, and spit upon, this time by Pilate's soldiers. The soldiers dress him as a comical king and mockingly pay homage to him. Jesus is treated without respect, honor, or status. He has lost those things associated with the mature adult male, and instead has the social standing of a child. He is treated like a fool, and is mocked with the very things that are true of him. In 15:21 another person is made to carry Jesus's cross. While Mark does not give details as to why this happens, it is plausible that it is because Jesus is too physically frail to carry the cross any longer. Jesus has lost the respect and admiration of the crowd, he is no longer eloquent or wise in his answers to his accusers, and now his strength has failed him. Narratively again he is portrayed as being stripped of the social standing of an adult, and instead acts as a child might: incapable of persuasive speech, physically frail, and without respect.[86]

As he is crucified, everyone around treats him with scorn, abuse, and mockery. Even those criminals crucified with him abuse him (15:32). Jesus is seen as mentally incompetent, morally inferior, and physically frail—all characteristics associated with childhood. Jesus has made a radical transition in reversal of cultural expectations. Finally, as Jesus dies, his final words are, "My God, my God, why have you abandoned me?" (15:34). Jesus references Psalm 22, which proclaims God, as well as acknowledges the petitioner's feeling of abandonment. At the moment of death, even God seems to have abandoned Jesus. He is utterly alone, without friends, comfort, or support. He has been stripped physically, socially, and emotionally of everything. Like a child, frail and alone, he has been seemingly rejected by his Father and his society, and will succumb to death, all in reversal of normal cultural expectations.[87] In terms of van Gennep's *rites of passage*, he has made a complete separation from his former life. Jesus's separation

---

[86] Mark McVann agrees, although characterizes this section as the liminal section of the passion-resurrection narrative. See McVann "Reading Mark Ritually: Honor-Shame and the Ritual of Baptism," *Semeia* 67 (1994): 193–5.

[87] James Francis makes a similar connection, noting that Jesus fails this one time to address God as "Father": "we may also note how the cry of derelication in Mk 15.34 is given added poignancy by this one recorded instance of Jesus' failure to address God as Father, whereby shame is expressed in a sense of the abandonment of all kinship." James Francis, "Children and Childhood in the New Testament," in *The Family in Theological Perspective* (ed. Stephen Barton; Edinburgh: T&T Clark, 1996), 68.

is not merely paralleling the *rites of passage*, however; he is also reversing the normal cultural expectation whereby a person leaves behind his childhood with its negative associations to gain adulthood and maturity. Here, instead, he is mirroring the *rites of passage* while inverting the normal fulfillment: he has become childlike once more.

By all appearances, Jesus has been completely abandoned, and he himself seems to feel abandoned. However, two things happen that signal God's continued faithfulness. First, the sanctuary veil rips from top to bottom. Mark makes no commentary on this event, but simply by narrating it, he communicates a momentous moment. There are two major ways to view this—that God has broken out of the Holy of Holies and a new access has been granted for people to come in. Either way, the act functions as a mysterious portent. Second, Mark narrates that darkness descends upon the land around noon ("the sixth hour"), and lasts for about three hours, at which point Jesus breathes his last. Mark does not explicitly narrate that the darkness lifts at the moment of Jesus's death, but this is the implication of the story.[88] While neither of these portents is explicated by Mark, the centurion standing guard at Jesus's death gives voice to the implications: "Truly this man was the Son of God!" (15:39).[89] As the final explicit reference to Jesus as a child, as God's son, this scene holds climactic importance: Jesus is acknowledged to have succeeded, to have enacted obedience to God, precisely in his moment of abject humiliation. The least is indeed the greatest.

The Resurrection

Throughout this chapter, it has been acknowledged that Mark's original narrative ends at 16:8. The other three Gospels have robust resurrection appearances by Jesus. Furthermore, the other three Gospels have a narrated scene of reconciliation with the disciples. Mark, on the other hand, simply narrates women who encounter an empty tomb and a young man "wearing a white robe" (16:5). These women had been watching as Jesus died, and watching as Joseph of Arimathea placed Jesus's body into a tomb and rolled a large stone to cover it (15:40-41, 46-47). They are told by the young man that Jesus has risen. Furthermore, he has a message from Jesus for the disciples and Peter: he is going ahead to Galilee, where they will see him (16:7). The women instead flee in terror, and stay silent.

Why does Mark choose to end his Gospel in this way, instead of a more definite ending of joy? Why do the disciples not have a final moment of pure faith? Why do we not see Jesus in his glory, triumphant?

---

[88] I posit this through analysis of the timing of the text: if darkness has descended for three hours starting at about noon, and Jesus breathes his last at three, then while the text doesn't say outright that the light shown through at three, it seems to imply it.

[89] Malbon, for instance asserts that "it is frequently argued that the Markan narrator delays the recognition of Jesus as 'Son of God' by a human character not the narrator [1:1] or unclean spirits [3:11]) until that moment when the true meaning of Jesus' sonship can be understood—the moment of Jesus' death on the cross (15:37, 39)" (Malbon, *In the Company of Jesus*, 59). Later she goes on to also assert that "it is frequently argued that the fact that it is a Roman centurion who recognizes the crucified Jesus as 'Son of God' suggest the surprising openness of the Christian faith to the Gentile world" (ibid., 60).

I argue that Mark consistently insists on the absence of the fully realized Kingdom of God. Mark is clear that it *will* appear, that it is coming. Mark also implies that it is already here now, but like the smallest of seeds, it looks insignificant. It is growing, but not fully here.[90] In fact, once again, the tripartite structure of the *rites of passage*, and particularly the coming-but-not-fully-realized nature of the liminal stage, consistently pairs with the trajectory of the narrative in Mark's Gospel.

This also holds true not only for Jesus's narrated death and subsequent resurrection but also for his predictions of his death. Each time he predicts his death, he predicts three things—the suffering he will undergo leading to his death, the three days that will elapse in between his death, and his subsequent resurrection. He also always speaks of himself as the "Son of Man" in these accounts. Between the three accounts, the predictions vary only in their level of detail about his sufferings. In 8:31 Jesus speaks of "great suffering" and his rejection by the "elders, chief priests and scribes." In the shortest of his predictions, 9:31, he predicts simply that he will be "betrayed" or "handed over" into "human hands." In the third prediction, in 10:33-34, Jesus says that he will be "handed over to the chief priests and scribes," who will condemn him to death, and then they, in turn, will "hand him over to the Gentiles" who will "ridicule him, spit on him, and whip him," in addition to killing him.

Each of these predictions also emphasizes his separation from those in power and a period of waiting after his death: his predictions consistently mention "three days." Finally, Jesus consistently mentions his resurrection: death is not the end. The predictions are especially weighted toward his humiliation in terms of narrative space. This is certainly not to say that the three-day waiting period and especially his resurrection are of less theological value. They absolutely are not. However, there is an insistence on the specifics of what will happen during his humiliation. Mark's Gospel time and again focuses on the difficulty of the separation from the past life, and of the longevity of the liminal, transformational period. Mark does not shy away from the danger and the pain of such a transformation. Much is lost before much is gained.

The same holds true in the narrative account of the actual event. Mark takes time and uses a multiplicity of details to describe Jesus's humiliation. He is falsely accused, mocked, spit upon, and reviled by the Jewish elders. They condemn him to death and send him to Pilate. Pilate, in turn, finds nothing wrong, but because of the crowd, has him crucified. His own soldiers revile, spit on, and whip him. Jesus feels the separation of God, crying out, "My God, my God, why have you forsaken me?" (15:43). In his hour of suffering, his disciples have fled, and everyone around him mocks and derides him, save the women looking on (15:40-41) and a centurion, who at Jesus's death proclaims that Jesus truly was the "Son of God" (15:39). Once Jesus dies, the in-between period provides a sense of waiting as well. The curtain in the temple is torn in two at the moment of Jesus's death. Joseph asks for the body, wraps it in linen, and lays it in a tomb. The women, who were watching at Jesus's crucifixion, also watch to see where

---

[90] Don Juel makes this argument as well: "the announcement from the empty tomb that Jesus has been raised—as he said he would—thus opens a gateway to the future. The disciples will surely see him. Whatever the obstacles, the harvest will come; the tiny seed will grow into a shrub large enough to provide nesting places for the birds; at the end of the birth pangs one can expect new life." Juel, *A Master of Surprise*, 115.

the body is placed. The resurrection story is shorter still. The women, having seen where Jesus was laid, come with prepared spices to anoint his body. As they worry over how to move the large stone covering the tomb, they see it has been rolled away, and are greeted by the "young man dressed in a white robe" (16:5), who tells them that Jesus is raised. They famously flee, and seem to fail to deliver the message to the disciples that the young man has entrusted to them.

The narrative of Jesus's passion is many times the length of the description of what happened after Jesus's death but before his resurrection. That, in turn, is longer than the account resurrection itself. This is compounded by the fact that, in Mark, the resurrected Jesus fails to appear on the scene.

This does not mean that Mark cares more for the suffering of Jesus than for the fact of his resurrection. Throughout Mark there is a certainty in Jesus's resurrection, as expressed in his passion predictions and confirmed by the young man at the tomb. Yet much like the failure to detail the Kingdom of God's full enactment, Mark neglects to describe the fullness of Jesus as the resurrected Christ. Throughout Mark there is a strong sense of a tripartite structure necessary to follow Christ and to enter the kingdom: separation from past life, a middle period of waiting, anxiety, and persecution, and a final glorious reincorporation as a transformed and changed person. Jesus's teachings about discipleship show this, his parables describe it, and his death and resurrection corroborate this as well. Yet this tripartite structure most often portrays the struggles of the first two stages, the dangers inherent in them, and the failures and rejections and lack of understanding. The third stage while promised and expected, remains elusive.

As for the disciples, they have been promised twice over that Jesus will meet them in Galilee. The disciples continuously represent fear, misunderstanding, and failure. Like the negative associations of children in the ancient world, they are consistently less than the ideal adult male. Mark, by portraying them this way, points to a crisis of belief: they stumble over Jesus's teachings, over Jesus's radical reorientation of the kingdom's values. They also serve as stumbling blocks to the implied reader: far from model recipients of the kingdom, the disciples seem to represent mostly failure. The reader is left in ignorance as to how, or if, the disciples are transformed. We continuously seem to be set up to mentally behave toward the disciples just as the disciples behave toward the children in Mark 10:13-16: we would like to indignantly push away those drawing near Jesus who (we think) are clearly unworthy. How can Jesus surround himself with such *children*? But just as Jesus rebukes the disciples in Mark 10:13-16, so too, I believe, Jesus rebukes the implied reader. The disciples throughout Mark are shown to be continuously aided by Jesus. Where they fear, he comforts. Where they fail to understand, he continuously teaches, and teaches again. Where they are faithless, he is faithful.[91] When Mark has Jesus engaging with the disciples, Jesus functions to enact God's inclusive love, caring for them as beloved children even when they stumble.

---

[91] This is a similar point to that which Elizabeth Struthers Malbon makes in *In the Company of Jesus*. She goes one step further: she insists that the narrative uses wording like "whoever" to expand the audience of Jesus's words and comfort: "what the Markan narrative says about discipleship it says to all. Both separately and together, the disciples and the crowd serve to open the story of Jesus and the narrative of mark outward to the larger group—whoever has ears to hear or eyes to read the Gospel of Mark" (Malbon, *In the Company of Jesus*, 99).

Moreover, Mark continues to teach the reader that we too will stumble. As often as we show attempts at exclusion and pushing away those we deem less than worth, Mark also has us identifying with the disciples in their incomprehension: what *does* Jesus mean? The demands of Jesus for the reader seem counterintuitive and hopelessly unattainable. Here again, God's consistent love, enacted by Jesus, gives the reader hope. In some ways Jesus alone emerges as not only the Father's faithful Son but—arguably— also the only one fully *adult* in the story.[92]

Children in the ancient world may have been believed to be morally incompetent, mentally inferior, and physically frail. But that did not mean that individual children were not loved and appreciated by their families. This truth can be seen in the healing narratives about children. Parents were willing to go to absolute lengths to help their helpless children: believing in the face of death, questioning and out-riddling Jesus himself, and exposing innermost ambiguity while pleading for help. God as parent exhibits absolute faithfulness to the Beloved Son. So too God, via Jesus, may be expected to exhibit absolute faithfulness to the disciples. As Juel puts it:

> To insist that the discordant ending offers no promise of resolution whatever is to do equal violence to the story. Jesus has promised an end. That end is not yet, but the story gives good reasons to remain hopeful even in the face of disappointment. The possibilities of eventual enlightenment for the reader remain in the hands of the divine actor who will not be shut in—or out.[93]

The economy of the kingdom is radically different from the structures of the ancient world. Honor, wealth, and even biological kinship are all rejected by Jesus both through his words and through his actions. The Kingdom of God inverts the social norms. Moreover, to enter the kingdom, a reversal must happen. Separation from the former way of life is the most difficult of tasks: to truly set aside a previous understanding of the world and its values is shown to be nearly impossible. Even when one believes this has happened, there is a protracted sense of waiting, of ambiguity and uncertainty, of backsliding and relearning. Transformation may be possible, but only with God (Mark 9:23, 10:27).

On the other hand, Jesus, while looking like an adult when narratively paired with the disciples, consistently looks decreasingly like the ideal adult male the closer he comes to the cross. Jesus becomes more and more childlike, and Mark shows this by ascribing to Jesus both traditionally positive and traditionally negative traits of children. Jesus is indeed God's child, and to become like a child, he must strip away signs of honor, family, status and bearing. Jesus is declared God's son by the centurion, and is declared raised from the dead by the young man at the tomb, but we the readers are left with the uneasy sense that the way may not be passable but for God's faithful love to us, God's children.

---

[92] Many thanks to Clift Black for this insight.
[93] Juel, *Master of Surprise*, 120.

Conclusion and Summary

This chapter has aimed to demonstrate that there is merit in viewing discipleship through the lens of ancient conceptions of a child. Scholars of Mark have long noted two difficulties in the narrative of Mark. First, the disciples seem to move from a mixture of successes and failures to almost exclusively failures. Second, the narrative attention on Jesus himself in the latter half of Mark focuses on suffering and denial, as opposed to the first half of Mark, where he is represented as a powerful preacher and healer. I have proposed that both of these narrative representations can be illuminated by examining them according to the characteristics associated with children. While scholars note that Jesus is referred to as the "Son of God" and "Son of Man," these are usually examined by way of their titles, rather than their familial relational attributes. When one takes seriously the idea that the model recipient of the kingdom is a child, and that one needs to transform into a child to receive the kingdom, then the descent from respected to despised, from powerful to weak, from confident to confused, and from in control to utterly dependent begins to fit a pattern. The narrative continuously asserts that the kingdom's society is radically different from the traditional society of the ancient world. It insists that humility and service mark the true leaders. Mark is equally committed to the mystery of the kingdom. God may be trustworthy, but God's actions are subtle and often difficult to discern. The narrative ends with hope, but not with surety.

A central motif of funerary inscriptions is that the child has lost all the potential that others put their hope in him. They had great expectations for the daughter's marriage, for the grandchildren she would bear. They had great hopes for the son, who would become a grand orator, who would become a student of the Law, who would bring military glory or hope. Death has dashed all these hopes: the potential of the child will never be realized.

The abrupt and enigmatic ending of Mark insists that the reader rely on hope still. Not even death has cut short the hopes that the Parent had for the Child. Jesus, dying in loneliness and more childlike than he has ever appeared before, has risen. Certain hopes are entirely probable: Mark proclaims that Jesus's promises are trustworthy. But the concrete hopes that the disciples had for a king, that the people had for a rebellious military leader, that Jesus's parents had for a dutiful son—these hopes are left to be grieved.

Likewise, the disciples are left as children. They never overcome their bewilderment, confusion, or fear. The reader must make sense of the disciples as children: decidedly showing a lack of potential in the narrative that may well contrast with other stories the reader may have heard about the disciples speaking with power and authority. In this narrative once again there is hope, but a hope mysterious. The only reason we may think this is true is because of the word of Jesus, because of a hope that he sees a potential in them that no one else seems to. The reader must trust the narrator, must trust Jesus.

6

Conclusions and Looking Forward

In this book, I have sought to fill a gap in scholarship by examining children within the Gospel of Mark. Mark 10:13-16 features a story about Jesus welcoming and embracing children, and chiding his disciples who stopped them from coming to him. All of this is unusual in an ancient world context. Most surprisingly, however, Jesus goes further: insisting not only that children have a place in the Kingdom of God but that "whoever does not receive the Kingdom of God as a child will never enter it" (10:15). While this phrase is often repeated glibly in church settings, few scholars have examined in depth what the passage intends vis a vis qualities of children. Recent scholarship has settled on a general sense that the passage invokes a metaphorical sense of the "dependence" of children on their caregivers that adults should emulate in regard to God. I have argued that this sense of "dependence" is a piece of what is intended, but that it is incomplete. Rather, the image invokes a sense of fundamental transformation. Anthropologists such as Arnold van Gennep argue that cultures have sets of rituals (e.g. birth, marriage, death) grouped under the category *rites of passage*, whereby a person is protected through a societal transition from one status to another. Within this grouping of *rites of passage* van Gennep links both coming-of-age rites and rites welcoming new members of an organization into its fold as "initiation rites." These rites both protected a person from the danger of such a transition and effected the change from one state to another. Children, according to ancient sensibilities, were distinct from and inferior to the adult male. A transformation was needed via a *rite of passage* for a child to become an adult. I have argued throughout that a helpful lens for understanding Mark 10:13-16's requirement to enter Kingdom of God "as a child" involves a transformation that both mirrors and reverses this rite. God's kingdom requires fundamental transformation from the old way of life, the latter of which is both distinct from and inferior to that of the kingdom. And yet God's kingdom looks radically different from traditional societal understandings of the world—so different, in fact, that the qualities usually associated with children are a better model than those commonly assumed to be held by adult males.

In Chapter 1, I surveyed scholarship on children in the ancient world. Studies on children are still relatively new, with interest springing up only in the last three or four decades. Full-length monographs remain even more elusive, with most scholarship on children relegated to edited volumes on the family. Many of these, in fact, study children only as ancillary to the family system, focusing much more on husband/wife dynamics. A few, including Beryl Rawson, study children as such, and ask questions ranging from children's pastimes, to depictions of children in art, to qualities associated with children. Jewish studies on children are rare, although the last few years have produced a few full-length works devoted to children in the Hebrew Bible, and the Ancient Near East. Children in the New Testament fare slightly better—there are both a more robust group of articles on various aspects of children in the New Testament and a few full-length monographs devoted to children in the New Testament, the Gospels, or Mark specifically. Judith Gundry and Sharon Betsworth both represent the scholarship closest to my own, concerning themselves with literary representations of children in Mark, and how those characteristics align with the Kingdom of God.

Chapters 2 and 3 work together to give a sense of children in the ancient world, as well as their transition to adulthood. Chapter 2 uses a sociohistorical lens to examine references to children in Greco-Roman and Jewish literature roughly contemporaneous to the writing of Mark. I look at how children are described, what qualities they exhibit, and how and when adults are compared to children. In general, children are thought of as incomplete and inferior to the adult male. Children are not as strong, moral, or intelligent as the adult male was perceived to be and are lumped together with other "inferior" categories of humans: women and slaves. Children had a few positive characteristics, but these were generally a limited sense that children were charming and endearing in their speech and antics—but were entertaining as a spectacle or show. Children were enjoyed, but not admired, and to say that adult male was "childish" was almost universally an insult. The singular exception surrounded the idea of a child's potential to grow up and change. This sense was generally relegated to funerary inscriptions: the child *failed* to grow up and achieve his or her potential. A few philosophers take up the subject of a child's potential to change and grow in an oblique way, concerning themselves with whether the child always had a "spark" or seed of maturity that needed to develop or whether a final moment serves to transform the child almost as once, as placing a keystone in an arch.

In Chapter 3, I take up the idea of the transition of childhood to adulthood. Using anthropological figures like van Gennep and Turner, I apply the idea of *rites of passage* to the ancient world. Anthropologists argue that these *rites of passage* follow a consistent tripartite format and function to socially and even ontologically transition a person from one state to another. There was indeed a formal transition from childhood to adulthood, at least for well-born Roman males—the *toga virilis* ceremony, which follows this tripartite structure. Similarly, the wedding ceremony (already a recognized *rite of passage*) functioned as the transition from childhood to adulthood of girls, as marriage in the ancient world happened quite young for women. These two chapters then argue two important things: that children were not considered to be estimable in themselves but that a socially recognized mechanism allowed for their transition into adulthood.

Chapters 4 and 5 then transition to studying the Markan text. Mark 10:13-16 represents a shocking cultural twist whereby Jesus holds up a child as admirable, and worth of emulation. I argue that the passage is playing with imagery that both mirrors and inverts the cultural sense of the transformation a child undergoes to become an adult. I argue that this inversion and mirroring can be seen in three intertwining stands throughout the Gospel. Throughout Mark, there is a struggle to account for the Kingdom of God, and how its appearance is not as striking or impressive as anticipated, without diminishing its true potential and power. Simultaneously throughout Mark there is a struggle to account for the kingdom member—what does a true disciple look like? Jesus himself, much like the kingdom, in certain regard is not as striking or impressive as anticipated, particularly the further the narrative goes. And finally, the disciples, far from being bastions of power and insight, are bumbling and unreliable, and are increasingly erratic as the narrative continues. In all three cases, I argue that the structure of a *rite of passage*, as well as the understood qualities of children, helps inform what is happening. The kingdom, like a child, begins small and insignificant, overlooked by many. And yet eventually it grows and develops into a remarkable harvest. Similarly, when it comes to discipleship, or to enter the Kingdom of God, a transformation needs to happen, a transformation that involves separation, liminality, and reincorporation. Furthermore, the qualities sought after and hoped for in the kingdom look like the qualities of children—serving others, trying to be last and least, being comfortable with a lack of social regard. Jesus begins his ministry with power and authority, and the crowds and people throng to him in hopes of his power. But Jesus increasingly insists on a path of humility, suffering, and dishonor, a path that leads him to abandonment by everyone, even seemingly God, and a humiliating death as a criminal. Mark's open-ended conclusion leaves the reader sure of Jesus's resurrection, but little else: the narrative pushes for dependence and faith rather than knowledge and assurance. The disciples as well function to remind the implied reader that "the least of these," the ones who seem incompetent and unknowing, will be first in the kingdom. The disciples themselves must learn this lesson: a child should be their model of humility; a child should be their model for entrance into the kingdom. So too the implied reader is instructed. Mark's narrative is most comfortable in the middle period, the period of liminality, where one is no longer but not quite, where one is already but not yet: separated from their old life, and old way of being, but not fully incorporated into the new reality. The narrative is aware of the before period, and insistent on the arrival of future period, and yet will not settle into a proclamation of an easy transition from one to the next. In fact, as Don Juel argues, the narrative attempts to unsettle, allowing only for trust in the promises of Jesus.

Looking Forward

I argued that the idea of *rites of passage* function as a helpful rubric by which to view Mark's structure. I have also argued that understanding the way children were viewed in the ancient world is another helpful lens by which to view Mark's meaning. While I have stuck carefully to a few key passages and themes, there are many areas of scholarship left to be gleaned.

Key passages in Jesus's own ministry as described via the Gospels would benefit from being explored via the *rites of passage*. The baptism in particular, both in Mark and the other gospels, shows great promise. The tripartite structure of separation, liminality, and reincorporation is present, as well as a disquieting sense ambiguity expressed by John the Baptist over why Jesus need be baptized at all. Jesus then goes to the wilderness to be tempted before reentering society to preach.[1] John the Baptist himself merits further study—his intentional segregation from society and living in the wastelands as well as his dietary fare all signal not only a separation from society (which is commonly noted) but also a liminal quality. His power is well known by those around him, and people come out to the wilderness to him, submitting to his authority.

Mark furthermore insists on the ways in which Jesus upturns society for the sake of the kingdom. Family structures, ideological values, and even religious institutions (viz. Jesus upturning the tables in the temple) are upended. Jesus consistently insists that the kingdom has a different and often polar opposite structure and set of values than that of those around him. Part of the violence of Mark is the struggle of the disciples to comprehend and be willing to upturn society in the way Jesus describes. Furthermore, this comes with a deep sense of danger. Jesus is killed for his radical beliefs, and Mark 8-10 detail the danger of living in the in-between—of living kingdom values while the kingdom has not come in its fullness.

It would be profitable to apply this anthropological concept to a wide range of New Testament passages on the Kingdom of God. Paul frequently struggles to account for how the reign of God is already-but-not-yet, present but still to come. J. Albert Harrill[2] uses the *toga virlis* ceremony to frame Paul's concept of "putting on Christ" in Galatians. Other such work could yield interesting results. Other New Testament works, such as Revelation, could also benefit from such a lens: Revelation 19 recounts the marriage of the Bride to the Lamb, describing the celebration after a long wait, where she is given special symbolic garments. In this passage in Revelation, the emphasis is on the glorious and final reincorporation of the church into the kingdom. This perspective is different from the Markan material but nonetheless pinpoints a typical *rite of passage* to help visually and emotionally paint a picture.

On the level of scholarship on children in the New Testament as well, my research provides the springboard for future endeavors. A set of passages that merit attention are the healing narratives in Mark that concern themselves with children. While touched on in this book, more work can and should be done on the dangerous liminality that these children exhibit—their closeness and vulnerability to death and spirits, the helplessness of those around them to save them, and their own narrative and situational powerlessness. Jesus is able to heal them in the face of disbelief, doing what can only be described as miraculous. It would be profitable to explore the way in which Jesus is powerful: when it comes to children in Mark, Jesus is consistently defying expectations and equally consistently showing tenderness and mercy.

While *The Child in the Bible* has explored many avenues with regard to the child's function in biblical literature, these articles as well as my own research can be paired

---

[1] Mark McVann has analyzed the parallel passage in Matthew in just these terms. Mark McVann, "One of the Prophets: Matthew's Testing Narrative as a Rite of Passage," *Biblical Theology Bulletin* 23.1 (1993): 14–20.

[2] J. Albert Harrill, "Coming of Age and Putting on Christ: The Toga Virilis Ceremony, Its Paraenesis, and Paul's Interpretation of Baptism in Galatians," *Novum Testamentum*, 44.33 (2002): 252–77.

together to delve even deeper into cursory ideas. For instance, a greater search in the line of Beverly Gaventa or Reider Aasgaard's topics—Paul's use of "child" and "childhood" within his letters—would be incredibly profitable. In particular, a detailed look at 1 Corinthians 13:8-13 through the eyes of childhood would give new life to this exceptionally well-known passage. In the last verses Paul struggles to account for the ways in which key "good" things like knowledge and prophecy are only partial and not complete. In a series of images like seeing face to face instead of through a dark mirror, or an adult putting aside childhood, he argues that perfection will replace the imperfect. While the passage certainly adheres to as standard sense that adulthood is superior to childhood, it also struggles to account for the *telos* of things like faith and hope. Contextualizing this intricate series of metaphors within a robust sense of childhood might breathe new life into an already beloved passage.

Finally, these concepts could be beneficial in the world of practical theology and religious ministry. Children in today's society enjoy both consistent praise of being "the hope of the future" while simultaneously being relegated to the sidelines of the present. In general, those who work with children, whether children's ministers or school teachers, are similarly praised but not supported. While the ancient understandings of children would shock and horrify most modern thinkers, there is nonetheless a striking similarity in the ways in which children are understood today: underdeveloped physically, mentally, morally. While these characteristics today aren't paired with the same impatient scorn as in the ancient world, nonetheless there seems to be lingering implicit biases which leave children and their caregivers and educators marginalized. While youth in the church and in broader religious faith have begun to be studied seriously,[3] children have still been largely ignored. Furthermore, there is a deep theological message that is ideally located toward a consumer culture that presupposes scarcity and suspicion. This message is that of the ideal of countercultural transformation wherein the least are elevated and the greatest are humbled, and a child is the model recipient of the Kingdom of God.

---

[3] Here I think, in particular, of Christian Smith's seminal study "The National Study of Youth and Religion" and Kenda Creasy Dean's academic study of youth ministry which responds to the study.

Bibliography

Aasgaard, Reidar. "Children in Antiquity and Early Christianity: Research History and Central Issues." *Familia* 33 (2006): 23–46.

Aasgaard, Reidar. "Like a Child: Paul's Rhetorical Use of Childhood." Pages 249–77 in *The Child in the Bible*. Edited by Marcia J. Bunge, Terence E. Fretheim, and Beverly Roberts Gaventa. Grand Rapids: Eerdmans, 2008.

Aeschylus. *Oresteia: Agamemnon. Libation-Bearers. Eumenides*. Edited and translated by Alan H. Sommerstein. Loeb Classical Library 146. Cambridge: Harvard University Press, 2009.

Ambrozic, Aloysius M. *The Hidden Kingdom: A Redaction-Critical Study of the References to the Kingdom of God in Mark's Gospel*. Washington: Catholic Biblical Association of America, 1972.

Anderson, Sheryl. "Maturity, Delinquency and Rebellion." Pages 111–34 in *Children of God: Towards a Theology of Childhood*. Edited by Angela Shier-Jones. Peterborough: Epworth, 2007.

Apuleius. *Metamorphoses (The Golden Ass)*. Edited and translated by John Arthur Hanson. 2 vols. Loeb Classical Library. Cambridge: Harvard University Press, 1989–96.

Ariès, Philippe. *Centuries of Childhood: A Social History of Family Life*. Translated by Robert Baldick. New York: Vintage Books, 1962.

Aristotle. *Problems, Volume I: Books 1–19*. Edited and translated by Robert Mayhew. Loeb Classical Library 316. Cambridge: Harvard University Press, 2011.

Arrian. Translated by Peter Astbury Brunt. 2 vols. Loeb Classical Library. Cambridge: Harvard University Press, 1976–83.

Augustine. *Confessions*. Translated by Edward Bouverie Pusey. Uhrichsville: Barbour, 1984.

Augustine. *Expositions on the Psalms 99–120*. Edited by Boniface Ramsey, trans. Maria Boulding. Hyde Park, New York: New City Press, 2003.

Bailey, James. "Experiencing the Kingdom as a Little Child: A Rereading of Mark 10: 13–16." *WW* 15.1 (1995): 58–67.

Bakke, O. M. *When Children Became People: The Birth of Childhood in Early Christianity*. Minneapolis: Augsburg Fortress, 2005.

Balch, David L. and Carolyn Osiek, eds. *Early Christian Families in Context: An Interdisciplinary Dialogue*. Grand Rapids: Eerdmans, 2003.

Balla, Peter. *The Child-Parent Relationship in the New Testament and Its Environment*. Peabody: Hendrickson, 2006.

Balz, Horst. *Exegetical Dictionary of the New Testament: Volume 3*. Wm. B. Eerdmans Publishing, 1993.

Barclay, John C. "The Family as the Bearer of Religion in Judaism and Early Christianity." Pages 66–80 in *Constructing Early Christian Families: Family as Social Reality and Metaphor*. Edited by Halvor Moxnes. London: Routledge, 1997.

Bartlett, David L. "Adoption in the Bible." Pages 375–98 in *The Child in the Bible*. Edited by Marcia J. Bunge, Terence E. Fretheim, and Beverly Roberts Gaventa. Grand Rapids: Eerdmans, 2008.

Barton, Stephen, ed. *The Family in Theological Perspective*. Edinburgh: T&T Clark, 1996.
Baxter, Jane Eva, ed. *Children in Action: Perspectives on The Archaeology of Childhood*. Berkeley: University of California Press for the American Anthropological Association, 2005.
Best, Ernest. *Disciples and Discipleship: Studies in the Gospel According to Mark*. Edinburgh: T&T Clark, 1986.
Best, Ernest. *Following Jesus: Discipleship in the Gospel of Mark*. Sheffield: Journal for the Study of the Old Testament Press, 1981.
Best, Ernest. *Mark: The Gospel as Story*. Edinburgh: T&T Clark, 1984.
Betsworth, Sharon. *Children in Early Christian Narratives*. New York: Bloomsbury, 2015.
Betsworth, Sharon. *The Reign of God is Such as These: A Socio-Literary Analysis of Daughters in the Gospel of Mark*. New York: T&T Clark, 2010.
Bierkan, Andrew T., Charles P. Sherman, and Emile Stocquart. "Marriage in Roman Law." *YLJ* 16.5 (1907): 312–14.
Black, C. Clifton. *Mark*. Abingdon New Testament Commentaries. Nashville: Abingdon Press, 2011.
Bonner, Stanley F. *Education in Ancient Rome: From the Elder Cato to the Younger Pliny*. Berkeley: University of California Press, 1977.
Booth, Alan D. "Punishment, Discipline, and Riot in the Schools of Antiquity." *Echos du Monde Classique* 17 (1973): 107–14.
Borg, Marcus. *Rereading the Bible Again for the First Time*. San Francisco: Harper, 2002.
Bradly, Keith. "Children and Dreams." Pages 43–51 in *Childhood, Class and Kin in the Roman World*. Edited by Suzanne Dixon. London: Routledge, 2001.
Bradly, Keith. *Discovering the Roman Family: Studies in Roman Social History*. New York: Oxford University Press, 1991.
Bradly, Keith. "Images of Childhood: The Evidence of Plutarch." Pages 183–96 in *Plutarch's Advice to the Bride and Groom and A Consolation to His Wife: English Translations, Commentary, Interpretive Essays, and Bibliography*. Edited by Sarah B. Pomeroy. New York: Oxford University Press, 1999.
Bradly, Keith. "Wet-Nursing at Rome: A Study in Social Relations." Pages 201–29 in *The Family in Ancient Rome: New Perspectives*. Edited by Beryl Rawson. Ithaca: Cornell University Press, 1986.
Browning, Don S. and Marcia J. Bunge, eds. *Children and Childhood in World Religions*. New Brunswick: Rutgers University Press, 2009.
Brueggemann, Walter. "Vulnerable Children, Divine Passion, and Human Obligation." Pages 399–422 in *The Child in the Bible*. Edited by Marcia J. Bunge, Terence E. Fretheim, and Beverly Roberts Gaventa. Grand Rapids: Eerdmans, 2008.
Bryan, Jocelyn. "Being and Becoming: Adolescence." Pages 135–58 in *Children of God: Towards a Theology of Childhood*. Edited by Angela Shier-Jones. Peterborough: Epworth, 2007.
Bunge, Marcia J., Terence E. Fretheim, and Beverly Roberts Gaventa, eds. *The Child in the Bible*. Grand Rapids: Eerdmans, 2008.
Bunge, Marcia J., Terence E. Fretheim, Beverly Roberts Gaventa, and John Wall. "Christianity." Pages 83–149 in *Children and Childhood in World Religion*. Edited by Don S. Browning and Marcia J. Bunge. New Brunswick: Rutgers University Press, 2009.
Bunge, Marcia J., Terence E. Fretheim, Beverly Roberts Gaventa, and John Wall, ed. *The Child in Christian Thought*. Grand Rapids: Eerdmans, 2001.

Burguiere, Andre, Christiane Klapisch-Zuber, Martine Segalen, and Francois Zonabend, eds. *A History of the Family*. Vols. 1-2. Cambridge: Belknap, 1996.
Burkill, T. Alec. "The Historical Development of the Story of the Syrophoenician Woman (Mark vii: 24-31)." *Novum Testamentum* 9.3 (1967): 161-77.
Bush, Archie C. and Joseph J. McHugh, "Patterns of Roman Marriage." *Ethnology* 14.1 (1975): 25-45.
Campbell, Ken M. ed. *Marriage and Family in the Biblical World*. Downers Grove: InterVarsity, 2003.
Carey, Greg. *Sinners: Jesus and His Earliest Followers*. Waco: Baylor University Press, 2009.
Caroll, John T. "Children in the Bible." *Interpretation* 55 (2001): 121-34.
Caroll, John T "'What Then Will This Child Become?': Perspectives on Children in the Gospel of Luke." Pages 177-94 in *The Child in the Bible*. Edited by Marcia J. Bunge, Terence E. Fretheim, and Beverly Roberts Gaventa. Grand Rapids: Eerdmans, 2008.
Carp, Teresa C. "'Puer senex' in Roman and Medieval Thought." *Latomus* 39.3 (1980): 736-9.
Catullus, Tibullus. Catullus. Tibullus. Pervigilium Veneris. Translated by F. W. Cornish, J. P. Postgate, J. W. Mackail. Revised by G. P. Goold. Loeb Classical Library 6. Cambridge: Harvard University Press, 1913.
Celsus. *On Medicine, Volume I: Books 1-4*. Translated by W. G. Spencer. Loeb Classical Library 292. Cambridge: Harvard University Press, 1935.
Chapin, Anne P. "Boys Will Be Boys: Youth and Gender Identity in the Theran Frescoes." Pages 229-56 in *Constructions of Childhood in Ancient Greece and Italy*. Edited by Ada Cohen and Jeremy B. Rutter. Vol. 41 of *Hesperia Supplements*. Princeton: The American School of Classical Studies at Athens, 2007.
Chariton. *Callirhoe*. Edited and translated by G. P. Goold. Loeb Classical Library 481. Cambridge: Harvard University Press, 1995.
Cicero. Translated by Harry Caplan et al. 29 vols. Loeb Classical Library. Cambridge: Harvard University Press, 1954-99.
Clement of Alexandria. Translated by William Wilson. Edinburg: T&T Clark, 1867.
Cohen, Ada and Jeremy B. Rutter, eds. *Constructions of Childhood in Ancient Greece and Italy*, Vol. 41 of *Hesperia Supplements*. Princeton: The American School of Classical Studies at Athens, 2007.
Cohen, Shaye J. D. "Introduction." Pages 1-8 in *The Jewish Family in Antiquity*. Edited by Shaye J. D. Cohen. Atlanta: Scholars, 1993.
Cohen, Shaye J. D., ed. *The Jewish Family in Antiquity*. Atlanta: Scholars, 1993.
Collins, Adela Yarbro. *Mark: A Commentary*. Hermenia; Minneapolis: Fortress, 2007.
Columella. *On Agriculture, Volume I: Books 1-4*. Translated by Harrison Boyd Ash. Loeb Classical Library 361. Cambridge: Harvard University Press, 1941.
Corbier, Mireille. "Child Exposure and Abandonment." Pages 52-73 in *Childhood, Class and Kin in the Roman World*. Edited by Suzanne Dixon. London: Routledge, 2001.
Cotter, Wendy. *The Christ of the Miracle Stores*. Grand Rapids: Baker Academic, 2010.
Cribiore, Raffaella. *Gymnastics of the Mind: Greek Education in Hellenistic and Roman Egypt*. Princeton: Princeton University Press, 2001.
Crossan, John Dominic. "The Seed Parables of Jesus." *Journal of Biblical Literature* 92.2 (1973): 244-66.
Culpepper, R. Alan. *Mark*. Smyth & Helwys Bible Commentary. Macon: Smyth & Helwys, 2007.

Dahl, Nils. "Parables of Growth." Pages 141–66 in *Jesus in the Memory of the Early Church*. Minneapolis: Augsburg, 1976.
Danove, Paul. "The Narrative Rhetoric of Mark's Ambiguous Characterization of the Disciples." *Journal for the study of the New Testament* 70 (1998): 21–37.
Deeks, David and Angela Shier-Jones, "Moulding and Shaping: Education." Pages 63–83 in *Children of God: Towards a Theology of Childhood*. Edited by Angela Shier-Jones Peterborough: Epworth, 2007.
Demetrius. *On Style*. Translated by Stephen Halliwell, W. Hamilton Fyfe, Doreen C. Innes, W. Rhys Roberts. Revised by Donald A. Russell. Loeb Classical Library. Cambridge: Harvard University Press, 1995.
DeVries, Dawn. "'Be Converted and Become as Little Children': Friedrich Schleiermacher on the Religious Significance of Childhood." Pages 329–49 in *The Child in Christian Thought*. Edited by Marcia J. Bunge. Grand Rapids: Eerdmans, 2001.
Dio Cassius. *Roman History*. Translated by Earnest Cary, Herbert B. Foster. 9 vols. Loeb Classical Library. Cambridge: Harvard University Press, 1914–27.
Diodorus Siculus. *Library of History, Volume II: Books 2.35-4.58*. Translated by C. H. Oldfather. Loeb Classical Library 303. Cambridge: Harvard University Press, 1935.
Dixon, Suzanne, ed. *Childhood, Class and Kin in the Roman World*. London: Routledge, 2001.
Dixon, Suzanne. *The Roman Family*. Baltimore: Johns Hopkins University Press, 1992.
Dixon, Suzanne. "The Sentimental Ideal of the Roman Family." Pages 99–113 in *Marriage, Divorce, and Children in Ancient Rome*. Edited by Beryl Rawson. Oxford: Oxford University Press, 1991.
Dobb, David and Christopher Faraone, eds. *Initiation in Ancient Greek Rituals and Narratives*. London: Routledge, 2003.
Dodd, C. H. "The Kingdom of God." Pages 175–94 in *The Parables of the Kingdom*. New York: Charles Scribner's Sons, 1961.
Dolansky, Fanny. "Coming of Age in Rome: The History and Social Significance of Assuming the *Toga Virilis*." Master's dissertation, University of Victoria, 1999.
Donahue, John R. *The Theology and Setting of Discipleship in the Gospel of Mark*. Milwaukee: Marquette University Press, 1983.
Douglas, Mary. *Purity and Danger: An Analysis of Concepts of Pollution and Taboo*. England: Penguin Books, 1970.
Dowd, Sharyn Echols. *Prayer, Power and the Problem of Suffering: Mark 11: 22-25 in the Context of Markan Theology*. Atlanta: Scholars Press, 1988
Drury, John. *The Parables in the Gospels*. New York: Crossroad, 1985.
Ellis, Robinson. *Poems and Fragments of Catullus*. London: Bradbury, Evans and Co., 1871.
Engels, D. "The Problem of Female Infanticide in the Greco-Roman World." *Classical Philology* 75 (1980): 112–20.
Epictetus. *Discourses*. Translated by W. A. Oldfather. 2 vols. Loeb Classical Library. Cambridge: Harvard University Press, 1925-8.
Eubanks, Larry L. "Mark 10: 13-16." *Review & Expositor* 91.3 (1994): 401–5.
Evans, Elizabeth C. *Physiognomics in the Ancient World*. Philadelphia: American Philosophical Society, 1969.
Eyben, Emiel. "Family Planning in Greco-Roman Antiquity." *Ancient Society* 11/12 (1980): 5–28.
Eyben, Emiel. "Fathers and Sons." Pages 114–43 in *Marriage, Divorce, and Children in Ancient Rome*. Edited by Beryl Rawson. Oxford: Oxford University Press, 1991.

Fantham, Elaine. "Sex, Status and Survival in Hellenistic Athens: A Study of Women in New Comedy." *Phoenix* 29 (1975): 44–74.

Fass, Paula S., ed. chief. *Encyclopedia of Children and Childhood in History and Society, Vols. I-III*. New York: Macmillan Reference USA, 2004.

Fewell, Danna Nolan. *The Children of Israel: Reading the Bible for the Sake of Our Children*. Nashville: Abingdon, 2003.

Forster, E.M. *A Room With A View*. Norfolk: New Directions, 1922.

Fossier, Robert. "The Feudal Era (Eleventh–Thirteenth Century)." Pages 407–29 in *A History of the Family, Volume I*. Edited by Andre Burguiere, Christiane Klapisch-Zuber, Martine Segalen, and Francois Zonabend. Cambridge: Belknap, 1996.

Francis, James. "Children and Childhood in the New Testament." Pages 65–85 in *The Family in Theological Perspective*. Edited by Stephen Baron. Edinburgh: T&T Clark, 1996.

Frank, Richard I. "Augustus' Legislation on Marriage and Children." *Cal Studies in Classical Antiquity* 8 (1975): 41–52.

Fretheim, Terence. "'God Was with the Boy' (Genesis 21:20): Children in the Book of Genesis." Pages 3–23 in *The Child in the Bible*. Edited by Marcia J. Bunge, Terence E. Fretheim, and Beverly Roberts Gaventa. Grand Rapids: Eerdmans, 2008.

Galen. *Method of Medicine*. Edited and translated by Ian Johnston, G. H. R. Horsley. 3 vols. Loeb Classical Library. Cambridge: Harvard University Press, 2011.

Galen. *On the Natural Faculties*. Translated by A. J. Brock. Loeb Classical Library 71. Cambridge: Harvard University Press, 1916.

Garroway, Kristine Hendrickson. *Children in the Ancient Near Eastern Household*. Winona Lake: Eisenbrauns, 2014.

Gaventa, Beverly Roberts. "Finding a Place for Children in the Letters of Paul." Pages 233–48 in *The Child in the Bible*. Edited by Marcia J. Bunge, Terence E. Fretheim, and Beverly Roberts Gaventa. Grand Rapids: Eerdmans, 2008.

Golden, Mark. *Children and Childhood in Classical Athens*. Baltimore: Johns Hopkins University Press, 1993.

Golden, Mark. "Did the Ancients Care When Their Children Died?" *Greece and Rome* 35.2 (1988): 152–63.

Greek Anthology. Translated by W. R. Paton. 5 vols. Revised by Michael A. Tueller. Loeb Classical Library. Cambridge: Harvard University Press, 1918–2014.

Grey, Matthew J. "Becoming as a Little Child: Elements of Ritual Rebirth in Ancient Judaism and Early Christianity." *Studia Antiqua* 1 (2001): 63–85.

Gundry-Volf, Judith. "Children in the Gospel of Mark, with Special Attention to Jesus's Blessing of the Children (Mark 10: 13-16)and the Purpose of Mark." Pages 143–76 in *The Child in the Bible*. Edited by Marcia J. Bunge, Terence E. Fretheim, and Beverly Roberts Gaventa. Grand Rapids: Eerdmans, 2008.

Gundry-Volf, Judith. "The Least and the Greatest: Children in the New Testament." Pages 29–60 in *The Child in Christian Thought*. Edited by Marcia J. Bunge. Grand Rapids: Eerdmans, 2001.

Gundry-Volf, Judith. "Mark 9: 33-37." *Interpretation* 53 (1999): 57–61.

Gundry-Volf, Judith. "Putting *The Moral Vision of the New Testament* into Focus: A Review." *Bulletin for Biblical Research* 9 (1999): 277–87.

Gundry-Volf, Judith. "To Such as These Belongs the Reign of God: Jesus and Children." *Theology Today* 56 (1999): 469–80.

Hanson, K. C. "The Galilean Fishing Economy and the Jesus Tradition." *Biblical Theology Bulletin* 27 (1997): 99–111.

Harrill, J. Albert. "Coming of Age and Putting on Christ: The Toga Virilis Ceremony, Its Paraenesis, and Paul's Interpretation of Baptism in Galatians." *Novum Testamentum* 44.3 (2002): 252–77.

Harris, W. V. "Child-Exposure in the Roman Empire." *The Journal of Roman Studies* 84 (1994): 1–22.

Hawley, Richard. "Practicing What You Preach: Plutarch's Sources and Treatment." Pages 116–27 in *Plutarch's Advice to the Bride and Groom and A Consolation to His Wife: English Translations, Commentary, Interpretive Essays, and Bibliography*. Edited by Sarah B. Pomeroy. New York: Oxford University Press, 1999.

Hersch, Karen K. *The Roman Wedding: Ritual and Meaning in Antiquity*. New York: Cambridge University Press, 2010.

Hopkins, M. K. "The Age of Roman Girls at Marriage." *Population Studies* 18.3 (1965): 309–27.

Horn, Cornelia B. and Robert R. Phenix, eds. *Children in Late Ancient Christianity*. Tübingen: Mohr Siebeck, 2009.

Howard, Melanie. "Mothers in Mark: A Socio-Literary Exploration of Maternal Imagery and the Value-Reproductive Role of Mothers in the Gospel of Mark." Ph.D. diss., Princeton Theological Seminary, 2015.

Huber, Lynn R. *Like a Bride Adorned: Reading Metaphor in John's Apocalypse*. New York: T&T Clark, 2007.

Humphrey, Edith. *The Ladies and the Cities*. Journal for the Study of the Pseudepigrapha Supplement Series 17. Sheffield: Sheffield Academic Press, 1995.

Hurtado, Larry W. "Following Jesus in the Gospel of Mark—and Beyond." Pages 9–29 in *Patterns of Discipleship in the New Testament*. Edited by Richard N Longenecker. Grand Rapids: Eerdmans, 1996.

Interpretation 55.2 (2001).

Ivanovska, Inta. "Baptized Infants and Pagan Rituals: Cyprian *versus* Augustine." Pages 46–73 in *Children in Late Ancient Christianity*. Edited by Christian Laes, Katarina Mustakallio, and Ville Vuolanto. Interdisciplinary Studies in Ancient Culture and Religion 15. Walpole: Peeters, 2015.

Jensen, David H. *Graced Vulnerability: A Theology of Childhood*. Cleveland: Pilgrim, 2005.

Jeremias, Joachim. *The Parables of Jesus*. Translated by S.H. Hooke. New York: Charles Scribner's Sons, 1962.

Jindřich Mánek, "Fishers of Men." *Novum Testamentum* 2.2 (1957): 138–41.

"Joseph & Aseneth." Pages 473–503 in *The Apocryphal Old Testament*. Translated by David Cook and edited by H. F. D. Sparks. Oxford: Oxford University Press, 1984. Online http://www.markgoodacre.org/aseneth/translat.htm accessed on 4/5/2015.q

Josephus. *Jewish Antiquities*. Translated by H. St. J. Thackeray et al. 9 vols. Loeb Classical Library. Cambridge: Harvard University Press, 1930–65.

Juel, Donald. *A Master of Surprise: Mark Interpreted*. Minneapolis: Augsburg Fortress, 2002.

Jung, C. G. "The Psychology of the Child Archetype." Pages 113–31 in *Psyche & Symbol: A Selection from the Writings of C.G. Jung*. Edited by Violet S. deLaszlo. New York: Doubleday Anchor, 1958.

Jung, C. G. "The Special Phenomenology of the Child Archetype." Pages 132–47 in *Psyche & Symbol: A Selection from the Writings of C.G. Jung*. Edited by Violet S. deLaszlo. New York: Doubleday Anchor, 1958.

Juvenal. *Juvenal and Persius*. Edited and translated by Susanna Morton Braund. Loeb Classical Library 91. Cambridge: Harvard University Press, 2004.

Juvenal. *The Sixteen Satires*. Translated by Peter Green. London: Penguin Books, 2004.

Kelber, W. H. *The Kingdom in Mark: A New Place and a New Time*. Philadelphia: Fortress Press, 1974.

Kelber, W. H. "Mark 14: 32-42:Gethsemane; Passion Christology and Discipleship Failure." *Zeitschrift Für Die Neutestamentliche Wissenschaft Und Die Kunde Der Älteren Kirche* 63.3–4 (1972): 166–87.

Koepf-Taylor, Laurel W. *Give Me Children or I Shall Die: Children and Communal Survival in Biblical Literature*. Minneapolis: Fortress, 2013.

Kottsieper, Ingo. "'We have a Little Sister': Aspects of the Brother-Sister Relationship in Ancient Israel." Pages 49–80 in *Families and Family Relations*. Edited by Jan Willem and Athalya Brenner. Netherlands: Deo Publishing, 2000.

Kuss, Otto. "Zum Sinngehalt des Doppelgleichnisses vom Senfkorn und Sauerteig." *Studia Biblica et Orientalia* 40 (1959): 641–53.

Laes, Christian, Katarina Mustakallio, and Ville Vuolanto, eds. *Children and Family in Late Antiquity*. Interdisciplinary Studies in Ancient Culture and Religion 15. Walpole: Peeters, 2015.

Laes, Christian, Katarina Mustakallio, and Ville Vuolanto. "Desperately Different? *Delicia* Children in the Roman Household." Pages 298–326 in *Early Christian Families in Context, An Interdisciplinary Dialogue*. Edited by David L. Balch and Carolyn Osiek. Grand Rapids: Eerdmans, 2003.

Lapsley, Jacqueline E. "'Look! The Children and I Are as Signs and Portents in Israel': Children in Isaiah." Pages 82–102 in *The Child in the Bible*. Edited by Marcia J. Bunge, Terence E. Fretheim, and Beverly Roberts Gaventa. Grand Rapids: Eerdmans, 2008.

Lardinois, Roland. "The World Order and the Family Institution in India." Pages 566–600 in *A History of the Family, Volume I*. Edited by Andre Burguiere, Christiane Klapisch-Zuber, Martine Segalen, and Francois Zonabend. Cambridge: Belknap, 1996.

Lawton, Carol L. "Children in Classical Attic Votive Reliefs." Pages 41–60 in *Constructions of Childhood in Ancient Greece and Italy*. Edited by Ada Cohen and Jeremy B. Rutter. Vol. 41 of *Hesperia Supplements*. Princeton: The American School of Classical Studies at Athens, 2007.

Legasse, S. *Jesu et l'enfant: "Enfants", "petits" et "simples" dans la tradition synoptique*. Paris: Librairie Lecoffre, 1968.

Lewittes, Mendell. *Jewish Marriage: Rabbinic Law, Legend, and Custom*. London: Jason Aronson Inc., 1994.

Lindermann, Andreas. "Die Kinder und die Gottesherrschaft: Markus 10, 13-16 und die Stellung der Kinder in der späthellenistischen Gesellschaft und im Urchristentum." Pages 109–34 in *Die Evangelien und die Apostelgeschichte: Studien zu ihrer Theologie und zu ihrer Geschichte*. Wissenschaftliche Untersuchungen zum Neuen Testament 241. Tübingen: J. C. B. Mohr, 2009.

Livy. *History of Rome*. Translated by B. O. Foster et al. 14 vols. Loeb Classical Library. Cambridge: Harvard University Press, 1919–59.

Longenecker, Bruce W. *2 Esdras*. Sheffield: Sheffield Academic Press, 1995.

Longinus. *On the Sublime*. Translated by Stephen Halliwell, W. Hamilton Fyfe, Doreen C. Innes, W. Rhys Roberts. Revised by Donald A. Russell. Loeb Classical Library 199. Cambridge: Harvard University Press, 1995.

Lucretius. *On the Nature of Things*. Translated by W. H. D. Rouse. Revised by Martin F. Smith. Loeb Classical Library 181. Cambridge: Harvard University Press, 1924.

M'Bartenurach, Rabbeinu Ovadiah. *Mishnah A New Integrated Translation and Commentary.* Accessed Online 2/2/2017: http://www.emishnah.com/

Macrobius. *Saturnalia.* Edited and translated by Robert A. Kaster. 3 vols. Loeb Classical Library. Cambridge: Harvard University Press, 2011.

Malbon, Elizabeth Struthers. "Disciples/Crowds/Whoever: Markan Characters and Readers." *Novum Testamentum* 28.2 (1986): 104–30.

Malbon, Elizabeth Struthers. "Fallible Followers: Women and Men in the Gospel of Mark." *Semeia* 28 (1983): 29–48.

Malbon, Elizabeth Struthers. *In the Company of Jesus: Characters in Mark's Gospel.* Louisville: Westminster John Knox, 2000.

Malina, Bruce J. *The New Testament World: Insights from Cultural Anthropology.* Atlanta: John Knox Press, 1981.

Manning, C. E. *Seneca's "Ad Marciam."* Mnemosyne Supplement 69. Boston: Brill, 1981.

Marcus, Joel. "Blanks and Gaps in the Markan Parable of the Sower." *Biblical Interpretation* 5.3 (1997): 247–62.

Marcus, Joel. *Mystery of the Kingdom of God.* SBL Dissertation Series 90. Atlanta: Scholars Press, 1986.

Marcus, Joel. *Mark 1–8.* Anchor Bible 27. London: Doubleday, 2000.

Marcus, Joel. *Mark 8–16.* New Haven, Conn.: Yale University Press, 2009.

Marrou, H.I. *A History of Education in Antiquity.* Translated by George Lamb. New York: SHeed and Wrd, 1956.

Martial. *Epigrams.* Edited and translated by D. R. Shackleton Bailey. 3 vols. Loeb Classical Library. Cambridge: Harvard University Press, 1993.

Martin, Dale. *The Corinthian Body.* New Haven: Yale University Press, 1995.

Maurus Servius Honoratus. *Commentary on the Eclogues of Vergil.* Edited by Georgius Thilo. Accessed online on 3/12/2018: http://www.perseus.tufts.edu/hopper/text?doc=Perseus%3Atext%3A2007.01.0091%3Apoem%3D4%3Acommline%3D49.

Mc Vann, Mark Edward. "Baptism, Miracles, and Boundary Jumping in Mark." *Biblical Theology Bulletin* 21.4 (1991): 151–7.

Mc Vann, Mark Edward. *Dwelling Among the Tombs: Discourse, Discipleship, and the Gospel of Mark 4: 35-5:43.* PhD diss., Emory University, 1984.

Mc Vann, Mark Edward. "General Introductory Bibliography for Ritual Studies." *Semeia* 67 1994: 227–32.

Mc Vann, Mark Edward. "Introduction." *Semeia* 67 (1994): 7–12.

Mc Vann, Mark Edward. "One of the Prophets: Matthew's Testing Narrative as a Rite of Passage." *Biblical Theology Bulletin* 23.1 (1993): 14–20.

Mc Vann, Mark Edward. "The 'Passion' of John the Baptist and Jesus before Pilate: Mark's Warnings about Kings and Governors." *Biblical Theology Bulletin* 38.4 (2008): 152–7.

Mc Vann, Mark Edward. "Reading Mark Ritually: Honor-Shame and the Ritual of Baptism." *Semeia* 67 (1994): 179–98.

Müller, Peter. *In der Mitte der Gemeinde: Kinder im Neuen Testament.* Neukirchen-Vluyn: Neukirchener, 1992.

Myers, Ched. *Binding the Strong Man: A Political Reading of Mark's Story of Jesus.* Mary Knoll: Orbis Books, 1988.

Nathan, Geoffrey. *The Family in Late Antiquity: The Rise of Christianity and the Endurance of Tradition.* London: Routledge, 2000.

Neils, Jenifer and John H. Oakley, eds. *Coming of Age in Ancient Greece: Images of Childhood from the Classical Past.* New Haven: Yale University Press, 2003.

Neufeld, E. *Ancient Hebrew Marriage Laws: With Special References to General Semitic Laws and Customs.* London: Longmans, Green and Co., 1944.
Newey, Edmund. *Children of God: The Child as Source of Theological Anthropology.* Surrey: Ashgate, 2012.
Nicolaus of Damascus: *Life of Augustus*, fragment 127: 4.8-9(C.M.Hall). Accessed online on 3/1/2018: *http://www.attalus.org/translate/nicolaus1.html*
Osborne, B. A. E. "Peter: Stumbling-Block and Satan." *Novum Testamentum* 15 (1973): 187–90.
Ovid. *Fasti.* Translated by James G. Frazer. Revised by G. P. Goold. Loeb Classical Library 253. Cambridge: Harvard University Press, 1931.
Ovid. *Heroides. Amores.* Translated by Grant Showerman. Revised by G. P. Goold. Loeb Classical Library 41. Cambridge: Harvard University Press, 1914.
Padilla, Mark, ed. *Rites of Passage in Ancient Greece: Literature, Religion, Society.* Lewisburg: Bucknell University Press, 1999.
Parker, Julie Faith. *Valuable and Vulnerable: Children in the Hebrew Bible, Especially the Elisha Cycle.* Providence: Brown Judaic Studies, 2013.
Parsenios, George. *Departure and Consolation: The Johannine Farewell Discourses in Light of Greco-Roman Literature.* Boston: Brill, 2005.
Persius. *Juvenal and Persius.* Edited and translated by Susanna Morton Braund. Loeb Classical Library 91. Cambridge: Harvard University Press, 2004.
Peskowitz, Miriam. "Domesticity and the Spindle." Pages 118–34 in *Families and Family Relationships as Represented in Early Judaism and Early Christianities: Texts and Fictions.* Edited by Jan Willem Van Henten and Athalya Brenner. STAR 2. Leiden: Deo.
Philo. Translated by F. H. Colson, G. H. Whitaker. 10 vols. Loeb Classical Library. Cambridge: Harvard University Press, 1929–62.
Plato. *Plato in Twelve Volumes.* Translated by R. G. Bury. Cambridge: Harvard University Press; London: Heinemann, 1967–8.
Pliny the Elder. *Natural History.* Translated by H. Rackham et al. 10 vols. Loeb Classical Library. Cambridge: Harvard University Press, 1938–62.
Pliny the Younger. *Letters.* Translated by Betty Radice. 2 vols. Loeb Classical Library. Cambridge: Harvard University Press, 1969.
Plutarch. *Lives.* Translated by Bernadotte Perrin. 11 vols. Loeb Classical Library. Cambridge: Harvard University Press, 1914–26.
Plutarch. *Moralia.* Translated by Frank Cole Babbitt et al. 15 vols. Loeb Classical Library. Cambridge: Harvard University Press, 1927–69.
Plutarch. *Plutarch's Morals.* Translated from the Greek by several hands. Corrected and revised by. William W. Goodwin, PH. D. Boston: Little, Brown, and Company. Cambridge. Press Of John Wilson and son. 1874.
Pomeroy, Sarah B. *Families in Classical and Hellenistic Greece: Representations and Realities.* Oxford: Oxford University Press, 1997.
Pomeroy, Sarah B., ed. *Plutarch's Advice to the Bride and Groom and A Consolation to His Wife: English Translations, Commentary, Interpretive Essays, and Bibliography.* New York: Oxford University Press, 1999.
Pomeroy, Sarah B. "Reflections on Plutarch's, *A Consolation to His Wife*." Pages 75–84 in *Plutarch's Advice to the Bride and Groom and A Consolation to His Wife: English Translations, Commentary, Interpretive Essays, and Bibliography.* Edited by Sarah B. Pomeroy. New York: Oxford University Press, 1999.
Pomeroy, Sarah B. "'Technikia Kai Mousikia:' The Education of Women in the 4th Century and Hellenistic Period." *American Journal of Ancient History* 2 (1977): 51–68.

Powers, Jennifer Goodall. "Ancient Weddings." SUNY Albany, 1997. Accessed online 3/10/2018. https://archive.is/tdsYz

Propertius. *Elegies*. Edited and translated by G. P. Goold. Loeb Classical Library 18. Cambridge: Harvard University Press, 1990.

Quintilian. *The Orator's Education*. Edited and translated by Donald A. Russell. 5 vols. Loeb Classical Library. Cambridge: Harvard University Press, 2002.

Raemer, Ross. "Jewish Mothers and Daughters in the Greco-Roman World." Pages 89–112 in *The Jewish Family in Antiquity*. Edited by Shaye J. D. Cohen. Atlanta: Scholars, 1993.

Rahner, Karl. "Ideas for a Theology of Childhood." Pages 33–50 in *Theological Investigations, Volume VIII: Further Theology of the Spiritual Life II*. Translated by David Bourke. New York: Herder and Herder, 1971.

Rawson, Beryl. "Adult-Child Relationships in Roman Society." Pages 7–30 in *Marriage, Divorce, and Children in Ancient Rome*. Edited by Beryl Rawson. Oxford: Oxford University Press, 1991.

Rawson, Beryl. *Children and Childhood in Roman Italy*. Oxford: Oxford University Press, 2003.

Rawson, Beryl. "Children as Cultural Symbols: Imperial Ideology in the Second Century." Pages 21–42 in *Childhood, Class and Kin in the Roman World*. Edited by Suzanne Dixon. London: Routledge, 2001.

Rawson, Beryl. "Children in the Roman *Familia*." Pages 170–200 in *The Family in Ancient Rome: New Perspectives*. Edited by Beryl Rawson. Ithaca: Cornell University Press, 1986.

Rawson, Beryl. "Death, Burial, and Commemoration of Children in Roman Italy." Pages 277–97 in *Early Christian Families in Context, An Interdisciplinary Dialogue*. Edited by David L. Balch and Carolyn Osiek. Grand Rapids: Eerdmans, 2003.

Rawson, Beryl, ed. *The Family in Ancient Rome: New Perspectives*. Ithaca: Cornell University Press, 1986.

Rawson, Beryl. "Family Life among the Lower Classes at Rome in the First Two Centuries of the Empire." *Classical Philology* 61 (1966): 71–83.

Reardon, Bryan P. *Collected Ancient Greek Novels*. Berkeley: University of California Press, 1989.

Rhoads, David. "Jesus and the Syrophoenician Woman in Mark: A Narrative-Critical Study." *Journal of the American Academy of Religion* 62.2 (1994): 343–75.

Rose, H. J. *Roman Questions of Plutarch: A New Translation with Introductory Essays and Running Commentary*. New York: Biblo & Tannen, 1974.

Saller, Richard. "Corporal Punishment, Authority, and Obedience in the Roman Household." Pages 144–65 in *Marriage, Divorce, and Children in Ancient Rome*. Edited by Beryl Rawson. Oxford: Oxford University Press, 1991.

Saller, Richard. *Patriarchy, Property and Death in the Roman Family*. Cambridge: Cambridge University Press, 1994.

Satlow, Michael L. *Jewish Marriage in Antiquity*. Princeton: Princeton University Press, 2001.

Schnackenburg, R. *God's Rule and God's Kingdom*. Freiburg/Montreal: Herder/Palm, 1963.

Schreiber, Johannes. "Die Christologie des Markusevangeliums." *Zeitschrift für Theologie und Kirche* 58 (1961): 175–83.

Schroeder, Hans-Hartmut. *Eltern un Kinder in der Verkundigung Jesu: Eine hermeneutische und exegetische Untersuchung*. Theologische Forschung 53. Hamburg-Bergstedt: Reich, 1972.

Seneca the Younger. Translated by John W. Basore, Richard M. Gummere, et al. 11 vols. Loeb Classical Library. Cambridge: Harvard University Press, 1917–28.

Shaw, Brent D. "The Age of Roman Girls at Marriage: Some Reconsiderations." *The Journal of Roman Studies* 77 (1987): 30–46.

Shier-Jones, Angela ed. *Children of God: Towards a Theology of Childhood*. Peterborough: Epworth, 2007.

Shreeve, Esther. "Birth: Pain and Potential." Pages 21–40 in *Children of God: Towards a Theology of Childhood*. Edited by Angela Shier-Jones. Peterborough: Epworth, 2007.

Shweder, Richard A., Thomas R. Bidell, Anne C. Dailey, Suzanne D. Dixon, Peggy J. Miller, and John Modell eds. *The Child: An Encyclopedic Companion*. Chicago: University of Chicago Press, 2009.

Snodgrass, Klyne. *Stories with Intent*. Grand Rapids: Eerdmans, 2008.

Soranus, *Gynecology*. Translated by O Temkin. Baltimore: Johns Hopkins University Press: 1956.

Spitaler, P. "Welcoming a Child as a Metaphor for Welcoming God's Kingdom: A Close Reading of Mark 10.13-16." *Journal for the Study of the New Testament* 31.4 (2009): 423–46.

Statius. *Silvae*. Edited and translated by D. R. Shackleton Bailey. Revised by Christopher A. Parrott. Loeb Classical Library 206. Cambridge: Harvard University Press, 2015.

Steinberg, Naomi. *The World of the Child in the Hebrew Bible*. Sheffield: Sheffield Phoenix Press, 2013.

Strabo. *Geography*. Translated by Horace Leonard Jones. 8 vols. Loeb Classical Library. Cambridge: Harvard University Press, 1917–32.

Strange, William A. *Children in the Early Church: Children in the Ancient World, the New Testament and the Early Church*. Carlisle: Paternoster, 1996.

Suetonius. *Lives of the Caesars*. Translated by J. C. Rolfe. Introduction by K. R. Bradley. 2 vols. Loeb Classical Library. Cambridge: Harvard University Press, 1914–98.

Sweat, Laura. *Theological Role of Paradox*. Library of New Testament Studies 492. London: T&T Clark, 2013.

Tacitus. *Annals*. Translated by John Jackson. 3 vols. Loeb Classical Library. Cambridge, MA: Harvard University Press, 1931–7.

Tannehill, Robert C. "The Disciples in Mark: The Function of a Narrative Role." Pages 135–60 in *The Shape of the Gospel: New Testament Essays*. Eugene: Cascade Books, 2007.

Tannehill, Robert C. "The Disciples in Mark: The Function of a Narrative Role." *The Journal of Religion* 57.4 (1977): 386–405.

Theology Today 56 (2000).

Thompson, D.F.S. *Catullus*. Toronto: University of Toronto Press, 1997.

Thompson, Marinnae Meye. "Children in the Gospel of John." Pages 195–214 in *The Child in the Bible*. Edited by Marcia J. Bunge, Terence E. Fretheim, and Beverly Roberts Gaventa. Grand Rapids: Eerdmans, 2008.

Tolbert, Mary Ann. *Sowing the Gospel: Mark's Work in Literary-Historical Perspective*. Minneapolis: Augsburg Fortress, 1996.

Treggiari, Susan. "Marriage and Family in Roman Society." Pages 132–82 in *Marriage and Family in the Biblical World*. Edited by Ken M Campbell. Illinois: InterVarsity, 2003.

Treggiari, Susan. *Roman Marriage Iusti Coniuges from the Time of Cicero to the Time of Ulpian*. Oxford: Oxford University Press, 1991.

Turner, Victor Witter. "Betwixt and Between: The Liminal Period in *Rites de Passage*." Pages 93–111 in *The Forest of Symbols: Aspects of Ndembu Ritual*. Ithaca: Cornell University Press, 1967.

Turner, Victor Witter. "Liminality and *Communitas*." Pages 94–130 in *The Ritual Process: Structure and Anti-Structure*. Ithaca: Cornell University Press, 1969.

Tyson, Joseph B. "The Blindness of the Disciples in Mark." *Journal of Biblical Literature* 80.3 (1961): 261–8.

van Gennep, Arnold. *The Rites of Passage*. Translated by Monika Vizedom and Gabrielle Caffee. London: Routledge & Kegan Paul, 1960.

Van Henten, Jan Willem, and Athalya Brenner, eds. *Families and Family Relations*. Netherlands: Deo Publishing, 2000.

Via, Dan. *The Ethics of Mark's Gospel: In the Middle of Time*. Eugene: Wipf & Stock, 2005.

Weber, Hans Ruedi. *Jesus and the Children: Biblical Resources for Study and Preaching*. Atlanta: John Knox Press, 1994.

Weeden, Theodore J. "Heresy that necessitated Mark's Gospel." *Zeitschrift Für Die Neutestamentliche Wissenschaft Und Die Kunde Der Älteren Kirche* 59.3-4 (1968): 145–58.

Weeden, Theodore J. *Mark Traditions in Conflict*. Philadelphia: Fortress Press, 1971.

White, K. D. "The Parable of the Sower." *Journal of Theological Studies* 15 (1964): 300–7.

White, Keith and Haddon Willmer. *Entry Point: Towards Child Theology with Matthew 18*. London: WTL Publications, 2013.

White, Keith, and Haddon Willmer. "'He Placed a Little Child in the Midst': Jesus, the Kingdom, and Children." Pages 353–74 in *The Child in the Bible*. Edited by Marcia J. Bunge, Terence E. Fretheim, and Beverly Roberts Gaventa. Grand Rapids: Eerdmans, 2008.

Wiedemann, Thomas. *Adults and Children in the Roman Empire*. New York: Routledge, 1989.

Williams, Gordon. "Some Aspects of Roman Marriage Ceremonies and Ideals." *JoRS* 48 (1958): 16–29.

Wilson, Stephen M. *Making Men: The Male Coming-of-Age Theme in the Hebrew Bible*. New York: Exoford University Press, 2015.

Wood, D, ed. *The Church and Childhood*. Oxford: Blackwell, 1994.

Wypustek, Andrzej. *Images of Eternal Beauty in Funerary Verse Inscriptions of the Hellenistic and Greco-Roman Periods*. Boston: Brill, 2013.

Yarbrough, O. Larry. "Parents and Children in the Jewish Family of Antiquity." Pages 39–59 in *The Jewish Family in Antiquity*. Edited by Shaye J. D. Cohen. Atlanta: Scholars, 1993.

Zuck, Roy B. *Precious in His Sight: Childhood & Children in the Bible*. Grand Rapids: Baker Books, 1996.

Index

abandoned/abandonment/abandoning 5, 7, 100, 103, 117, 129, 130, 131, 139
adolescent/adolescence 6, 17, 34
adopted/adoption 10, 13, 117
Apuleius 76–7, 142
Aristotle 19, 31–2, 42
Augustan marriage laws 7, 51n139

boy/boyhood 4, 8, 10, 12, 25, 26, 30, 34, 36–41, 55, 47, 48–9, 51–2, 57, 66–8, 68–74 (*toga virilis*), 75, 77, 84, 87, 107–9 (the healing of the spirit possessed boy), 128

children
as valuable 9, 74
as vulnerable/ vulnerability of 9, 22, 57, 66, 84, 103, 105, 109.
nonadult 8n58, 99n45, 103
qualities of
negative 27–39
positive 39–48
Chariton 76n81, 77n86
Cicero 5, 7, 19, 27, 30, 4–45, 47, 69, 71, 76
coming of age 1, 3, 4n14, 8, 10, 44, 67, 68–74 (*toga virilis*), 74–84 (wedding ceremony), 87, 140n2

daughter 6, 22–24, 27, 40, 49, 53–5 (Plutarch's daughter in *Consolation to his Wife*), 77n88, 80, 81, 99n45, 103–6 (Jairus's daughter), 106–7 (Syrophoenician Woman's daughter), 108, 109, 124, 125, 135
death 2, 5, 12, 13, 23, 25, 27–9, 34–5, 40, 47–56 (death of children), 57, 60–1, 62, 65, 66, 67, 69, 72, 73, 77, 83, 84, 91, 103–6, 109, 116, 123–135 (Jesus's predictions of death), 137, 139, 140
Douglas, Mary 2, 58, 62, 65–7, 84

Epictetus 36, 121

father 6, 9, 12, 19, 21, 22, 28, 36, 40, 41, 49, 51, 52, 59, 69, 72, 73, 81, 82, 90, 98, 100, 105, 107–8, 110, 112, 120, 128, 130, 134. *See also God as father/parent*
funerary
inscriptions 4, 27, 48–52, 54, 56, 57, 83, 124, 135, 138
rites 26, 50, 53, 58, 65, 125. *See also Death*

Galen 31–2, 38n62–3
girl/girlhood 4, 7, 8, 12, 22, 26, 27, 40, 49–52, 54–5, 57, 59n6, 62, 68, 74–84 (wedding ceremony), 87, 103–6 (Jairus's daughter), 106–7 (Syrophoenician Woman's daughter), 109, 124, 138
God (Judeo-Christian) 14, 15, 18, 24, 26, 81, 90n9, 95, 96, 97, 98, 99, 100, 102, 111, 112, 114, 117, 119n62, 122, 124, 126, 128, 129, 130–4, 135, 137, 139
as parent/father 21, 24, 98, 99, 100, 103, 111, 112, 117, 120, 122, 126, 128, 130–4, 135
gods/goddesses (Greco-Roman): 35, 40, 50, 51, 70, 72, 73, 76, 78, 79

infanticide 20
Isaac 32, 33
Ishmael 32, 33

Jerusalem 97, 126
Jesus
child/son of God 20, 26, 100, 103, 112, 122, 123, 124, 131, 132, 135
and children 1, 2, 11, 12, 16, 18, 20, 22, 23, 24, 25, 26, 84, 87–100, 103–9, 117, 135, 137–8, 140

Son of Man 24, 26, 100, 112, 121, 123–7, 129, 132, 135
Jairus/Jairus's daughter 24, 103–6, 107, 108, 109
John the Baptist 123, 140
Josephus 79–80
Juvenal 30

Kingdom of God 1, 2, 20, 23, 24, 25, 56, 58, 63, 64, 84, 85, 87–100 (chapter 4), 101, 102, 116, 132–4, 137, 138, 139, 140

liminal/liminality 10, 16, 25, 58, 67, 68, 71, 72, 74, 77–8, 87, 98–101, 103–9 (children as liminal), 124, 130, 132, 139, 140
   as defined by Arnold van Gennep 58–61
   as defined by Victor Turner 61–5
Livy 33
Longinus 35
Lucretius 28, 34, 44

Macrobius 69–70
Manhood 10, 41, 57, 66, 68–74 (*toga virilis ceremony as transition from boyhood to manhood*)
marriage 2, 4, 5, 6, 7, 8, 9, 12, 22, 49–51, 55, 57, 58, 59, 68, 74–84 (wedding/marriage ceremony), 87, 105, 135, 137, 138, 140. *See also Wedding Ceremony*
masculinity 31 (Greco-Roman physiognomy)
maturation 10, 37, 48. *See also rites of passage, toga virilis, wedding ceremony*
menstrual/menstruation/menarche 59n6, 62, 83n116, 84
metaphor/metaphorical 1, 15, 16, 19, 23, 27, 28, 44, 45, 47, 52, 60, 64, 66, 76, 89n7, 90–1, 93, 95, 100, 106–7, 110, 118–19, 124–5, 126–7, 137, 141
mother/motherhood 4, 9, 22, 39, 40, 41, 42n88, 49–52, 54, 59, 60, 66, 75–7, 79, 81, 94–5, 98, 101, 106–7 (Syrophoenician mother), 110–12
Moses 10, 32n35, 33, 121

orphan(s) 10, 51
Ovid 40, 71–2

Paidion παιδίον 26, 40–1, 87–95, 96, 99n45, 105, 107, 108
parable 97, 99n45, 106, 113, 117n56, 120, 127, 133
parent 1, 2, 4–6, 8–10, 12, 14–5, 18, 20, 26–7, 43, 48–55 (parents mourning children), 57, 76n82, 77–9, 82, 83n113, 88–90, 99n45, 101–2, 103–9 (healing narratives of children in Mark), 111–12, 117, 120n66, 124, 128, 134–5. *See also God as parent*
Paul, apostle 15, 16, 28, 33, 38, 41, 47, 119, 127n84, 140, 141
Persius 70, 73
Philo 19, 27, 28, 29, 32–8, 41, 42, 52–5 (*Consolation to His Wife*), 69, 70, 75–9, 83, 89, 104, 124–5
Pliny
   the Elder 34–5, 40, 69
   the Younger 37n58, 40–1
play/playing, children 15–6, 33, 35, 36, 40, 52, 55
puberty 4n14, 17, 48n123, 59, 75, 83–4. *See also boy/boyhood, girl/girlhood*
purity 22, 62, 65, 78

Quintilian 19, 39, 40, 41–4, 48–9

reversal 2, 15, 26, 93, 95, 99, 123–4, 130, 134
rites of passage 2, 10, 17, 25–6, 55–6, 57–85 (Chapter 3), 87, 89, 91, 93, 95, 97–9, 100, 124, 130–2, 137–9, 140
ritual 2, 12, 20n153, 23, 50, 55, 59, 61n15, 62–3, 65–7, 75–7, 79, 82, 84–5, 130n86, 137. *See also rites of passage*

save(s) 41, 97, 107, 124, 140
Seneca 5, 27, 30, 34, 39–40, 42, 45–8, 52, 54n161, 72–3
slave(s)/slavery 5, 6, 10, 12, 13, 27, 30, 39, 42–4, 57, 69, 70, 116, 127, 129, 138
Statius 70n62, 73–4
Strabo 39

Synoptic Gospels/Synoptics 17, 18, 22, 91

teknon τέκνον 89n6, 97, 99n45, 106–7, 126n81
transformation 2, 26–7, 45–6, 56, 58, 61–2, 64–5, 84–5, 87, 90, 93, 95, 97, 100, 116, 117, 123, 132, 134, 137–9, 141
Turner, Victor 2, 25, 58, 61–5, 67, 84, 99, 138

van Gennep, Arnold 2, 10, 25, 56, 58–61, 64–8, 70, 74, 79, 82–5, 130, 137–8
wedding(s)/wedding ceremonies 26, 50, 67n42, 68, 74–84, 138. *See also Marriage*
   Greco-Roman practices 74–84
   Jewish practices 79–82
womanhood 41n83, 57, 68, 75, 84, 105

www.ingramcontent.com/pod-product-compliance
Lightning Source LLC
Chambersburg PA
CBHW061840300426
44115CB00013B/2457